Christmas

Taste of Home BOOKS

RDA ENTHUSIAST BRANDS, LLC
MILWAUKEE, WI

Contents

Taste of Home.

© 2023 RDA Enthusiast Brands, LLC.
1610 N. 2nd St., Suite 102, Milwaukee WI
53212-3906

International Standard Book Number:
D 978-1-62145-862-3
U 978-1-62145-863-0
International Standard Serial Number:
1948-8386
Component Number:
D 119600108H
U 119600110H

Executive Editor: Mark Hagen
Senior Art Director: Raeann Thompson
Editor: Hazel Wheaton
Art Director: Maggie Conners
Designer: Carrie Peterson
Deputy Editor, Copy Desk: Dulcie Shoener

Cover:
Photographer: Mark Derse
Food Stylist: Shannon Norris
Set Stylist: Stacey Genaw

Pictured on front cover:
Winning Cranberry Glazed Ham, p. 59;
Buttery Crescent Rolls, p. 62;
Pimiento Green Beans, p. 75

Pictured on back cover:
Peppermint Cheesecake, p. 92;
Roast Christmas Goose, p. 53;
Sweet Potato Spice Bread, p. 160

Holly illustration:
Shutterstock/Leigh Prather

Printed in U.S.A.
10 9 8 7 6 5 4 3 2 1

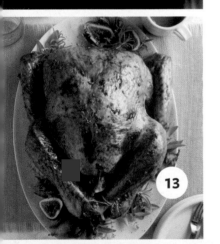

Create new traditions this year with Taste of Home Christmas

1. IT'S A SMALL (PLATE) WORLD
Take your family and friends around the world with this tantalizing collection of global flavors—perfect for a holiday cocktail party.

2. SET IT & FORGET IT
Holiday entertaining has never been easier than with these fabulous slow-cooker recipes. Do the prep, then catch up with your guests until it's time to finish and serve.

3. HOLIDAY FEASTS
Serve your loved ones a meal they'll always remember. A traditional goose, a vegetarian spread or filet mignon, these specially designed menus give you lots to choose from—plus plenty of a la carte options.

4. RED & GREEN HOLIDAY SIDES
Round out your serving plates with a festive finishing touch by creating mouthwatering side dishes in celebratory shades of red and green.

5. 5-STAR DESSERTS
For a truly showstopping finale to your holiday meal, look no further than this chapter, which spotlights some of our most impressive and highly rated desserts.

6. BREAKFAST IN BED
Before the rush of the holiday begins, take time to enjoy a quiet morning together. These indulgent breakfast and brunch recipe are perfectly portioned for two.

3

4

5

6

7

10

9

8

IT'S A SMALL (PLATE) WORLD

*Whether you're hosting a Christmas Eve get-together
or a sparkling New Year's Eve cocktail party,
take your guests around the world in one evening
with this tantalizing collection of global flavors.*

PERUVIAN CHICHA MORADA

Chicha morada is a nonalcoholic Peruvian beverage made by boiling purple corn, called maiz morado, *with water, pineapple rinds, cinnamon, cloves, sugar and lime. It can be traced back to the pre-colonial era in Peru and is considered a staple of the Peruvian cuisine. You can find maiz morado in specialty shops and online outlets.*
—Andrea Potischman, Menlo Park, CA

- -

PREP: 20 min. + chilling • **COOK:** 50 min. • **MAKES:** 8 servings

- 1   fresh pineapple
- 1   pkg. (15 oz.) dried purple corn on the cob
- 12 cups water
- ¾   cup sugar
- 3   cinnamon sticks (3 in.)
- 10 whole cloves
- ⅓   cup lime juice
- 1   medium green apple, chopped

1. Peel pineapple, removing any eyes from fruit. Reserve half the peel. Remove and discard core from fruit. Chop pineapple and reserve for garnish.
2. Remove corn from cobs; discard cobs. Place corn, water, pineapple peel, sugar, cinnamon and cloves in a Dutch oven. Bring to a boil; reduce heat. Simmer, uncovered, 50 minutes. Strain. Refrigerate until chilled, at least 1 hour. Stir in lime juice.
3. Serve over ice with apple and reserved chopped pineapple.
¾ CUP: 99 cal., 0 fat (0 sat. fat), 0 chol., 1mg sod., 26g carb. (24g sugars, 1g fiber), 0 pro.

POLENTA WITH SAUTEED MUSHROOMS & SPINACH

As a vegetarian, I love coming up with new dishes that non-vegetarians will enjoy as much as I do (and not miss the meat). This recipe is so good, everyone always asks for the recipe.
—Marcy Delpome, Stanhope, NJ

- -

PREP: 35 min. • **BAKE:** 40 min. • **MAKES:** 12 servings

- 1   tube (18 oz.) polenta, cut into ½-in. slices
- 3   Tbsp. olive oil, divided
- 1   lb. sliced fresh mushrooms
- 1   shallot, chopped
- ½   cup sherry
- 1   Tbsp. all-purpose flour
- ¼   tsp. salt
- ¼   tsp. pepper
- ½   cup vegetable broth
- 5   cups fresh baby spinach (about 5 oz.)

1. Preheat oven to 425°. Brush both sides of polenta slices with 1 Tbsp. oil; place on a 15x10x1-in. baking pan. Bake 20-25 minutes on each side or until crisp.
2. Meanwhile, in a large skillet, heat the remaining 2 Tbsp. oil over medium-high heat. Add mushrooms and shallot; cook and stir 12-14 minutes or until liquid has evaporated and the mushrooms start to brown. Add sherry; cook, stirring to loosen any browned bits from pan.
3. In a small bowl, mix flour, salt and pepper; stir in broth until smooth. Stir into pan. Cook and stir until thickened, 1-2 minutes. Add spinach; cook and stir over medium-low heat until slightly wilted, about 2 minutes.
4. Arrange polenta on a platter; top with mushroom mixture.
1 POLENTA SLICE WITH 3 TBSP. TOPPING: 97 cal., 4g fat (1g sat. fat), 0 chol., 295mg sod., 12g carb. (2g sugars, 1g fiber), 2g pro.

SANTORINI LAMB SLIDERS

I love lamb burgers, so I created a crowd-friendly slider version. The tzatziki sauce is best made a day or two in advance to allow the flavors to mingle, which also makes it extra-convenient for party planning.
—Cristina Certano, Colorado Springs, CO

- -

PREP: 30 min. + chilling • **GRILL:** 10 min.
MAKES: 10 servings

- 1 cup plain Greek yogurt
- ½ cup shredded peeled cucumber
- 1¼ tsp. salt, divided
- 1 lb. ground lamb
- 1 Tbsp. grated lemon zest
- 4 garlic cloves, minced and divided
- 2 tsp. dried oregano
- ¼ tsp. plus ⅛ tsp. pepper, divided
- 1 tsp. lemon juice
- 1 tsp. dill weed
- 10 mini buns or mini ciabatta buns
- 10 Bibb lettuce leaves or Boston lettuce leaves
- 1 medium red onion, thinly sliced
- 1 cup crumbled feta cheese

1. Line a strainer or colander with 4 layers of cheesecloth or 1 coffee filter; place over a bowl. Place yogurt in strainer; cover yogurt with sides of cheesecloth. Refrigerate for 2-4 hours. Meanwhile, place cucumber in a colander over a plate; sprinkle with ¼ tsp. salt and toss. Let stand for 30 minutes.
2. In a large bowl, combine lamb, lemon zest, 2 garlic cloves, oregano, ¾ tsp. salt and ¼ tsp. pepper, mixing lightly but thoroughly. Shape into ten ½-in.-thick patties. Refrigerate 30 minutes.

3. For sauce, remove yogurt from the cheesecloth to a bowl; discard strained liquid. Squeeze cucumber and blot dry with paper towels. Add the cucumber, lemon juice, dill, remaining 2 garlic cloves, remaining ¼ tsp. salt and remaining ⅛ tsp. pepper to yogurt, stirring until combined.
4. Grill burgers, covered, over medium heat for 3-4 minutes on each side or until a thermometer reads 160°. Grill buns over medium heat, cut sides down, for 30-60 seconds or until toasted. Serve burgers on buns with lettuce, red onion, feta and sauce.
1 SLIDER: *228 cal., 12g fat (5g sat. fat), 43mg chol., 531mg sod., 16g carb. (3g sugars, 1g fiber), 14g pro.*

TOSTONES

Although I grew up eating many different dishes from Puerto Rico, tostones have always been a favorite for me. I still make the fried snacks whenever I miss my family.
—Leah Martin, Gilbertsville, PA

- -

PREP: 15 min. + soaking
COOK: 5 min./batch • **MAKES:** 3 dozen

- 3 garlic cloves, minced
- 1 Tbsp. garlic salt
- ½ tsp. onion powder
- 6 green plantains, peeled and cut into 1-in. slices
- Oil for deep-fat frying

SEASONING MIX

- 1 Tbsp. garlic powder
- 1½ tsp. garlic salt
- ½ tsp. onion powder
- ½ tsp. kosher salt
- Optional: Guacamole and pico de gallo

1. In a large bowl, combine the garlic, garlic salt and onion powder. Add plantains; cover with cold water. Soak for 30 minutes.
2. Drain plantains; place on paper towels and pat dry. In a deep cast-iron or electric skillet, heat oil to 375°. Add the plantains, a few at a time, and cook until lightly browned, 30-60 seconds. Remove with a slotted spoon; drain on paper towels.
3. Place plantain slices between 2 sheets of aluminum foil. With the bottom of a glass, flatten to ½-in. thickness. Fry until golden brown, 2-3 minutes longer.
4. Combine seasoning mix ingredients; sprinkle over tostones. If desired, serve with guacamole and pico de gallo.
NOTE: *Plantains are a tropical fruit that resembles the banana, but unlike bananas, plantains are cooked before being eaten. They often are used in place of potatoes because of their starch content. Plantains can be baked in their skins, or peeled and sauteed or fried until tender.*
1 TOSTONE: *63 cal., 3g fat (0 sat. fat), 0 chol., 103mg sod., 10g carb. (2g sugars, 1g fiber), 0 pro.*

STEAMED BEEF & GINGER POT STICKERS

These dumplings have a hearty filling that's easy to make and a dipping sauce that's too irresistible to pass up. I prepare them in advance and freeze them.
—Trisha Kruse, Eagle, ID

- -

PREP: 1 hour • **COOK:** 5 min./batch
MAKES: 4 dozen

- 4 green onions, thinly sliced
- 2 Tbsp. reduced-sodium soy sauce
- 2 garlic cloves, minced
- 1 Tbsp. rice vinegar
- 1 Tbsp. minced fresh gingerroot
- ¼ tsp. coarsely ground pepper
- 1 lb. ground beef
- 48 pot sticker or gyoza wrappers

DIPPING SAUCE

- ¼ cup reduced-sodium soy sauce
- 2 Tbsp. rice vinegar
- 2 Tbsp. ketchup
- 1 Tbsp. minced fresh gingerroot
- 2 tsp. sesame oil
- 1 garlic clove, minced

1. In a large bowl, combine the first 6 ingredients. Add beef; mix lightly but thoroughly. Place a scant 1 Tbsp. filling in the center of each wrapper. (Cover the remaining wrappers with a damp paper towel until ready to use.)
2. Moisten wrapper edges with water. Fold over filling; seal edges, pleating the front side several times to form a pleated pouch. Stand pot stickers on a work surface to flatten bottoms; if desired, curve slightly to form crescent shapes.
3. In a 6-qt. stockpot, place a greased steamer basket over ¾ in. of water. In batches, place dumplings in the basket. Bring water to a boil. Reduce heat to maintain a low boil; steam, covered, 4-5 minutes or until cooked through.
4. Meanwhile, in a small bowl, combine sauce ingredients. Serve with dumplings.
FREEZE OPTION: *Place uncooked pot stickers on waxed paper-lined baking sheets; freeze until firm. Transfer to resealable freezer containers; return to freezer. To use, steam frozen pot stickers as directed, increasing time to 6-7 minutes or until cooked through. Serve with sauce.*
1 POT STICKER WITH ½ TSP. SAUCE: *37 cal., 1g fat (0 sat. fat), 6mg chol., 115mg sod., 4g carb. (1g sugars, 0 fiber), 2g pro.*

Holiday Helper

You can substitute wonton wrappers for pot sticker and gyoza wrappers. Stack 2 or 3 wonton wrappers on a work surface; cut into circles with a 3½-in. biscuit or round cookie cutter. Fill and wrap as directed.

BANH MI SKEWERS

I love banh mi sandwiches but wanted to make them a little easier to serve for a party. Skewers are a really fun twist! For easier prep on the day of the party, make the meatballs in advance and freeze them.
—Elisabeth Larsen, Pleasant Grove, UT

PREP: 45 min. + chilling
COOK: 10 min./batch • **MAKES:** 12 servings

1	cup white vinegar or rice vinegar
¼	cup sugar
½	tsp. salt
1	English cucumber, thinly sliced
2	medium carrots, thinly sliced
4	radishes, thinly sliced
1	cup mayonnaise
1	Tbsp. Sriracha chili sauce
2	Tbsp. minced fresh cilantro
2	green onions, thinly sliced
1	Tbsp. soy sauce
1	garlic clove, minced
¼	tsp. cayenne pepper
1½	lbs. ground pork
2	Tbsp. canola oil
1	French bread baguette (10½ oz.), cut into 24 slices

1. In a large bowl, combine vinegar, sugar and salt; whisk until sugar is dissolved. Add cucumber, carrots and radishes; let stand until serving. Combine mayonnaise and chili sauce; refrigerate until serving.
2. In another large bowl, combine the cilantro, green onions, soy sauce, garlic and cayenne. Add pork; mix lightly but thoroughly. Shape into 36 balls.
3. In a large skillet, heat oil over medium heat. Cook meatballs in batches until cooked through, turning occasionally.
4. Drain vegetable mixture. On 12 metal or wooden skewers, alternately thread vegetables, meatballs and baguette slices. Serve with Sriracha mayonnaise.
1 SKEWER WITH ABOUT 1 TBSP. SAUCE:
336 cal., 24g fat (5g sat. fat), 39mg chol., 416mg sod., 16g carb. (2g sugars, 1g fiber), 13g pro.

HORCHATA

A mixture of ground rice and almonds is accented with a hint of lime in this popular drink. Depending on your preference, you can use more or less water for a thinner or creamier beverage.
—James Schend, Pleasant Prairie, WI

PREP: 5 min. + standing • **PROCESS:** 10 min.
MAKES: 6 servings

¾	cup uncooked long grain rice
2	cups blanched almonds
1	cinnamon stick (3 in.)
1½	tsp. grated lime zest
4	cups hot water
1	cup sugar
1	cup cold water
	Optional: Ground cinnamon, lime slices and additional cinnamon sticks

1. Place rice in a blender; cover and process 2-3 minutes or until very fine. Transfer to a large bowl; add almonds, cinnamon stick, lime zest and hot water. Let stand, covered, at room temperature 8 hours.
2. Discard cinnamon stick. Transfer rice mixture to a blender; cover and process 3-4 minutes or until smooth. Add sugar; process until sugar is dissolved.
3. Place a strainer over a pitcher; line with double-layered cheesecloth. Pour rice mixture over cheesecloth; using a ladle, press mixture through strainer.
4. Stir in cold water. Serve over ice. If desired, sprinkle with cinnamon and serve with lime and cinnamon sticks.
¾ CUP: *134 cal., 3g fat (2g sat. fat), 12mg chol., 82mg sod., 25g carb. (21g sugars, 0 fiber), 3g pro.*

FINGER FOOD

When setting up for your party, you can arrange stunning boards for your appetizers. Supplement the small bites you've prepared with fresh fruit, meats, cheeses and other tasty bits.

For the board pictured on p. 6 and above, we started with Spiced Mango-Almond Tarts (opposite), Crisp Crab Wonton Cups (p. 20) and glasses of Peruvian Chicha Morada (p. 8), and chose a selection of easy nibbles to complement them.

When constructing a board, take care to balance different textures and flavors. In ours, red and green grapes and fresh figs provide sweetness while olives and cashews lend salt and crunch. We chose one soft but intense blue cheese and a milder hard cheese (Gouda), paired with some artisan crackers. Deli ham and dry-cured salami add something for meat lovers. As a final touch, we wrapped slices of prosciutto around thin, crisp breadsticks for a quick crunchy and salty appetizer.

AIR-FRIED PUMPKIN SHAKARPARAS

I grew up in an Indian-American household where shakarparas were a staple cookie for the holidays. My family makes the traditional version every year, and I wanted to put my own twist on it. I adapted the recipe by adding pumpkin and different spices and cooking them in an air fryer.
—Jessica Burke, Chandler, AZ

- -

PREP: 30 min. + standing
COOK: 5 min./batch • **MAKES:** 7½ dozen

- 2 cups all-purpose flour
- ¾ cup sugar
- ½ cup semolina flour
- 1 Tbsp. pumpkin pie spice
- 1 tsp. ground cloves
- ¼ tsp. baking powder
- ½ cup canned pumpkin
- 1 large egg, room temperature
- 1 Tbsp. butter, melted

1. In a large bowl, whisk first 6 ingredients. In another bowl, beat pumpkin, egg and butter until blended. Stir into the dry ingredients to form a soft dough.
2. Turn dough onto a floured surface; knead until smooth, about 12 times. Cover and let rest 15 minutes.
3. Divide into 4 portions. Roll each to ⅛-in. thickness. Cut into ½-in. diamonds.
4. Preheat air fryer to 375°. In batches, arrange diamonds in a single layer on greased tray in air-fryer basket. Cook until the edges are golden brown, 3-4 minutes. Remove to a wire rack to cool.

NOTE: *In our testing, we find cook times vary dramatically between brands of air fryers. As a result, we give wider than normal ranges on suggested cook times. Begin checking at the first time listed and adjust as needed.*

1 COOKIE: *23 cal., 0 fat (0 sat. fat), 2mg chol., 3mg sod., 5g carb. (2g sugars, 0 fiber), 1g pro.*

SPICED MANGO-ALMOND TART

There are many tarts in the world, but this one is extra gorgeous. I like to present it with a sprinkle of confectioners' sugar, some whipped cream and a few mint leaves.
—Lisa Speer, Palm Beach, FL

- -

PREP: 35 min. + freezing • **BAKE:** 25 min./batch
MAKES: 2 tarts (8 servings each)

    1   pkg. (17.3 oz.) frozen puff pastry, thawed
    ⅔ cup almond paste, divided
    2   large mangoes, peeled and thinly sliced
    2   Tbsp. lemon juice
    3   Tbsp. packed brown sugar
   1½ tsp. ground cinnamon
    ½ tsp. ground ginger
        Dash ground cloves

1. Preheat oven to 375°. Working with 1 puff pastry sheet at a time, unfold onto a large sheet of parchment dusted lightly with flour. Roll into a 10-in. square. Transfer pastry and paper to a baking sheet. Using a sharp knife, score a ½-in. border around edges of pastry (this will help the edge of the crust rise).
2. On a second sheet of parchment, roll ⅓ cup almond paste to ⅛-in. thickness. Peel off almond paste in pieces and arrange on puff pastry, keeping within edges of scored border.
3. In a large bowl, toss mangoes with lemon juice; arrange half the mangoes over almond paste. In a small bowl, mix brown sugar and spices; sprinkle half the mixture over mangoes. Place tart in freezer to chill, about 10 minutes. Repeat with the remaining ingredients to make a second tart.
4. Bake until crust is golden brown, 25-35 minutes. If baking 2 tarts at a time, switch position of pans halfway through baking. Serve warm.
1 PIECE: *232 cal., 11g fat (2g sat. fat), 0 chol., 103mg sod., 32g carb. (12g sugars, 4g fiber), 3g pro.*

JALAPENO POMEGRANATE COCKTAIL

This spicy and sweet sipper gives you a little fix of jalapeno flavor minus the heat. Start a couple of days ahead to flavor the vodka.
—Melissa Rodriguez, Van Nuys, CA

- -

PREP: 10 min. + chilling • **MAKES:** 8 servings

    2   jalapeno peppers, halved lengthwise and seeded
   1½ cups vodka
    6   to 8 cups ice cubes
    3   cups pomegranate juice
    3   cups Italian blood orange soda, chilled
        Lime wedges

1. For jalapeno vodka, place jalapenos and vodka in a glass jar or container. Refrigerate, covered, 2-3 days to allow flavors to blend. Strain before using.
2. For each serving, fill cocktail shaker three-fourths full with ice. Add 3 oz. pomegranate juice and 1½ oz. jalapeno vodka; cover and shake until condensation forms on outside of shaker, 10-15 seconds. Strain into a cocktail glass; top with 3 oz. soda. Serve with lime wedges.
1 CUP: *184 cal., 0 fat (0 sat. fat), 0 chol., 12mg sod., 22g carb. (22g sugars, 0 fiber), 0 pro.*

CURRIED CHICKEN BRUSCHETTA BITES

This curry-enhanced chicken is my go-to party food for cocktail parties, bridal showers and more. Whether made into bruschetta (as in this recipe) or simply served as a dip, it always goes fast!
—*Amy Freeze, Avon Park, FL*

TAKES: 30 min. • **MAKES:** 2 dozen

1   pkg. (8 oz.) cream cheese, softened
½   cup chopped celery
2   Tbsp. steak sauce
1   Tbsp. dried celery flakes
2   tsp. curry powder
1   tsp. garlic powder
3   cooked chicken breasts, cubed
½   cup slivered almonds, toasted
1   loaf (1 lb.) French bread, sliced thin
2   Tbsp. olive oil
2   Tbsp. minced fresh cilantro

1. Preheat oven to 425°. Pulse the first 6 ingredients in a food processor until well combined. Add chicken; pulse just until finely chopped. Stir in almonds.
2. Brush bread slices with olive oil; spread 2 Tbsp. chicken mixture on each slice. Place on a 15x10-in. pan; bake until bread is toasted and chicken is lightly browned, 8-10 minutes. Sprinkle with cilantro.
NOTE: *To toast nuts, bake in a shallow pan in a 350° oven for 5-10 minutes or cook in a skillet over low heat until lightly browned, stirring occasionally.*
1 APPETIZER: *129 cal., 6g fat (2g sat. fat), 19mg chol., 177mg sod., 11g carb. (2g sugars, 1g fiber), 6g pro.*

JICAMA WATERMELON SALAD

I discovered jicama at a Las Vegas buffet and fell for its crisp texture and the amazing sweet flavor. It stars in this unusual salad that's quick and easy.
—*Crystal Jo Bruns, Iliff, CO*

PREP: 15 min. + chilling • **MAKES:** 12 servings

1   miniature seedless watermelon (about 4 lbs.), peeled and cubed (about 8 cups)
2   medium ripe avocados, peeled and diced
2   cups shredded peeled jicama
¼   cup lime juice
½   tsp. Tajin seasoning
¼   tsp. salt

In a large bowl, combine all ingredients; toss to coat. Cover and chill at least 1 hour.
¾ CUP: *91 cal., 4g fat (0 sat. fat), 0 chol., 80mg sod., 16g carb. (11g sugars, 3g fiber), 1g pro.*
DIABETIC EXCHANGES: *1 fruit, 1 fat.*

Holiday Helper

If watermelon is unavailable in your area in December, substitute any other available melon. Or, omit the melon completely to make a marinated jicama salad.

GRUYERE & CARAMELIZED ONION TARTS

Garlic and onion is a match made in heaven, and I love creating new recipes to showcase the pair. Gruyere cheese adds impeccable flavor to this eye-catching starter. If you can't get Gruyere, substitute a good-quality Swiss cheese instead.
—Lisa Speer, Palm Beach, FL

PREP: 45 min. **BAKE:** 15 min.
MAKES: 2 dozen

- 1   large sweet onion, thinly sliced
- 2   Tbsp. olive oil
- 1   Tbsp. butter
- 3   garlic cloves, minced
- ¼   tsp. salt
- ¼   tsp. pepper
- 1   pkg. (17.3 oz.) frozen puff pastry, thawed
- 1   cup shredded Gruyere or Swiss cheese
- ¼   cup grated Parmesan cheese
- 2   Tbsp. minced fresh thyme

1. In a large skillet, saute onion in oil and butter until softened. Reduce heat to medium-low; cook, uncovered, for 40 minutes or until deep golden brown, stirring occasionally. Add garlic; cook 1 minute longer. Stir in salt and pepper.
2. Unfold each puff pastry sheet onto an ungreased baking sheet. Using a knife, score decorative lines around the edges of each pastry. Spread the onion mixture to within ½ in. of edges. Sprinkle with cheeses and thyme.
3. Bake at 400° for 12-15 minutes or until crust is golden brown. Cut each tart into 12 pieces. If desired, top with additional fresh thyme and grated Parmesan cheese. Serve warm.
1 PIECE: *142 cal., 9g fat (3g sat. fat), 7mg chol., 125mg sod., 13g carb. (1g sugars, 2g fiber), 3g pro.*

CAULIFLOWER CEVICHE

My 87-year-old mom showed me how to make this delicious vegetarian recipe that tastes so much like seafood ceviche. I often serve it with crackers on the side.
—Beatriz Barranco, El Paso, TX

- -

PREP: 20 min. + chilling • **MAKES:** 10 servings

1   **medium head cauliflower, finely chopped**
1   **cup ketchup**
1   **cup orange juice**
3   **medium tomatoes, chopped**
1   **medium onion, finely chopped**
½   **cup minced fresh cilantro**
¼   **tsp. salt**
¼   **tsp. pepper**
3   **medium ripe avocados, peeled and cubed**
    Optional: Lemon wedges, tortilla chip scoops and hot pepper sauce

1. In a large skillet, bring 1 cup water to a boil. Add cauliflower; cook, uncovered, just until crisp-tender, 5-8 minutes. Remove with a slotted spoon; drain and pat dry. Meanwhile, stir together ketchup and orange juice.
2. In a large bowl, combine cauliflower with tomatoes and onion. Add the ketchup mixture, cilantro, salt and pepper; toss to coat. Refrigerate, covered, at least 1 hour.
3. Stir in avocado cubes. If desired, serve with lemon wedges, tortilla chip scoops and hot pepper sauce.
1 SERVING: *129 cal., 7g fat (1g sat. fat), 0 chol., 387mg sod., 18g carb. (11g sugars, 5g fiber), 3g pro.*

Holiday Helper
Ceviche (pronounced suh-VEE-chay) is usually made with fresh, raw seafood. This version cleverly uses cauliflower instead for a refreshing vegetarian treat with a hint of sweetness. If you like things more savory, use tomato sauce instead of ketchup. Spice it up with a minced jalapeno or chipotle pepper.

HONEYED FIG & RICOTTA APPETIZERS

These sweet and creamy appetizers sound fancy, but they couldn't be simpler to make. Spiced-up ricotta cheese on top of crispy gingersnaps—how easy is that?
—Taste of Home *Test Kitchen*

- -

TAKES: 20 min. • **MAKES:** 2 dozen

½   **cup ricotta cheese**
1   **tsp. sugar**
¼   **tsp. ground cinnamon**
¼   **tsp. ground nutmeg**
24   **gingersnap cookies**
8   **dried figs**
¼   **cup honey**

1. Preheat oven to 350°. In a small bowl, combine the ricotta cheese, sugar, cinnamon and nutmeg. Spread 1 tsp. cheese mixture over each cookie. Arrange on a foil-lined baking sheet.
2. Cut each fig into 3 slices; place on cheese mixture. Drizzle fig slices with honey. Bake for 4-6 minutes or until heated through. Serve immediately.
1 APPETIZER: *66 cal., 1g fat (1g sat. fat), 2mg chol., 53mg sod., 13g carb. (8g sugars, 1g fiber), 1g pro.*

SPICY EDAMAME

Edamame (pronounced eh-duh-MAH-may) are young soybeans in their pods. They make a delicious addition to soups and salads, but we love them as a fun and tasty appetizer. In our Test Kitchen, we boiled and seasoned them with salt, ginger, garlic powder and red pepper flakes. Serve them in the pods and let guests peel them open to reveal the delicious beans!
—Taste of Home *Test Kitchen*

- -

TAKES: 20 min. • **MAKES:** 6 servings

1   **pkg. (16 oz.) frozen edamame pods**
2   **tsp. kosher salt**
¾   **tsp. ground ginger**
½   **tsp. garlic powder**
¼   **tsp. crushed red pepper flakes**

Place edamame in a large saucepan and cover with water. Bring to a boil. Cover and cook until tender, 4-5 minutes; drain. Transfer to a large bowl. Add the seasonings; toss to coat.
1 SERVING: *52 cal., 2g fat (0 sat. fat), 0 chol., 642mg sod., 5g carb. (1g sugars, 2g fiber), 4g pro.*

CRISP CRAB WONTON CUPS

Chinese mustard, five-spice powder and wasabi give these appetizers a spicy Asian flavor. I first made them with leftover Dungeness crab, but a good-quality canned crabmeat works well.
—Margee Berry, White Salmon, WA

TAKES: 30 min. • **MAKES:** 40 appetizers

40 wonton wrappers
1 pkg. (8 oz.) cream cheese, softened
¼ cup sweet-and-sour sauce
1 large egg, room temperature
⅓ cup chopped green onions
½ tsp. Chinese-style mustard
¼ tsp. prepared wasabi or horseradish
    Dash Chinese five-spice powder
1 cup lump crabmeat, drained
2 Tbsp. black sesame seeds

1. Press each wonton wrapper into a greased miniature muffin cup. Bake at 350° until golden brown, 6-7 minutes.
2. In a small bowl, beat the cream cheese, sweet-and-sour sauce and egg. Stir in the onions, mustard, wasabi and five-spice powder. Fold in crab. Spoon 1 Tbsp. crab mixture into each cup. Sprinkle with sesame seeds.
3. Bake until heated through, 10-12 minutes longer. If desired, top with additional chopped green onions.
1 APPETIZER: 52 cal., 2g fat (1g sat. fat), 14mg chol., 96mg sod., 6g carb. (1g sugars, 0 fiber), 2g pro.

THREE-CHEESE FONDUE

I got this easy recipe from my daughter, who lives in France. It's become my go-to fondue, and I make it often for our family.
—Betty Mangas, Toledo, OH

TAKES: 30 min. • **MAKES:** 4 cups

2 cups dry white wine
4 tsp. cherry brandy
2 Tbsp. cornstarch
⅛ tsp. ground nutmeg
⅛ tsp. paprika
    Dash cayenne pepper
½ lb. each Emmenthaler, Gruyere and
    Jarlsberg cheeses, finely shredded
    Cubed French bread baguette,
    boiled red potatoes and/or tiny whole pickles

1. In a large saucepan, whisk together the first 6 ingredients until smooth. Heat mixture over medium heat until slightly thickened, stirring constantly, 5-7 minutes.
2. Reduce heat to low; gradually add ½ cup cheese, stirring constantly with a figure-8 motion, until the cheese is melted (cheese will separate from wine mixture). Gradually add the remaining cheese, allowing cheese to melt between additions. Cook and stir until thickened and mixture is blended and smooth, 4-5 minutes.
3. Transfer to a fondue pot (or a 3-qt. slow cooker on its lowest setting). Serve with bread cubes, potatoes and/or pickles.
¼ CUP: 191 cal., 12g fat (7g sat. fat), 37mg chol., 151mg sod., 3g carb. (1g sugars, 0 fiber), 12g pro.

AUSTRIAN NUT COOKIES

These are my family's favorite cookies. You can sprinkle the almonds on top or arrange them in a pinwheel fashion so the cookie looks like a little flower.
—Marianne Weber, South Beach, OR

PREP: 30 min. + chilling • **BAKE:** 10 min./batch + cooling
MAKES: 10 sandwich cookies

  1   **cup all-purpose flour**
  ⅔   **cup finely chopped almonds**
  ⅓   **cup sugar**
  ½   **cup butter, softened**
  ¼   **cup seedless raspberry jam**
FROSTING
  1   **oz. unsweetened chocolate, melted and cooled**
  ⅓   **cup confectioners' sugar**
  2   **Tbsp. butter, softened**
      Slivered almonds, optional

1. Combine flour, chopped almonds and sugar. Mix in butter until dough is just combined. On a floured surface, roll dough to ⅛-in. thickness. Cut with a 2-in. round cutter and place 1 in. apart on greased baking sheets. Cover and refrigerate 1 hour.
2. Uncover and bake at 375° for 7-10 minutes or until the edges are lightly browned. Remove to wire racks to cool completely. Spread jam on half of the cookies; top with another cookie.
3. For frosting, combine chocolate, confectioners' sugar and butter. Spread on tops of cookies. Decorate with slivered almonds if desired.
1 COOKIE: *277 cal., 18g fat (9g sat. fat), 31mg chol., 92mg sod., 28g carb. (16g sugars, 2g fiber), 4g pro.*

BAKED COCONUT MOCHI SQUARES

My family has been making simple baked mochi for years—and the treats never last more than a day. We love the warm, rich, gooey texture that comes from sweet rice flour baked with coconut milk, butter, sugar and coconut flakes. As the mixture bakes, it creates a beautiful crispy golden crust atop the squares.
—Thac Nguyen, Ottawa, ON

PREP: 15 min. • **BAKE:** 50 min. + cooling • **MAKES:** 35 servings

  2   **cups sugar**
  2   **cups canned coconut milk**
  1   **cup whole milk**
  5   **large eggs, room temperature**
  ½   **cup butter, melted**
  2   **tsp. vanilla extract**
  2½ **cups sweet white rice flour**
  1   **tsp. baking powder**
  1½ **cups sweetened shredded coconut**

1. Preheat oven to 350°. Line a 13x9-in. baking pan with parchment; grease paper. Set pan aside.
2. In a large bowl, beat sugar, coconut milk, milk, eggs, butter and vanilla until well blended. In another bowl, whisk rice flour and baking powder; gradually beat into sugar mixture. Stir in coconut.
3. Transfer to prepared baking pan. Bake until golden brown, 50-55 minutes. Cool in pan on a wire rack. Lifting with the parchment, remove from pan. Cut into bars.
1 BAR: *175 cal., 7g fat (5g sat. fat), 34mg chol., 62mg sod., 25g carb. (14g sugars, 0 fiber), 2g pro.*

SET IT & FORGET IT

Holiday entertaining has never been easier than with these fabulous slow-cooker recipes. Do the prep work, set the cooker, then catch up with family and friends until it's time to finish and serve.

RANCH MUSHROOMS

I got this recipe from my sister-in-law, and it has become a family favorite. The mushrooms don't last long once people know I have made them.
—Jackie McGee, Byron, MN

- -

PREP: 10 min. • **COOK:** 3 hours • **MAKES:** 16 servings (4 cups)

- 1½ lbs. whole fresh mushrooms
- 1 cup butter, melted
- 1 envelope ranch salad dressing mix
  Optional: Chopped fresh dill weed or parsley

Place mushrooms in a 4- or 5-qt. slow cooker. In a small bowl, whisk butter and ranch mix; pour over mushrooms. Cook, covered, on low until mushrooms are tender, about 3 hours. Serve with a slotted spoon. If desired, sprinkle with dill or parsley.
¼ CUP: 21 cal., 1g fat (1g sat. fat), 3mg chol., 47mg sod., 2g carb. (1g sugars, 0 fiber), 1g pro.

LAZY-DAY CRANBERRY RELISH

This no-fuss condiment simmers away while I do other holiday preparations. It's especially delicious served with turkey.
—June Formanek, Belle Plaine, IA

- -

PREP: 5 min. • **COOK:** 6 hours + chilling • **MAKES:** 3 cups

- 2 cups sugar
- 1 tsp. grated orange zest
- 1 cup orange juice
- 4 cups fresh or frozen cranberries, thawed

1. In a 1½-qt. slow cooker, mix sugar, orange zest and juice until sugar is dissolved; stir in cranberries.
2. Cook, covered, on low 6 hours. Mash berries; transfer to a bowl. Cool slightly. Refrigerate, covered, until cold.
¼ CUP: 154 cal., 0 fat (0 sat. fat), 0 chol., 1mg sod., 40g carb. (37g sugars, 1g fiber), 0 pro.

CHEESY MEATBALLS

This delicious appetizer combines the flavor of homemade meatballs with the convenience of a slow-cooked party food. My beef, sausage and cheese recipe has a big fan following.
—Jill Hill, Dixon, IL

- -

PREP: 1 hour • **COOK:** 4 hours • **MAKES:** about 9 dozen

- 1 large egg
- ½ cup 2% milk
- 2 Tbsp. dried minced onion
- 4 Tbsp. chili powder, divided
- 1 tsp. salt
- 1 tsp. pepper
- 1½ cups crushed Ritz crackers (about 1 sleeve)
- 2 lbs. ground beef
- 1 lb. bulk pork sausage
- 2 cups shredded Velveeta
- 3 cans (10¾ oz. each) condensed tomato soup, undiluted
- 2½ cups water
- ½ cup packed brown sugar

1. Preheat oven to 400°. In a large bowl, whisk egg, milk, minced onion, 2 Tbsp. chili powder, and the salt and pepper; stir in crushed crackers. Add beef, sausage and cheese; mix lightly but thoroughly.
2. Shape mixture into 1-in. balls. Place meatballs on greased racks in 15x10x1-in. baking pans. Bake until browned, 15-18 minutes.
3. Meanwhile, in a 5- or 6-qt. slow cooker, combine soup, water, brown sugar and remaining 2 Tbsp. chili powder. Gently stir in meatballs. Cook, covered, on low until meatballs are cooked through, 4-5 hours.
1 MEATBALL: 52 cal., 3g fat (1g sat. fat), 11mg chol., 134mg sod., 4g carb. (2g sugars, 0 fiber), 3g pro.

PUMPKIN PIE HOT CHOCOLATE

Spiked hot chocolate is the ultimate holiday cocktail. Made in a slow cooker and perfect for feeding a crowd, this creamy twist on a classic is a must-make for the season!
—Becky Hardin, St. Peters, MO

- -

PREP: 10 min. • **COOK:** 2 hours
MAKES: 10 servings

- 4   cups whole milk
- 2   cups heavy whipping cream
- 1   can (14 oz.) sweetened condensed milk
- 1   pkg. (12 oz.) semisweet chocolate chips
- 1   cup vodka
- 1   cup canned pumpkin
- 1   Tbsp. pumpkin pie spice
  Optional garnishes: Miniature marshmallows and whipped cream

In a 4-qt. slow cooker, combine all ingredients except garnishes. Cook, covered, on low, for 2 hours, stirring occasionally, until mixture is hot and chocolate is melted. If desired, garnish with marshmallows or whipped cream.
1 CUP: *575 cal., 34g fat (21g sat. fat), 77mg chol., 111mg sod., 52g carb. (47g sugars, 3g fiber), 9g pro.*

Holiday Helper
- To lighten this up, use a low-fat or dairy-free milk, such as almond, soy or oat, instead of the whole milk. Or, use half-and-half or fat-free sweetened condensed milk instead of heavy cream. Changing more than one ingredient will change the flavor dramatically, so try the original recipe before making alterations.
- This recipe calls for vodka, but you can use bourbon, brandy, Irish cream or a chocolate liqueur, too.

UPSY-DAISY PLUM PUDDING

Baking is not my favorite thing to do, but for the holidays, a sweet plum pudding is always in order. So, I created one in my slow cooker. My family thinks it is the best ever—hopefully you'll agree.
—Judy Batson, Tampa, FL

- -

PREP: 25 min. • **COOK:** 4 hours
MAKES: 8 servings

- 7 oz. medium red plums, halved, pitted and sliced
- 1 cup frozen unsweetened blackberries, thawed
- 2 Tbsp. mixed berry jelly
- ½ cup butter, softened
- ½ cup sugar
- 2 large eggs, room temperature
- 1 cup self-rising flour
- ⅓ cup ground almonds
- ⅛ tsp. almond extract
  Sweetened whipped cream, optional

1. Pour 1 in. water into a 6-qt. slow cooker. Layer two 24-in. pieces of foil; roll up lengthwise to make a 1-in.-thick roll. Shape into a ring; place in the slow cooker to make a rack.

2. Toss plums and blackberries with jelly; arrange in the bottom of greased 2-qt. baking dish. For batter, in a large bowl, cream butter and sugar until light and fluffy, 5-7 minutes. Add eggs, 1 at a time, beating well after each addition. Add flour to creamed mixture just until moistened. Stir in almonds and extract. Spread batter over the fruit mixture; cover with foil.

3. Fold an 18x12-in. piece of foil lengthwise into thirds, making a sling. Use the sling to lower the baking dish onto the foil rack, not allowing sides to touch slow cooker. Cook, covered, on high until a toothpick inserted in the center comes out clean, about 4 hours.

4. Use the sling to remove the baking dish from slow cooker. Run a knife around the edge of the baking dish; invert onto a serving plate. Serve warm. Top with sweetened whipped cream if desired.

1 PIECE: *283 cal., 15g fat (8g sat. fat), 77mg chol., 296mg sod., 34g carb. (20g sugars, 2g fiber), 4g pro.*

KASHMIRI LAMB CURRY STEW

When I was growing up, I was taught that spicy foods are for lovers. So when I married, this was the first meal I made for my husband. Every time we have a disagreement, I make this dish.
—Amber El, Pittsburgh, PA

- -

PREP: 25 min. + marinating • **COOK:** 8 hours
MAKES: 11 servings (2¾ qt.)

- 1 cup plain yogurt
- 2 Tbsp. ghee or butter, melted
- ¼ cup lemon juice
- 4 tsp. curry powder
- 1 Tbsp. cumin seeds
- 1 tsp. each coriander seeds, ground ginger, ground cloves, ground cardamom, sugar and salt
- ½ tsp. each ground cinnamon and pepper
- 3 lbs. lamb stew meat, cut into 1-in. cubes
- 1 large onion, sliced
- 1 medium sweet potato, quartered
- 1 medium Yukon Gold potato, quartered
- 1 large tomato, chopped
- 1 cup frozen peas and carrots
- 3 garlic cloves, minced
- 2 dried hot chiles
- ½ cup chicken broth
- 1½ Tbsp. garam masala
  Optional: Hot cooked basmati rice, sliced green onion, mango chutney and raisins

1. In a large dish, combine yogurt, ghee and lemon juice; add curry powder, cumin seeds, coriander, ginger, cloves, cardamom, sugar, salt, cinnamon and pepper. Add lamb, vegetables, garlic and chiles; turn to coat. Cover and refrigerate up to 24 hours.

2. Transfer the lamb mixture and marinade to a 6-qt. slow cooker; stir in broth and garam masala. Cook, covered, on low until meat is tender, 8-9 hours. If desired, serve with rice, green onion, mango chutney and raisins.

NOTE: *This meal may also be made with boneless chicken or cubed beef.*

1 CUP: *261 cal., 10g fat (4g sat. fat), 89mg chol., 384mg sod., 15g carb. (5g sugars, 3g fiber), 28g pro.*
DIABETIC EXCHANGES: *4 lean meat, 1 starch.*

SLOW-COOKED GINGERED PEARS

My slow cooker allows me to serve a special dessert without much effort. These tender pears feature a surprise filling of candied ginger and pecans.
—Catherine Mueller, St. Paul, MN

PREP: 35 min. • **COOK:** 4 hours • **MAKES:** 6 servings

- ½ cup finely chopped crystallized ginger
- ¼ cup packed brown sugar
- ¼ cup chopped pecans
- 1½ tsp. grated lemon zest
- 6 medium Bartlett or Anjou pears
- 2 Tbsp. butter, cubed
  Optional: Vanilla ice cream and caramel ice cream topping

1. Combine the ginger, brown sugar, pecans and lemon zest. Using a melon baller or long-handled spoon, core pears to within ¼ in. of bottom. Spoon ginger mixture into the center of each.
2. Place pears upright in a 5-qt. slow cooker. Top each with butter. Cover and cook on low for 4-5 hours or until tender. Serve with ice cream and caramel topping if desired.
1 FILLED PEAR: *263 cal., 8g fat (3g sat. fat), 10mg chol., 43mg sod., 52g carb. (32g sugars, 6g fiber), 1g pro.*

MOIST CORN SPOON BREAD

Enjoy this easy take on a southern specialty by using the ultra-convenient slow cooker. It's an excellent side dish for Christmas, Thanksgiving, Easter or any special feast.
—Taste of Home *Test Kitchen*

PREP: 20 min. • **COOK:** 4 hours • **MAKES:** 8 servings

- 1 pkg. (8 oz.) cream cheese, softened
- 2 Tbsp. sugar
- 2 large eggs, beaten
- 1 cup 2% milk
- 2 Tbsp. butter, melted
- ½ tsp. salt
- ¼ tsp. cayenne pepper
- ⅛ tsp. pepper
- 2 cups frozen corn
- 1 can (14¾ oz.) cream-style corn
- 1 cup yellow cornmeal
- 1 cup shredded Monterey Jack cheese
- 3 green onions, thinly sliced
  Optional: Coarsely ground pepper and thinly sliced green onions

1. In a large bowl, beat cream cheese and sugar until smooth. Gradually beat in eggs. Beat in the milk, butter, salt, cayenne and pepper until blended. Stir in the next 5 ingredients.
2. Pour into a greased 3-qt. slow cooker. Cover and cook on low for 4-5 hours, until a toothpick inserted in the center comes out clean. If desired, top with additional pepper and green onions.
1 SERVING: *350 cal., 18g fat (11g sat. fat), 54mg chol., 525mg sod., 38g carb. (8g sugars, 3g fiber), 12g pro.*

SPICY KALE & HERB PORCHETTA

Serve this classic Italian specialty as a main entree or with crusty artisan bread as a sandwich. Use the liquid from the slow cooker with your favorite seasonings to make a sauce or gravy.
—Sandi Sheppard, Norman, OK

- -

PREP: 30 min. + chilling • **COOK:** 5 hours
MAKES: 12 servings

1½ cups packed torn fresh kale leaves (no stems)
¼ cup chopped fresh sage
¼ cup chopped fresh rosemary
¼ cup chopped fresh parsley
2 Tbsp. kosher salt
1 Tbsp. crushed fennel seed
1 tsp. crushed red pepper flakes
4 garlic cloves, halved
1 boneless pork shoulder roast (about 6 lbs.), butterflied
2 tsp. grated lemon zest
1 large sweet onion, thickly sliced
¼ cup white wine or chicken broth
1 Tbsp. olive oil
3 Tbsp. cornstarch
3 Tbsp. water

1. In a blender or food processor, pulse the first 8 ingredients until finely chopped. In a 15x10x1-in. baking pan, open roast flat. Spread herb mixture evenly over meat to within ½ in. of edges; sprinkle lemon zest over herb mixture.
2. Starting at a long side, roll up pork jelly-roll style. Using a sharp knife, score fat on the outside of roast. Tie at 2-in. intervals with kitchen string. Secure ends with toothpicks. Refrigerate, covered, at least 4 hours or overnight.
3. In a 6-qt. slow cooker, combine onion and wine. Place the porchetta seam side down on top of onion. Cook, covered, on low for 5-6 hours or until tender. Remove toothpicks. Reserve cooking juices.
4. In a large skillet, heat oil over medium heat. Brown porchetta on all sides; remove from heat. Tent with foil. Let stand 15 minutes.

5. Meanwhile, strain and skim fat from the cooking juices. Transfer to a large saucepan; bring to a boil. In a small bowl, mix cornstarch and water until smooth; stir into juices. Return to a boil, stirring constantly; cook and stir until thickened, 1-2 minutes. Cut string on roast and slice. Serve with gravy.

1 SERVING: *402 cal., 24g fat (8g sat. fat), 135mg chol., 1104mg sod., 5g carb. (1g sugars, 1g fiber), 39g pro.*

Holiday Helper

To butterfly the pork shoulder, make a cut starting 1 in. from the bottom of the roast and stopping 1 in. from the other side (it's easier to do this with the roast on its side). Lay the roast open like a book. Make a lateral cut into the thicker piece, taking care not to cut all the way through; unfold and lay flat. You can pound the pork lightly to help even it out. You can also ask the butcher to butterfly it for you.

VERY VANILLA SLOW-COOKER CHEESECAKE

Cinnamon and vanilla give this cheesecake so much flavor, and making it in the slow cooker creates a silky, smooth texture that's hard to resist. You can top it off with fresh fruit (the kiwi and cranberries give a festive red & green look), toasted nuts or a drizzle of chocolate ganache—whatever you like!

—Krista Lanphier, Milwaukee, WI

- -

PREP: 40 min. • **COOK:** 2 hours + chilling
MAKES: 6 servings

- ¾ cup graham cracker crumbs
- 1 Tbsp. sugar plus ⅔ cup sugar, divided
- ¼ tsp. ground cinnamon
- 2½ Tbsp. butter, melted
- 2 pkg. (8 oz. each) cream cheese, softened
- ½ cup sour cream
- 2 to 3 tsp. vanilla extract
- 2 large eggs, room temperature, lightly beaten
- Optional toppings as desired

1. Grease a 6-in. springform pan; place on a double thickness of heavy-duty foil (about 12 in. square). Wrap foil securely around pan.

2. Pour 1 in. water into a 6-qt. slow cooker. Layer two 24-in. pieces of foil. Starting with a long side, roll up foil to make a 1-in.-wide strip; shape into a circle. Place in bottom of slow cooker to make a rack.

3. In a small bowl, mix cracker crumbs, 1 Tbsp. sugar and the cinnamon; stir in butter. Press onto bottom and about 1 in. up sides of the prepared pan.

4. In a large bowl, beat cream cheese and remaining ⅔ cup sugar until smooth. Beat in sour cream and vanilla. Add eggs; beat on low speed just until combined. Pour into crust.

5. Place springform pan on the foil circle without touching slow-cooker sides. Cover slow cooker with a double layer of white paper towels; place lid securely over towels. Cook, covered, on high 2 hours.

6. Do not remove lid; turn off slow cooker and let cheesecake stand, covered, in slow cooker 1 hour.

7. Remove springform pan from slow cooker; remove foil around pan. Cool cheesecake on a wire rack 1 hour longer. Loosen sides from pan with a knife. Refrigerate overnight, covering when completely cooled. If desired, garnish with kiwi and cranberries as shown.

NOTE: *6-in. springform pans are available from Wilton Industries. Call 800-794-5866 or visit wilton.com.*

TO MAKE AHEAD: *Cheesecake may be stored in the refrigerator 4-6 days before serving. Wrap securely before chilling; top just before serving.*

1 PIECE: *565 cal., 41g fat (24g sat. fat), 180mg chol., 351mg sod., 41g carb. (33g sugars, 1g fiber), 10g pro.*

SLOW-COOKER CLAM & VEGETABLE CHOWDER

New England clam chowder has always been one of my favorite soups—I love mine heavy on the vegetables. It's made even better when I can put everything in my slow cooker and forget about it for hours. This is a perfect recipe for feeding a crowd.
—Erica Schmidt, Kansas City, KS

- -

PREP: 25 min. • **COOK:** 4½ hours
MAKES: 16 servings (4 qt.)

- 2 lbs. diced red potatoes
- 1 lb. sliced fresh carrots
- 5 thick-sliced bacon strips, cooked and crumbled
- 2 medium onions, chopped
- 2 celery ribs, chopped
- 2 cans (10 oz. each) whole baby clams
- 6 cups water
- 6 garlic cloves, minced
- 1 Tbsp. Worcestershire sauce
- 1 tsp. beef bouillon granules
- ¾ tsp. each dried thyme, salt and pepper
- 2 cups whole milk
- ¼ cup all-purpose flour

1. In a 5- or 6-qt. slow cooker, combine all ingredients except milk and flour. Cook, covered, on high until potatoes and carrots are tender, about 4 hours.
2. In a small bowl, mix milk and flour until smooth; gradually stir into chowder. Cook, covered, on high until thickened, about 30 minutes.

1 CUP: *127 cal., 3g fat (1g sat. fat), 23mg chol., 527mg sod., 18g carb. (4g sugars, 2g fiber), 8g pro.*
DIABETIC EXCHANGES: *1 starch, 1 lean meat, ½ fat.*

ITALIAN OYSTER CRACKERS

My friends and family love these crackers that are easily made in the slow cooker. They make a perfect topping for thick, creamy soups. I often leave them in the slow cooker and we eat them warm.
—Angela Lively, Conroe, TX

- -

PREP: 10 min. • **COOK:** 1 hour
MAKES: 8 servings

- 2 pkg. (9 oz. each) oyster crackers
- ¼ cup canola oil
- 3 garlic cloves, minced
- 1 envelope Italian salad dressing mix
- 1 tsp. dill weed
- ¼ cup butter, melted
- ½ cup grated Parmesan cheese

1. Combine crackers, oil, garlic, Italian dressing mix and dill weed in a 6-qt. slow cooker. Cook, covered, on low 1 hour.
2. Drizzle melted butter over crackers; sprinkle with cheese. Stir to coat.
3. Transfer mixture to a baking sheet; let stand until cool.

¾ CUP: *407 cal., 20g fat (6g sat. fat), 20mg chol., 1057mg sod., 49g carb. (2g sugars, 2g fiber), 8g pro.*

Holiday Helper
These crackers keep nicely, so you can make them ahead if you like. Store in an airtight container.

SLOW-COOKER CHRISTMAS PUNCH

Indulge in this warm pineapple punch made in the slow cooker. We use cinnamon and Red Hots to give it that cozy spiced flavor and welcome-home aroma.
—Angie Goins, Tazewell, TN

- -

PREP: 5 min. • **COOK:** 3 hours
MAKES: 10 servings

- 4   cups unsweetened pineapple juice
- 4   cups cranberry juice
- ⅓   cup Red Hots
- 2   cinnamon sticks (3 in.)
    Fresh cranberries and additional cinnamon sticks

In a 3- or 4-qt. slow cooker, combine the first 4 ingredients. Cook, covered, on low until heated through and candies are melted, 3-4 hours. Garnish individual servings with cranberries and additional cinnamon sticks.

¾ CUP: 129 cal., 0 fat (0 sat. fat), 0 chol., 4mg sod., 33g carb. (28g sugars, 0 fiber), 1g pro.

CRANBERRIES AS A CENTERPIECE

Looking for a simple centerpiece for your holiday gathering? You can make one with a bag of fresh cranberries, a clear glass cylinder vase and a bouquet of flowers from the grocery store.

Just pour the cranberries into the vase and top them off with enough water to fill about two-thirds of the vessel.

Use a sharp knife to trim the stems of the flowers at an angle. Then add them to the vase, starting with the largest and heaviest blooms and ending with the smallest and lightest.

Then, make changes as needed until you're happy with your arrangement.

BEST EVER ROAST BEEF

This is the best roast beef I've ever had. It's great for family dinners and suitable for company. Cube leftover meat and save any extra sauce to add to fried rice.
—Caroline Flynn, Troy, NY

PREP: 15 min. • **COOK:** 7 hours • **MAKES:** 12 servings

- 1   boneless beef chuck roast (4 lbs.), trimmed
- 1   large sweet onion, chopped
- 1⅓ cups plus 3 Tbsp. water, divided
- 1   can (10½ oz.) condensed French onion soup
- ½   cup packed brown sugar
- ⅓   cup reduced-sodium soy sauce
- ¼   cup cider vinegar
- 6   garlic cloves, minced
- 1   tsp. ground ginger
- ¼   tsp. pepper
- 3   Tbsp. cornstarch

1. Cut roast in half. Transfer to a 5-qt. slow cooker; add onion and 1⅓ cups water. In a small bowl, combine the soup, brown sugar, soy sauce, vinegar, garlic, ginger and pepper; pour over top. Cover and cook on low until meat is tender, 7-8 hours.
2. Remove meat to a serving platter and keep warm. Skim fat from cooking juices; transfer to a small saucepan. Bring liquid to a boil. Combine cornstarch and remaining water until smooth; gradually stir into the pan. Bring to a boil; cook and stir until thickened, 2 minutes. Serve with roast.
4 OZ. COOKED BEEF WITH ¼ CUP GRAVY: 324 cal., 15g fat (6g sat. fat), 99mg chol., 451mg sod., 15g carb. (11g sugars, 1g fiber), 31g pro.

SWEET POTATO & SAUSAGE STUFFING

I love this easy version of a holiday favorite. Slow-cooking the stuffing means that my oven is free for other dishes.
—Kallee Krong-McCreery, Escondido, CA

PREP: 20 min. • **COOK:** 3 hours • **MAKES:** 8 servings

- 8   oz. bulk pork sausage
- 6   cups dry bread cubes
- 2   cups mashed sweet potatoes
- 1   cup chopped onion
- 1   cup chopped celery
- ¼   cup butter, melted
- 2   tsp. poultry seasoning
- 1   tsp. salt
- 1   tsp. dried tarragon
- ½   tsp. pepper

1. In a large skillet, cook sausage over medium heat until no longer pink, 4-6 minutes, breaking into crumbles; drain and set aside. In a large bowl, combine bread, sweet potatoes, onion and celery. Add sausage to mixture, stirring to combine. Stir in butter, poultry seasoning, salt, tarragon and pepper.
2. Transfer to a greased 6-qt. slow cooker. Cook, covered, on low for 3-4 hours or until heated through, stirring once.
¾ CUP: 334 cal., 14g fat (6g sat. fat), 31mg chol., 856mg sod., 47g carb. (8g sugars, 5g fiber), 10g pro.

> ### Holiday Helper
> This recipe can also be baked in a preheated 350° oven. Transfer stuffing mixture to a greased 8x8-in. baking dish and bake until golden brown, 30-40 minutes.

SLOW-COOKED LASAGNA WITH HOMEMADE SAUCE

I got this recipe from a friend who made it using store-bought marinara sauce. I created a homemade sauce for my rendition, and it's been a hit whenever I serve it—especially at potlucks and bring-a-dish gatherings.
—Sheryl Oganowski, Naples, FL

PREP: 2 hours • **COOK:** 4 hours
MAKES: 10 servings

- 1 **lb. ground turkey**
- 1 **lb. bulk Italian sausage**
- ¾ **cup chopped sweet onion**
- 3 **garlic cloves, minced**
- 3 **cans (15 oz. each) tomato sauce**
- 1 **can (28 oz.) crushed tomatoes, undrained**
- 2 **Tbsp. sugar**
- 3 **Tbsp. dried parsley flakes, divided**
- 2 **tsp. dried basil**
- 3 **tsp. dried oregano, divided**
- ½ **tsp. salt, divided**
- ¼ **cup dry red wine or beef broth**
- 3 **cups shredded part-skim mozzarella cheese**
- 2½ **cups ricotta cheese**
- 1 **cup grated Parmesan cheese**
- 1 **large egg, room temperature, lightly beaten**
- 1 **pkg. (9 oz.) no-cook lasagna noodles**

1. In a Dutch oven, cook the turkey, sausage, onion and garlic over medium heat until meat is no longer pink; drain. Stir in the tomato sauce, crushed tomatoes, sugar, 2 Tbsp. parsley, basil, 2 tsp. oregano and ¼ tsp. salt. Bring to a boil. Reduce heat; simmer, uncovered, for 1 hour. Add wine; cook 20 minutes longer.
2. Meanwhile, in a large bowl, combine the cheeses, egg and the remaining 1 Tbsp. parsley, 1 tsp. oregano and ¼ tsp. salt.
3. Spread 2¼ cups meat mixture into a 6-qt. slow cooker. Arrange 5 noodles over sauce, breaking to fit if necessary. Spread 1⅓ cups cheese mixture over noodles. Repeat layers twice. Top with remaining meat mixture.
4. Cook, covered, on low until the noodles are tender, 4-5 hours.
1 PIECE: *577 cal., 30g fat (13g sat. fat), 127mg chol., 1607mg sod., 42g carb. (13g sugars, 5g fiber), 39g pro.*

CHICKEN CASSOULET SOUP

After my sister spent a year in France as an au pair, I created this lighter, easier version of traditional French cassoulet for her. It uses chicken instead of the usual duck.
—Bridget Klusman, Otsego, MI

PREP: 35 min. • **COOK:** 6 hours
MAKES: 7 servings (about 2¾ qt.)

- ½ **lb. bulk pork sausage**
- 5 **cups water**
- ½ **lb. cubed cooked chicken**
- 1 **can (16 oz.) kidney beans, rinsed and drained**
- 1 **can (15 oz.) black beans, rinsed and drained**
- 1 **can (15 oz.) garbanzo beans or chickpeas, rinsed and drained**
- 2 **medium carrots, shredded**
- 1 **medium onion, chopped**
- ¼ **cup dry vermouth or chicken broth**
- 5 **tsp. chicken bouillon granules**
- 4 **garlic cloves, minced**
- 1½ **tsp. minced fresh thyme or ½ tsp. dried thyme**
- ¼ **tsp. fennel seed, crushed**
- 1 **tsp. dried lavender flowers, optional**
- ½ **lb. bacon strips, cooked and crumbled**
  Additional fresh thyme, optional

1. In a large skillet, cook sausage over medium heat until no longer pink; drain.
2. Transfer sausage to a 4- or 5-qt. slow cooker. Add the water, chicken, beans, carrots, onion, vermouth, bouillon, garlic, thyme, fennel and, if desired, lavender. Cover and cook on low for 6-8 hours or until heated through.
3. Divide among bowls; sprinkle with bacon. If desired, top individual servings with additional fresh thyme.
NOTE: *Look for dried lavender flowers in spice shops. If using lavender from the garden, make sure it hasn't been treated with chemicals.*
1½ CUPS: *494 cal., 23g fat (7g sat. fat), 77mg chol., 1821mg sod., 34g carb. (6g sugars, 9g fiber), 34g pro.*

STUFFED TURKEY WITH MOJO SAUCE

I love Latin food so I created this recipe that combines wonderful spices and fresh ingredients. This is a traditional turkey recipe with a healthier twist because it uses chicken sausage instead of chorizo.
—Melissa Lauer, San Antonio, TX

- -

PREP: 45 min. • **COOK:** 5 hours + standing
MAKES: 8 servings (about 1 cup sauce)

1	medium green pepper, finely chopped
1	medium onion, finely chopped
2	garlic cloves, minced
2	tsp. ground coriander
1	tsp. ground cumin
⅛	tsp. cayenne pepper
1	lb. uncooked chicken sausage links, casings removed
1	fresh boneless turkey breast (4 lbs.)
¼	tsp. salt
¼	tsp. pepper

MOJO SAUCE

1	cup orange juice
½	cup fresh cilantro leaves
¼	cup minced fresh oregano or 4 tsp. dried oregano
¼	cup lime juice
4	garlic cloves, minced
1	tsp. ground cumin
½	tsp. pepper
¼	tsp. salt
⅛	tsp. cayenne pepper
1	cup olive oil

1. In a bowl, combine the first 6 ingredients. Crumble sausage over mixture and mix lightly but thoroughly.
2. With skin side down, pound turkey breast with a meat mallet to ½-in. thickness. Sprinkle with salt and pepper. Spread sausage mixture over turkey to within 1 in. of edges. Roll up jelly-roll style, starting with a short side; tie at 1½- to 2-in. intervals with kitchen string.
3. In a large skillet, brown turkey on all sides. Place in a 5-qt. oval slow cooker.
4. In a blender, combine the first 9 sauce ingredients; cover and process until blended. While processing, gradually add oil in a steady stream. Pour over turkey.
5. Cook, covered, on low for 5 hours or until a thermometer inserted in center reads 165°. Remove from slow cooker; cover and let stand for 10 minutes before slicing. Discard string.
6. Meanwhile, skim fat from cooking juices; transfer juices to a small saucepan. Bring to a boil; cook until liquid is reduced by half. Serve with turkey.

1 PIECE WITH 2 TBSP. SAUCE: *719 cal., 46g fat (9g sat. fat), 174mg chol., 515mg sod., 7g carb. (4g sugars, 1g fiber), 66g pro.*
BAKE OPTION: *Place turkey roll in a 13x9-in. baking dish. Pour sauce over top. Bake, uncovered, at 400° for 70-80 minutes or until a thermometer inserted in center reads 165°. (Cover with foil during the last 20 minutes if turkey browns too quickly.) Remove from oven; cover and let stand for 10 minutes before slicing. Discard string. Skim fat from juices; serve with turkey.*

SPICY STUFFED BANANA PEPPERS

Banana peppers can be tricky: Sometimes they are hot and sometimes they are not. If you want to be on the safe side, I suggest using Bianca peppers, a sweeter type of pepper, instead.
—*Danielle Lee, West Palm Beach, FL*

PREP: 45 min. • **COOK:** 3½ hours
MAKES: 4 servings

- 6 Tbsp. water
- 3 Tbsp. uncooked red or white quinoa, rinsed
- ½ lb. bulk spicy Italian sausage
- ½ lb. lean ground beef (90% lean)
- ½ cup tomato sauce
- 2 green onions, chopped
- 2 garlic cloves, minced
- 1½ tsp. Sriracha chili sauce
- ½ tsp. chili powder
- ¼ tsp. salt
- ⅛ tsp. pepper
- 16 mild banana peppers
- 2 cups reduced-sodium spicy V8 juice

1. In a small saucepan, bring water to a boil. Add quinoa. Reduce heat; simmer, covered, until the liquid is absorbed, 12-15 minutes. Remove from heat; fluff with a fork.
2. In a large bowl, combine sausage, beef, tomato sauce, green onions, garlic, chili sauce, chili powder, salt, pepper and cooked quinoa. Cut and discard tops from peppers; remove seeds. Fill peppers with the meat mixture.
3. Stand peppers upright in a 4-qt. slow cooker. Pour V8 juice over top. Cook, covered, on low until peppers are tender, 3½-4½ hours.
4 STUFFED PEPPERS: *412 cal., 22g fat (7g sat. fat), 74mg chol., 965mg sod., 29g carb. (11g sugars, 13g fiber), 26g pro.*

Holiday Helper
If you have trouble locating banana peppers, try Bianca peppers or regular bell peppers instead.

SLOW-COOKER CRAB & GREEN ONION DIP

This creamy dip reminds me of my dad, who took us crabbing as kids. Our fingers were tired after those excursions, but eating the fresh crab was always worth it.
—*Nancy Zimmerman, Cape May Court House, NJ*

PREP: 10 min. • **COOK:** 3 hours
MAKES: 16 servings (4 cups)

- 3 pkg. (8 oz. each) cream cheese, cubed
- 2 cans (6 oz. each) lump crabmeat, drained
- 4 green onions, chopped
- ¼ cup 2% milk
- 2 tsp. prepared horseradish
- 2 tsp. Worcestershire sauce
- ¼ tsp. salt
  Baked pita chips and assorted fresh vegetables

In a greased 3-qt. slow cooker, combine the first 7 ingredients. Cook, covered, on low for 3-4 hours or until heated through, stirring occasionally. Serve with chips or fresh vegetables.
¼ CUP: *167 cal., 15g fat (8g sat. fat), 68mg chol., 324mg sod., 2g carb. (2g sugars, 0 fiber), 7g pro.*

HOLIDAY FEASTS

When your loved ones take their seats at the holiday table, serve them a meal that will make the occasion memorable. From a traditional goose to a full vegetarian spread, these specially designed menus give you plenty to choose from.

Filet Mignon Feast

SPICE-CRUSTED STEAKS WITH CHERRY SAUCE

If you're hosting meat lovers, these impressive cast-iron skillet steaks are guaranteed to please. They're perfect for a special-occasion dinner without too much fuss.
—Taste of Home *Test Kitchen*

- -

PREP: 20 min. + chilling • **COOK:** 45 min. • **MAKES:** 4 servings

- ½ cup dried cherries
- ¼ cup port wine, warmed
- 3½ tsp. coarsely ground pepper
- 1 tsp. brown sugar
- ¾ tsp. garlic powder
- ¾ tsp. paprika
- ¾ tsp. ground coffee
- ½ tsp. kosher salt
- ¼ tsp. ground cinnamon
- ¼ tsp. ground cumin
- ⅛ tsp. ground mustard
- 4 beef tenderloin steaks (1¼ in. thick and 6 oz. each)
- 1 Tbsp. canola oil
- 1 large shallot, finely chopped
- 1 Tbsp. butter
- 1 cup reduced-sodium beef broth
- 1 tsp. minced fresh thyme
- ½ cup heavy whipping cream
     Crumbled blue cheese, optional

1. Preheat oven to 350°. In a small bowl, combine cherries and wine; set aside. In a shallow dish, combine the pepper, brown sugar, garlic powder, paprika, coffee, salt, cinnamon, cumin and mustard. Add 1 steak at a time and turn to coat. Cover and refrigerate for 30 minutes.

2. Place oil in a 10-in. cast-iron or other ovenproof skillet; tilt to coat bottom. Heat oil over medium-high heat; sear steaks, 2 minutes on each side. Bake, uncovered, until meat reaches desired doneness (for medium-rare, a thermometer should read 135°; medium, 140°; medium-well, 145°), about 15 minutes. Remove steaks and keep warm.

3. Wipe skillet clean; saute shallot in butter until crisp-tender. Add broth and thyme. Bring to a boil; cook until liquid is reduced by half, about 8 minutes. Stir in cream; bring to a boil. Cook until thickened, stirring occasionally, about 8 minutes.

4. Stir in the reserved cherry mixture. Serve sauce over steaks. If desired, sprinkle with blue cheese.

1 STEAK WITH 3 TBSP. SAUCE: *506 cal., 28g fat (13g sat. fat), 124mg chol., 381mg sod., 20g carb. (13g sugars, 1g fiber), 39g pro.*

Holiday Helper

Because the serving size is a steak per person, this recipe is very easy to scale up or down. You can bake them all at the same time, or in batches to different levels of doneness to suit your guests' individual tastes.

GREEN BEAN BUNDLES

I found this recipe in a rural newspaper years ago and have made it often. The bean bundles are excellent with chicken or beef. Sometimes I'll arrange them around a mound of wild rice to make an appetizing side dish.
— *Virginia Stadler, Nokesville, VA*

- -

TAKES: 25 min. • **MAKES:** 8 servings

- 1 lb. fresh green beans, trimmed
- 8 bacon strips, partially cooked
- 1 Tbsp. finely chopped onion
- 3 Tbsp. butter
- 1 Tbsp. white wine vinegar
- 1 Tbsp. sugar
- ¼ tsp. salt

1. Cook the beans until crisp-tender. Wrap about 10 beans in each bacon strip; secure with a toothpick. Place on a foil-covered baking sheet. Bake at 400° until bacon is done, 10-15 minutes.

2. In a skillet, saute onion in butter until tender. Add vinegar, sugar and salt; heat through. Remove bundles to a serving bowl or platter; pour sauce over and serve immediately.

1 BUNDLE: *186 cal., 17g fat (7g sat. fat), 27mg chol., 286mg sod., 5g carb. (3g sugars, 2g fiber), 3g pro.*

ROSEMARY ROASTED SWEET POTATOES

We love sweet potatoes, and these are simply the best we've ever made. This is our go-to recipe time and again. Roasting them brings out all of the wonderful sweetness!
—*Kristin Stone, Little Elm, TX*

PREP: 10 min. • **BAKE:** 30 min. • **MAKES:** 4 servings

2   large sweet potatoes, peeled and cut into ¾-in. rounds
1   Tbsp. olive oil
1   tsp. dried rosemary, crushed
½   tsp. salt
½   tsp. chili powder
½   tsp. pepper
⅛   tsp. cayenne pepper

Preheat oven to 425°. Place all ingredients in a large bowl; toss to coat. Line a 15x10x1-in. baking pan with foil; grease foil. Place sweet potatoes in a single layer in prepared pan. Bake, covered, for 20 minutes. Uncover and bake until golden brown, 10-12 minutes longer, turning once.
1 SERVING: *209 cal., 4g fat (1g sat. fat), 0 chol., 322mg sod., 42g carb. (17g sugars, 5g fiber), 3g pro.*

BLUE CHEESE WALNUT TART

This simple yet elegant tart gives any get-together a touch of class. It can be served as a light lunch entree but also makes a distinctive and delicious appetizer. The unbaked tart keeps in the freezer for up to three months, so it's a great make-ahead option. Just remove from the freezer 30 minutes before baking, and add about 15 minutes to the baking time.
—*Erin Chilcoat, Central Islip, NY*

PREP: 30 min. + cooling • **BAKE:** 15 min. • **MAKES:** 12 servings

1   sheet refrigerated pie crust
1   pkg. (8 oz.) cream cheese, softened
⅓   cup crumbled blue cheese
1   garlic clove, minced
¼   cup heavy whipping cream
1   large egg
¼   tsp. cayenne pepper
¼   tsp. coarsely ground pepper
⅓   cup chopped roasted sweet red peppers
3   Tbsp. chopped walnuts, toasted
2   Tbsp. minced fresh parsley

1. Press crust onto the bottom and up the side of an ungreased 9-in. fluted tart pan with removable bottom; trim edge. Bake at 425° for 8-10 minutes or until lightly browned. Cool completely on a wire rack.
2. In a large bowl, beat cream cheese, blue cheese and garlic until blended. Add cream, egg, cayenne and pepper; beat well. Spread mixture into crust. Sprinkle with red peppers, walnuts and parsley. Bake, uncovered, at 375° for 15-20 minutes or until the center is set.
1 PIECE: *197 cal., 16g fat (8g sat. fat), 51mg chol., 208mg sod., 10g carb. (1g sugars, 0 fiber), 4g pro.*

TIE IT WITH TWINE

For a quick and easy way to add a special touch to holiday place settings, tie napkins and utensils into pretty bundles with traditional baker's twine—which comes in a perfectly appropriate peppermint-stripe pattern.

GARLIC & OREGANO BREAD

Bakery bread is tempting when you're planning a feast, but this overnight loaf is so easy and special! Just stir up the dough. No kneading. No sweating.
—Megumi Garcia, Milwaukee, WI

- -

PREP: 30 min. + rising • **BAKE:** 50 min.
MAKES: 1 loaf (16 pieces)

- 1½ tsp. active dry yeast
- 1¾ cups water (70° to 75°)
- 3½ cups plus 1 Tbsp. all-purpose flour, divided
- 2 tsp. salt
- 1 Tbsp. cornmeal or additional flour
- ½ cup garlic cloves, peeled and quartered
- ¼ cup 2% milk
- 2 Tbsp. minced fresh oregano

1. In a small bowl, dissolve yeast in water. In a large bowl, mix 3½ cups flour and the salt. Using a rubber spatula, stir in the yeast mixture to form a soft, sticky dough. Do not knead. Cover and let rise at room temperature for 1 hour.

2. Punch down dough. Turn onto a lightly floured surface. Pat into a 9-in. square. Fold dough into thirds, forming a 9x3-in. rectangle. Fold rectangle into thirds, forming a 3-in. square. Turn dough over; place in a greased bowl. Cover; let rise at room temperature until almost doubled, about 1 hour.

3. Punch down dough and repeat the folding process. Return dough to bowl; refrigerate, covered, overnight.

4. Dust bottom of a disposable foil roasting pan with cornmeal. In a small microwave-safe bowl, combine garlic and milk; microwave on high for 45 seconds.

Drain garlic, discarding milk. Turn dough onto a floured surface; knead in the garlic and oregano. Shape dough into a 6-in. round loaf.

5. Transfer loaf to prepared pan; dust top with remaining 1 Tbsp. flour. Cover pan; let dough rise at room temperature until it expands to a 7½-in. loaf, about 1¼ hours.

6. Preheat oven to 500°. Using a sharp knife, make a slash (¼ in. deep) across top of loaf. Cover pan tightly with foil. Bake on lowest oven rack for 25 minutes.

7. Reduce oven setting to 450°. Remove foil; bake 25-30 minutes longer or until deep golden brown. Remove loaf to a wire rack to cool.

1 PIECE: 112 cal., 0 fat (0 sat. fat), 0 chol., 297mg sod., 23g carb. (0 sugars, 1g fiber), 3g pro.
DIABETIC EXCHANGES: 1½ starch.

ROASTED BALSAMIC BRUSSELS SPROUTS WITH PANCETTA

I always loved Brussels sprouts growing up, so I decided as an adult to bring them home to our family table. I've been making them ever since. This dressed-up version is perfect for a special occasion!
—*Brenda Washnock, Negaunee, MI*

PREP: 15 min. • **BAKE:** 30 min. • **MAKES:** 6 servings

- 2 lbs. fresh Brussels sprouts, trimmed and halved
- 3 Tbsp. olive oil, divided
- ½ tsp. salt
- ¼ tsp. pepper
- 2 oz. sliced pancetta or bacon strips, chopped
- 2 garlic cloves, minced
- 1 Tbsp. balsamic vinegar
- ⅓ cup dried cranberries
- ½ cup pine nuts, toasted

1. Preheat oven to 400°. Place Brussels sprouts in a 15x10x1-in. baking pan; toss with 2 Tbsp. oil, salt and pepper. Roast until lightly charred and tender, 30-35 minutes, stirring halfway.
2. Meanwhile, in a large skillet, heat the remaining 1 Tbsp. oil over medium-high heat. Add pancetta; cook and stir 4-6 minutes or until crisp. Add garlic; cook 1 minute longer. Remove from heat; stir in vinegar.
3. In a large bowl, combine Brussels sprouts, cranberries and pancetta mixture; toss to combine. Sprinkle with pine nuts.
NOTE: *To toast nuts, bake in a shallow pan in a 350° oven for 5-10 minutes or cook in a skillet over low heat until lightly browned, stirring occasionally.*
¾ **CUP:** *253 cal., 18g fat (3g sat. fat), 8mg chol., 407mg sod., 20g carb. (8g sugars, 6g fiber), 8g pro.*

MAPLE-APPLE CLAFOUTI

This fruit pudding could not be easier to make. A traditional comfort food in France, it is often made with cherries. I use apples and maple syrup to give it a midwestern flair.
—*Bridget Klusman, Otsego, MI*

PREP: 20 min. • **BAKE:** 40 min. • **MAKES:** 8 servings

- 4 medium tart apples, thinly sliced
- 2 Tbsp. lemon juice
- 4 large eggs
- 1¼ cups 2% milk
- ½ cup maple syrup
- 1 tsp. vanilla extract
- ½ cup all-purpose flour
- ½ tsp. ground cinnamon
  Dash salt
  Additional maple syrup, optional

1. Preheat oven to 375°. Toss apples with lemon juice; place in a greased 2-qt. baking dish. In a large bowl, whisk eggs, milk, syrup and vanilla until combined. In another bowl, combine flour, cinnamon and salt; add to egg mixture. Pour batter over apples.
2. Bake until puffed and lightly browned, 40-50 minutes. Serve warm, or cool on a wire rack. If desired, serve with additional maple syrup.
1 PIECE: *177 cal., 3g fat (1g sat. fat), 96mg chol., 75mg sod., 32g carb. (22g sugars, 2g fiber), 5g pro.*
DIABETIC EXCHANGES: *1½ starch, ½ fruit, ½ fat.*

Holiday Helper

Hot out of the oven, this is a showstopper, all puffed up and golden brown. As it sits, it will deflate a bit. So if you're looking to impress, take it from the oven right to the table.

Vegetarian Feast

VEGAN SQUASH SOUP WITH NAAN CROUTONS

This butternut squash soup is creamy and full of flavor—you won't miss the meat or dairy! The added can of pumpkin helps to make the soup creamy and smooth, while the coconut milk adds a light sweetness.
—Audrey Fell, Nashville, TN

PREP: 45 min. • **COOK:** 25 min. • **MAKES:** 8 servings (about 2¾ qt.)

1 large butternut squash, peeled and cut into 1-in. cubes (about 8 cups)
3 Tbsp. olive oil, divided
1 tsp. salt, divided
¼ tsp. pepper
1 medium onion, chopped
1 Tbsp. minced fresh gingerroot
2 garlic cloves, minced
1 tsp. ground turmeric
½ tsp. ground cumin
1 carton (32 oz.) reduced-sodium vegetable broth
1 can (15 oz.) pumpkin
1 can (13.66 oz.) coconut milk
2 naan flatbreads, cut into 1-in. squares
Optional: Minced fresh cilantro, crushed red pepper flakes and plain soy yogurt

1. Preheat oven to 400°. Place squash in a shallow roasting pan; drizzle with 1 Tbsp. oil. Sprinkle with ½ tsp. salt and the pepper. Roast until tender, 25-30 minutes, turning once. Reduce oven setting to 350°.
2. In a Dutch oven, heat 1 Tbsp. oil over medium-high heat. Add onion; cook and stir until tender, 5-7 minutes. Add ginger, garlic, turmeric, cumin and remaining ½ tsp. salt; cook 1 minute longer. Stir in broth, pumpkin and roasted squash. Bring to a boil; reduce heat. Simmer, uncovered, 15-20 minutes to allow flavors to blend. Add coconut milk; cook 5 minutes longer. Cool slightly. In a blender, cover and process soup in batches until smooth. Return pureed mixture to pan; cook and stir until heated through.
3. Meanwhile, place naan on a baking sheet. Drizzle with the remaining 1 Tbsp. oil; toss to coat. Bake at 350° until crispy, 12-15 minutes, stirring once. Serve soup with naan croutons and toppings of your choice.
1⅓ CUPS: 249 cal., 14g fat (9g sat. fat), 1mg chol., 506mg sod., 29g carb. (8g sugars, 7g fiber), 4g pro.

> ### Holiday Helper
> Don't have coconut milk on hand? Try using half-and-half cream as a substitute.

CILANTRO LIME WHITE BEAN SALAD

Enjoy a little taste of summer in the middle of winter with this healthy, cool salad for lunch! I buy the bulgur from the bulk section so I have just the right amount for this meal.
—Renee Hagens, Pittsburgh, PA

PREP: 15 min. + standing • **MAKES:** 6 servings

¾ cup bulgur
1½ cups boiling water
1 can (15 oz.) cannellini beans, rinsed and drained
1 plum tomato, seeded & chopped
⅓ cup finely chopped red onion
⅓ cup roasted sweet red peppers, drained and chopped
¼ cup minced fresh cilantro
¼ cup lime juice
¼ cup olive oil
½ tsp. salt
¼ tsp. pepper
1 medium ripe avocado, peeled & chopped

1. Place bulgur in a large bowl; stir in boiling water. Let stand, covered, until bulgur is tender and most of the liquid is absorbed, about 30 minutes. Drain well, pressing out excess water. Let it cool completely.
2. Add beans, tomato, onion, peppers and cilantro; gently toss to combine. In a small bowl, whisk lime juice, oil, salt and pepper. Drizzle over bulgur mixture; gently toss to coat. Refrigerate. Top with avocado just before serving.
⅔ CUP: 245 cal., 13g fat (2g sat. fat), 0 chol., 341mg sod., 28g carb. (1g sugars, 7g fiber), 6g pro.

MUSHROOM & LEEK STRUDEL

This elegant dish is almost effortless and can be used as an appetizer or a main course—just up the serving size. Use fresh herbs if possible, and feel free to sub in whole wheat phyllo.
—Lisa Diehl, Edina, MN

- -

PREP: 50 min. + cooling
BAKE: 20 min. + standing
MAKES: 2 strudels (12 pieces each)

- 2 Tbsp. butter, divided
- 2 lbs. fresh mushrooms, finely chopped, divided
- 1 medium leek (white portion only), chopped, divided
- 2 garlic cloves, minced
- ¼ cup white wine
- ¼ cup heavy whipping cream
- 2 Tbsp. minced fresh parsley
- 1 Tbsp. minced fresh thyme or 1 tsp. dried thyme
- ½ tsp. salt
- ¼ tsp. pepper

ASSEMBLY

- 12 sheets phyllo dough (14x9 in.)
- ¾ cup butter, melted
- 4 Tbsp. grated Parmesan cheese, divided

1. In a large skillet, heat 1 Tbsp. butter over medium-high heat. Add half the mushrooms and half the leek. Cook and stir until mushrooms are lightly browned and leek is tender; remove from pan. Repeat with remaining butter, mushrooms and leek, adding garlic during the last minute of cooking. Return all to pan.
2. Stir in the wine and cream; cook for 1-2 minutes or until the liquid is almost evaporated. Stir in herbs, salt and pepper. Remove from pan; cool completely.
3. Preheat oven to 375°. Place 1 sheet of phyllo dough on a work surface; brush with butter. Layer with 5 additional phyllo sheets, brushing each layer. (Keep remaining phyllo covered with a damp towel to prevent it from drying out.)
4. Spoon half the mushroom mixture down the center third of phyllo dough to within 1 in. of ends. Sprinkle filling with 2 Tbsp. cheese. Fold up short sides to enclose filling. Roll up jelly-roll style, starting with a long side.
5. Transfer roll to a parchment-lined 15x10x1-in. baking pan, seam side down. Brush with butter. Repeat with remaining ingredients to make a second strudel. Bake 18-22 minutes or until golden brown.
6. Let stand 10 minutes before slicing. Serve warm.
1 PIECE: *100 cal., 8g fat (5g sat. fat), 22mg chol., 135mg sod., 6g carb. (1g sugars, 1g fiber), 2g pro.*

BLOOD ORANGE AVOCADO SALAD

My refreshing side salad is such a nice addition to our holiday dinner. The citrus keeps the avocado from turning brown while the salad is chilling, making it perfect to prepare as part of a multicourse dinner.
—Nancy Heishman, Las Vegas, NV

- -

PREP: 30 min. + chilling • **MAKES:** 10 servings

- ⅓ cup orange juice
- ⅓ cup extra virgin olive oil
- 3 Tbsp. lime juice
- 2 Tbsp. honey
- 1 Tbsp. minced Italian parsley
- ¼ tsp. ground cardamom
- ¼ tsp. kosher salt
- ¼ tsp. coarsely ground pepper
- 4 medium ripe avocados, peeled and sliced
- 4 large red grapefruit, sectioned
- 2 medium blood oranges, peeled and sliced
- ½ cup finely chopped red onion
- ⅓ cup pomegranate seeds
- ⅓ cup crumbled feta cheese

For dressing, whisk together the first 8 ingredients. In a serving dish, combine avocados, grapefruit and oranges; sprinkle with onion and pomegranate seeds. Drizzle with dressing. Top with cheese. Refrigerate, covered, 1 hour before serving.

1 CUP: *241 cal., 16g fat (3g sat. fat), 2mg chol., 89mg sod., 24g carb. (17g sugars, 6g fiber), 3g pro.*
DIABETIC EXCHANGES: *3 fat, 1 fruit, ½ starch.*

Holiday Helper
This recipe is extremely versatile. Use regular oranges if you can't find blood oranges, and skip the cardamom if you don't have it on hand. In place of pomegranates, try dried cranberries or finely chopped walnuts.

APPLE QUINOA SPOON BREAD

My cousin is a strict vegetarian, so creating satisfying veggie dishes is my yearly challenge. This spoon bread stands as an amazing holiday side, but the addition of hearty, healthy quinoa and vegetables can also make it a well-rounded casserole.
—Christine Wendland, Browns Mills, NJ

- -

PREP: 25 min. • **BAKE:** 25 min.
MAKES: 9 servings

- ⅔ cup water
- ⅓ cup quinoa, rinsed
- 1 Tbsp. canola oil
- 1 small apple, peeled and diced
- 1 small onion, finely chopped
- 1 small parsnip, peeled and diced
- ½ tsp. celery seed
- 1¼ tsp. salt, divided
- 1 Tbsp. minced fresh sage
- ¾ cup yellow cornmeal
- ¼ cup all-purpose flour
- 1 Tbsp. sugar
- 1 tsp. baking powder
- 1 large egg, room temperature
- 1½ cups 2% milk, divided

1. Preheat oven to 375°. In a small saucepan, bring water to a boil. Add quinoa. Reduce heat; simmer, covered, until liquid is absorbed, 12-15 minutes. Fluff with a fork; cool slightly.
2. Meanwhile, in a large skillet, heat oil over medium heat; saute apple, onion and parsnip with celery seed and ½ tsp. salt until softened, 4-5 minutes. Remove from heat; stir in sage.
3. Whisk together cornmeal, flour, sugar, baking powder and remaining ¾ tsp. salt. In a second bowl, whisk together egg and 1 cup milk. Add to the cornmeal mixture, stirring just until moistened. Fold in the quinoa and the apple mixture.
4. Transfer to a greased 8-in. square baking dish. Pour remaining ½ cup milk over top. Bake, uncovered, until the edges are golden brown, 25-30 minutes. Let stand 5 minutes before serving. If desired, sprinkle with additional minced sage.

1 SERVING: *153 cal., 4g fat (1g sat. fat), 24mg chol., 412mg sod., 26g carb. (6g sugars, 2g fiber), 5g pro.*
DIABETIC EXCHANGES: *1½ starch, 1 fat.*

HOLIDAY SWEET POTATO CHEESECAKE

Family and friends can't seem to get enough of this deliciously different cheesecake that combines my two favorite desserts— sweet potato pie and cheesecake. I think the dessert tastes best if made 24 to 48 hours prior to serving.
—Melanie Bauder, Manlius, NY

PREP: 40 min. • **BAKE:** 55 min. + chilling • **MAKES:** 12 servings

- 1¾ cups graham cracker crumbs
- ⅓ cup butter, melted
- ¼ cup sugar

CHEESECAKE FILLING

- 2 pkg. (8 oz. each) cream cheese, softened
- ½ cup sugar
- 1 tsp. vanilla extract
- 2 large eggs, room temperature, lightly beaten

SWEET POTATO FILLING

- 1 cup mashed sweet potatoes (about ¾ lb.)
- ½ cup sugar
- ½ cup evaporated milk
- ¼ cup butter, melted
- 1 large egg
- ½ tsp. vanilla extract
- ⅛ tsp. each ground cinnamon, cloves and nutmeg
- ⅛ tsp. salt

TOPPING

- ¾ cup sour cream
- 3 Tbsp. sugar
- 1½ tsp. vanilla extract
  Glazed chopped pecans, optional

1. Preheat oven to 325°. Place a greased 9-in. springform pan on a double thickness of heavy-duty foil (about 18 in. square). Securely wrap foil around pan. In a small bowl, combine the cracker crumbs, butter and sugar. Press onto the bottom and 1½ in. up the side of prepared pan. Place pan on a baking sheet. Bake for 10 minutes. Cool on a wire rack.
2. For cheesecake filling, beat cream cheese and sugar until smooth. Beat in vanilla. Add eggs; beat on low speed just until combined. Pour into crust.
3. For sweet potato filling, combine sweet potatoes with sugar, evaporated milk, butter, egg, vanilla, spices and salt. Spoon over the cheesecake batter. Place springform pan in a large baking pan; add 1 in. hot water to larger pan. Bake until center is just set and top appears dull, 50-55 minutes.
4. For topping, combine the sour cream, sugar and vanilla. Spread over cheesecake. Bake just until set, 5-10 minutes longer. Remove springform pan from water bath. Cool on a wire rack for 10 minutes.
5. Carefully run a knife around the edge of the pan to loosen; cool 1 hour longer. Refrigerate overnight. Remove side of pan. Sprinkle cheesecake with pecans if desired.
1 PIECE: *489 cal., 31g fat (17g sat. fat), 131mg chol., 350mg sod., 45g carb. (34g sugars, 1g fiber), 7g pro.*

CARROT PUREE

The flavor of carrots pairs beautifully with anything from roasted meat to grilled fish; this puree takes them to an elegant new level. Cook the carrots fully to ensure a velvety-smooth puree.
—Gina Myers, Spokane, WA

PREP: 20 min. • **COOK:** 40 min. • **MAKES:** 4 servings

- 2 Tbsp. olive oil
- 2 lbs. carrots, peeled and chopped
- 2 shallots, chopped
- 4 garlic cloves, minced
- 1 tsp. fresh thyme leaves
- ½ tsp. salt
- ¼ tsp. pepper
  Optional: Additional olive oil and thyme leaves

1. In a Dutch oven, heat oil over medium heat. Add carrots and shallots; cook and stir until carrots are crisp-tender, 12-15 minutes. Stir in garlic and thyme; cook 1 minute longer.
2. Add water to cover carrots; bring to a boil. Reduce heat; simmer, uncovered, for 20-25 minutes or until the carrots are very tender.
3. Drain; cool slightly. Place carrot mixture, salt and pepper in a food processor; process until smooth. If desired, garnish with additional olive oil and thyme leaves.
⅔ CUP: *172 cal., 7g fat (1g sat. fat), 0 chol., 455mg sod., 26g carb. (11g sugars, 7g fiber), 3g pro.*

Goose Feast

ROAST CHRISTMAS GOOSE

I have such fond childhood memories of my mother serving this golden brown Christmas goose. To flavor the meat, Mom stuffed the bird with peeled and quartered fruit that she discarded after baking.
—Rosemarie Forcum, Heathsville, VA

- -

PREP: 10 min. • **BAKE:** 2¼ hours + standing
MAKES: 8 servings

1	domestic goose (10 to 12 lbs.)
	Salt and pepper
1	medium apple, peeled and quartered
1	medium navel orange, peeled and quartered
1	medium lemon, peeled and quartered
1	cup hot water

1. Preheat oven to 350°. Sprinkle the goose cavity with salt and pepper. Place the apple, orange and lemon in the cavity. Place goose breast side up on a rack in a large shallow roasting pan. Prick skin well with a fork. Pour water into pan.
2. Bake, uncovered, for 2¼-3 hours or until a thermometer reads 180°. If necessary, drain fat from pan as it accumulates. Cover goose with foil and let stand for 20 minutes before carving. Discard fruit.

4 OZ. COOKED GOOSE: 376 cal., 26g fat (8g sat. fat), 108mg chol., 84mg sod., 4g carb. (3g sugars, 1g fiber), 30g pro.

Holiday Helper

A goose gives up a lot of fat while it cooks, so don't forget to prick the skin to allow that fat to escape. Use a fork (as directed above), the tip of a sharp knife or even a clean needle to make sure you penetrate the skin but not the flesh. As the fat renders, it will rise to the top of the water in the pan; skim it off and keep it. Goose fat is rich and delicious—it's great for roasting vegetables. In many cases, it can even stand in for butter!

FROZEN GRAND MARNIER SOUFFLES

This delicious no-bake frozen souffle is perfect as a light, sweet finish to a heavy dinner and will impress just about everyone. It's a fantastic make-ahead dessert!
—Andrea Potischman, Menlo Park, CA

- -

PREP: 30 min. + freezing • **MAKES:** 8 servings

6	large egg yolks
½	cup sugar
¼	cup orange liqueur
2	Tbsp. water
2	tsp. orange juice
1	tsp. grated orange zest
1½	cups heavy whipping cream
1	Tbsp. confectioners' sugar
	Additional grated orange zest

1. In the top of a double boiler or in a metal bowl over simmering water, whisk egg yolks and sugar until blended. Stir in liqueur, water, orange juice and zest. Cook over low heat until mixture is just thick enough to coat a metal spoon and a thermometer reads at least 160°, about 10 minutes, stirring constantly but gently. Do not allow to boil. Immediately transfer to a bowl.
2. Place bowl in an ice-water bath for a few minutes, stirring custard occasionally. Cool to room temperature. In a large bowl, beat cream until it begins to thicken. Add confectioners' sugar; beat until stiff peaks form. Gently fold into cooled custard mixture.
3. Transfer to eight 4-oz. ramekins; smooth tops. Freeze until firm, at least 4 hours or overnight. Garnish with additional orange zest.

1 SOUFFLE: 258 cal., 20g fat (12g sat. fat), 189mg chol., 18mg sod., 17g carb. (16g sugars, 0 fiber), 3g pro.

GERMAN POTATO DUMPLINGS

Potato dumplings (called Kartoffel Kloesse in Germany) are a delightful addition to any feast. The browned butter sauce is delectable.
—*Arline Hofland, Deer Lodge, MT*

PREP: 40 min. • **COOK:** 10 min. • **MAKES:** 8 servings

- 3 lbs. medium potatoes (about 10), peeled and quartered
- 1 cup all-purpose flour
- 3 large eggs, lightly beaten
- ⅔ cup dry bread crumbs
- 1 tsp. salt
- ½ tsp. ground nutmeg
- 12 cups water

BROWNED BUTTER SAUCE
- ½ cup butter, cubed
- 1 Tbsp. chopped onion
- ¼ cup dry bread crumbs

1. Place potatoes in a Dutch oven; add water to cover. Bring to a boil. Reduce heat; cook, uncovered, 15-20 minutes or until tender. Drain; transfer to a large bowl.
2. Mash potatoes. Stir in flour, eggs, bread crumbs, salt and nutmeg. Shape into sixteen 2-in. balls.
3. In a Dutch oven, bring 12 cups water to a boil. Carefully add dumplings. Reduce heat; simmer, uncovered, 7-9 minutes or until a toothpick inserted in center of dumplings comes out clean.
4. Meanwhile, in a small heavy saucepan, heat butter and onion over medium heat. Heat 5-7 minutes or until butter is golden brown, stirring constantly. Remove from heat; stir in bread crumbs. Serve with dumplings.
2 DUMPLINGS WITH 2 TBSP. SAUCE: *367 cal., 14g fat (8g sat. fat), 100mg chol., 524mg sod., 51g carb. (2g sugars, 5g fiber), 9g pro.*

PRESSURE-COOKER CINNAMON APPLESAUCE

Homemade applesauce is a breeze in the Instant Pot. A few minutes of prep and a short cook time will put this cinnamon applesauce on the table very quickly!
—*Ally Billhorn, Wilton, IA*

PREP: 20 min. • **COOK:** 5 min. • **MAKES:** 12 servings (8 cups)

- 5 lbs. apples (about 15 medium), peeled and chopped
- 1 cup water
- ⅓ cup sugar
- 2 tsp. ground cinnamon
- ½ tsp. ground nutmeg
- ⅛ tsp. salt

1. Combine all ingredients in a 6-qt. electric pressure cooker. Lock lid; close pressure-release valve. Adjust to pressure-cook on high for 5 minutes. Let pressure release naturally.
2. Mash apples with a potato masher or use an immersion blender until blended to your desired consistency. Serve warm or store in an airtight container in the refrigerator.
⅔ CUP: *101 cal., 0 fat (0 sat. fat), 0 chol., 25mg sod., 26g carb. (22g sugars, 3g fiber), 0 pro.*

TAKE A BOUGH

An easy way to add seasonal charm to your feast table is to use material left over from decking the hall!

Cuttings from your Christmas tree or stray pieces from the garland that drapes your mantelpiece will keep green and fresh when set in decorative glasses and other vintage containers filled with water.

The greenery pairs well with simple candles and rustic pedestals found at craft and hobby stores. Try setting clusters of containers at different heights for a more sophisticated look.

RED CABBAGE WITH BACON

If you've braised or marinated red cabbage, or served it raw, try it steamed, then toss with bacon and a tangy sauce. We serve it with pork or chicken.
—*Sherri Melotik, Oak Creek, WI*

- -

TAKES: 25 min. • **MAKES:** 6 servings

- 1 **medium head red cabbage (about 2 lbs.), shredded**
- 8 **bacon strips, chopped**
- 1 **small onion, quartered and thinly sliced**
- 2 **Tbsp. all-purpose flour**
- ¼ **cup packed brown sugar**
- ½ **cup water**
- ¼ **cup cider vinegar**
- 1 **tsp. salt**
- ⅛ **tsp. pepper**

1. In a large saucepan, place steamer basket over 1 in. of water. Place cabbage in basket. Bring water to a boil. Reduce heat to maintain a simmer; steam, covered, just until tender, 6-8 minutes.

2. Meanwhile, in a large skillet, cook bacon over medium heat until crisp, stirring occasionally. Remove with a slotted spoon; drain on paper towels. Discard drippings, reserving 2 Tbsp. in pan.

3. Add onion to the drippings; cook and stir over medium-high heat until tender, 4-6 minutes. Stir in flour and brown sugar until blended. Gradually stir in water and vinegar. Bring to a boil, stirring constantly; cook and stir until thickened, 1-2 minutes. Stir in cabbage, bacon, salt and pepper.

¾ CUP: *188 cal., 9g fat (3g sat. fat), 15mg chol., 635mg sod., 23g carb. (15g sugars, 3g fiber), 6g pro.*

Holiday Helper

Dark brown and light brown sugar are generally interchangeable in recipes so you can use whichever you like. The big difference is that dark brown sugar contains more molasses, so if you prefer a bolder flavor, go for dark. For a milder flavor, stick with light.

WARM APPLE & PISTACHIO SPINACH SALAD

This salad started off as part of a recipe from Barton Seaver (in the book For Cod and Country*), one of the first to push for cooking with sustainable seafood. My tweaks and additions, including ricotta, ginger and Dijon, resulted in something amazing that goes well with just about any entree, seafood or not. This is a salad worthy of a dinner party, yet it's super quick and easy to make.*
—Justine Kmiecik, Crestview, FL

TAKES: 25 min. • **MAKES:** 6 servings

- 3 Tbsp. butter
- 2 cups chopped crisp apples, unpeeled (about 2 medium apples)
- 1 tsp. grated fresh gingerroot
- 1 cup shelled roasted pistachios
- 2 tsp. Dijon mustard
- 1 pkg. (5 oz.) fresh baby spinach
- 1 cup whole-milk ricotta cheese
- 2 Tbsp. honey
  Coarsely ground pepper

1. In a large skillet, melt butter over medium-high heat. Add apples and ginger; cook and stir until the apples soften and begin to caramelize, 3-5 minutes. Stir in pistachios and Dijon mustard. Reduce heat; simmer for 5 minutes, stirring occasionally.

2. Place the spinach on a serving platter. Pour two-thirds of the apple mixture over spinach. Add spoonfuls of ricotta cheese; top with the remaining apple mixture. Drizzle with honey. Add fresh pepper to taste.

1 SERVING: *278 cal., 19g fat (8g sat. fat), 32mg chol., 243mg sod., 20g carb. (14g sugars, 4g fiber), 10g pro.*

Holiday Helper
Because the warm apple mixture works to soften the crisp spinach, it's best to assemble this salad right before serving for the best flavor and texture. The apple mixture can be kept warm in the skillet over low heat until you're ready to serve.

SMOKED TROUT & HEARTS OF PALM BITES

I've had great luck finding hearts of palm in the canned vegetable section of my grocery store. If you're not as lucky, use quartered artichoke hearts instead—you'll still end up with a great-tasting dish.
—Lori Stefanishion, Drumheller, AB

TAKES: 25 min. • **MAKES:** 2 dozen

- 1 can (14 oz.) hearts of palm, drained
- 4 oz. cream cheese, softened
- 24 bagel chips
- 6 oz. smoked trout, broken into 24 portions
- 3 Tbsp. capers, drained

Cut hearts of palm widthwise into thin slices. Spread bagel chips with half of the cream cheese; layer with hearts of palm and trout. Garnish with the remaining cream cheese and capers.

NOTE: *Hearts of palm are the immature buds from a small bush native to the Middle East and Mediterranean regions that are either brined in vinegar or packed in coarse salt to preserve.*

1 APPETIZER: *91 cal., 4g fat (1g sat. fat), 11mg chol., 158mg sod., 11g carb., 1g fiber, 4g pro.*

More Choices for Christmas Menus

Use the recipes on these pages to complement the three set feast menus, or create your own dinner plan to suit your guests' preferences— from appetizer to dessert!

WINNING CRANBERRY GLAZED HAM

A friend shared the recipe for this tender ham with me. I've served it at reunions, weddings, graduations, baptisms and holiday gatherings. It's a delicious way to please a crowd.
—Sue Seymour, Valatie, NY

PREP: 15 min. + marinating • **BAKE:** 2½ hours
MAKES: 16 servings

- 2 cans (16 oz. each) whole-berry cranberry sauce
- 1 cup orange juice
- ⅓ cup steak sauce
- 2 Tbsp. canola oil
- 2 Tbsp. prepared mustard
- 2 Tbsp. brown sugar
- 1 fully cooked bone-in ham (7 to 9 lbs.)

1. In a large bowl, combine cranberry sauce, orange juice, steak sauce, oil, mustard and brown sugar. Score the surface of the ham with shallow diagonal cuts, making diamond shapes.

2. Place ham in a 2-gallon resealable bag. Add half the cranberry mixture; seal bag and turn to coat. Cover and refrigerate for 8 hours or overnight, turning several times. Cover and refrigerate remaining cranberry mixture.

3. Preheat oven to 325°. Drain the ham, discarding marinade. Place ham on a rack in a foil-lined roasting pan; cover with foil. Bake for 1¾ hours.

4. Place the reserved cranberry mixture in a small saucepan; heat through. Uncover ham; brush with cranberry mixture.

5. Bake until a thermometer reads 140°, 45-60 minutes longer, brushing with the cranberry mixture every 15 minutes. Warm the remaining cranberry mixture; serve with ham.

4 OZ. COOKED HAM: *264 cal., 7g fat (2g sat. fat), 87mg chol., 1164mg sod., 22g carb. (15g sugars, 1g fiber), 29g pro.*

Holiday Helper

When serving a bone-in ham, plan for ½ lb. ham per guest. So, if you're scaling this recipe down to serve 8, pick up a 4-lb. bone-in ham. (For boneless, figure ⅓ lb. per person.)

ROASTED POTATOES, CARROTS & LEEKS

Simply seasoned and flavored with garlic, this fantastic side dish will complement just about any entree. The colorful veggies are easy to prepare and look attractive on a holiday buffet—but you'll want to keep this recipe in mind for meals all year long.
—Janice Mitchell, Aurora, CO

PREP: 20 min. • **BAKE:** 45 min.
MAKES: 12 servings

- 2 lbs. small red potatoes, quartered
- 1 lb. fresh baby carrots
- 3 Tbsp. butter, melted
- 1 Tbsp. olive oil
- 1 tsp. salt
- ¼ tsp. pepper
- 6 medium leeks (white portions only), halved lengthwise, cleaned and cut into 1-in. lengths
- 2 garlic cloves, minced

1. Preheat oven to 425°. Scrub and quarter potatoes; place in a large bowl. Add the carrots, melted butter, oil, salt and pepper; toss to coat. Arrange in a single layer in 2 ungreased 15x10x1-in. baking pans.

2. Bake 25 minutes. Add leeks and garlic; bake until tender, stirring occasionally, 20-25 minutes longer.

¾ CUP: *131 cal., 4g fat (2g sat. fat), 8mg chol., 260mg sod., 22g carb. (4g sugars, 3g fiber), 2g pro.*
DIABETIC EXCHANGES: *1 starch, 1 fat.*

FIVE-SPICE PUMPKIN PIE

This recipe is a classic with a special spiced-up twist. Just half a teaspoon of five-spice powder adds an intriguing flavor without being overwhelming.
—Shawn Barto, Palmetto, FL

PREP: 30 min. + chilling
BAKE: 50 min. + cooling
MAKES: 8 servings

- 1¼ cups all-purpose flour
- ⅛ tsp. salt
- ½ cup shortening
- 1 Tbsp. vodka
- 1 to 2 Tbsp. ice water
- 1 large egg
- 1 Tbsp. water

FILLING
- 1 can (15 oz.) pumpkin
- 1 cup evaporated milk
- ¾ cup packed brown sugar
- 2 large eggs
- 1 tsp. ground cinnamon
- 1 tsp. vanilla extract
- ½ tsp. salt
- ½ tsp. Chinese five-spice powder

1. Mix flour and salt; cut in shortening until crumbly. Tossing with a fork, gradually add enough vodka and enough ice water for dough to hold together when pressed. Shape into a disk; wrap and refrigerate 1 hour or overnight.
2. Preheat oven to 425°. On a lightly floured surface, roll dough to a ⅛-in.-thick circle; transfer to a 9-in. pie plate. Trim crust to ½ in. beyond rim of plate; flute edge. In a small bowl, whisk egg with water. Brush over crust; refrigerate until ready to fill.
3. Beat filling ingredients until blended; transfer to crust. Bake on a lower oven rack for 15 minutes. Reduce oven setting to 350°; bake until a knife inserted in the center comes out clean, 35-40 minutes

longer. (Cover edges with foil during the last 15 minutes to prevent overbrowning if necessary.) Cool completely on a wire rack. Store in the refrigerator.
1 PIECE: *345 cal., 16g fat (5g sat. fat), 64mg chol., 244mg sod., 43g carb. (25g sugars, 2g fiber), 6g pro.*

Holiday Helper
To add decorative cutouts, double the dough amount and divide in half. Use one half for the crust; roll the other to ⅛-in. thickness and cut out with 1- to 1½-in. leaf-shaped cookie cutters. Use a sharp knife to score veins on cutouts. Bake on an ungreased baking sheet at 400° until golden brown, 6-8 minutes. Remove to a wire rack to cool. Arrange around edge of finished pie..

BROCCOLI WITH SMOKED ALMONDS

This dish makes for a colorful, attractive side. Almonds and pimientos add a little pizazz to your plate.
—Gertrudis Miller, Evansville, IN

TAKES: 15 min. • **MAKES:** 4 servings

- 5 cups frozen broccoli florets, thawed
- ½ tsp. minced garlic
- 1 Tbsp. olive oil
- ½ cup water
- ¼ tsp. salt
- ⅓ cup smoked or roasted salted almonds, coarsely chopped
- 1 jar (2 oz.) sliced pimientos, drained

1. In a large skillet, saute broccoli and garlic in oil over medium-high heat until garlic is golden brown, 2 minutes. Add water and salt; bring to a boil. Reduce heat; cover and cook until broccoli is tender, 2-3 minutes.
2. Add almonds and pimientos. Cook, uncovered, until water is evaporated, 1 minute.
¾ **CUP:** *155 cal., 11g fat (1g sat. fat), 0 chol., 226mg sod., 9g carb. (3g sugars, 4g fiber), 5g pro.*
DIABETIC EXCHANGES: *2 fat, 1 vegetable.*

POTS DE CREME

Looking for an easy dessert recipe that's still guaranteed to impress? Served in pretty stemmed glasses, this classic chocolate custard really sets the tone.
—Connie Dreyfoos, Cincinnati, OH

PREP: 15 min. + chilling • **MAKES:** 5 servings

- 1 large egg
- 2 Tbsp. sugar
- Dash salt
- ¾ cup half-and-half cream
- 1 cup semisweet chocolate chips
- 1 tsp. vanilla extract
- Optional: Whipped cream and assorted fresh fruit

1. In a small saucepan, combine the egg, sugar and salt. Whisk in cream. Cook and stir over medium heat until mixture reaches 160° and coats the back of a metal spoon.
2. Remove from heat; whisk in chocolate chips and vanilla until smooth. Pour into small dessert dishes. Refrigerate, covered, 8 hours or overnight. If desired, garnish with whipped cream and fruit.
⅓ **CUP:** *246 cal., 15g fat (9g sat. fat), 55mg chol., 66mg sod., 28g carb. (25g sugars, 2g fiber), 4g pro.*

CHESTNUT DRESSING

I enjoyed this stuffing when I spent my first Thanksgiving with my husband, Mike. It's a family recipe his mother has been making for years. Italian seasoning and chestnuts add flavor and texture.
—Sharon Brunner, Mohnton, PA

PREP: 25 min. • **BAKE:** 20 min.
MAKES: 18 servings (9 cups)

- 4 celery ribs, chopped
- 1 large onion, chopped
- 1½ cups butter, cubed
- 3 cups chestnuts, shelled and coarsely chopped
- 3 Tbsp. Italian seasoning
- 10 slices Italian bread (¾ in. thick), cubed

1. Preheat oven to 350°. In a large skillet, saute the celery and onion in butter over medium-high heat, 2-3 minutes, or until tender. Add the chestnuts and Italian seasoning. Bring to a boil. Reduce heat; simmer, uncovered, for 10 minutes. Add bread cubes and stir to coat.
2. Transfer to an ungreased 13x9-in. baking dish. Bake, uncovered, until golden brown, 20-25 minutes.
½ **CUP:** *223 cal., 16g fat (10g sat. fat), 40mg chol., 213mg sod., 18g carb. (3g sugars, 2g fiber), 2g pro.*

BUTTERY CRESCENT ROLLS

I typically double the recipe for these buttery rolls because they never last very long. You can shape them any way you like.
—Kelly Kirby, Mill Bay, BC

PREP: 35 min. + rising • **BAKE:** 10 min.
MAKES: 2 dozen

1	Tbsp. active dry yeast
1	tsp. plus ⅓ cup sugar
½	cup warm water (110° to 115°)
½	cup butter, softened
½	cup warm 2% milk (110° to 115°)
1	large egg, room temperature
¾	tsp. salt
4	cups all-purpose flour

1. In a large bowl, dissolve yeast and 1 tsp. sugar in warm water. Add butter, milk, egg, salt, remaining sugar and 2 cups flour. Beat until smooth. Stir in enough remaining flour to form a soft dough.
2. Turn onto a floured surface; knead until smooth and elastic, 6-8 minutes. Place in a greased bowl, turning once to grease the top. Cover and let rise in a warm place until doubled, about 1 hour.
3. Punch dough down. Turn onto a lightly floured surface; divide in half. Roll each portion into a 12-in. circle; cut each circle into 12 wedges. Roll up wedges from the wide end and place point side down 2 in. apart on greased baking sheets. Curve ends to form crescents. Cover and let rise in a warm place until doubled, about 30 minutes.
4. Preheat oven to 350°. Bake until golden brown, 10-12 minutes. Remove from pans to wire racks.
1 ROLL: *128 cal., 4g fat (3g sat. fat), 19mg chol., 107mg sod., 19g carb. (4g sugars, 1g fiber), 3g pro.*

Holiday Helper

To fit homemade rolls into your busy schedule, try placing the dough in the refrigerator for its first rise; it'll take about 8 hours instead of 1. Then shape it, and let it do its second rise at the normal temperature and time. The dough may be easier to shape if it comes to room temperature first.

SHRIMP IN CREAM SAUCE

Looking for an extra-special Christmas Eve entree to delight your busy crowd? My family enjoys this rich shrimp dish on the holiday. I serve it over golden egg noodles.
—Jane Birch, Edison, NJ

TAKES: 30 min. • **MAKES:** 8 servings

2	Tbsp. butter, melted
⅓	cup all-purpose flour
1½	cups chicken broth
4	garlic cloves, minced
1	cup heavy whipping cream
½	cup minced fresh parsley
2	tsp. paprika
	Salt and pepper to taste
2	lbs. large uncooked shrimp, peeled and deveined
	Hot cooked noodles or rice

1. Preheat oven to 400°. In a small saucepan, melt butter; stir in flour until smooth. Gradually add broth and garlic. Bring to a boil; cook and stir until thickened, 2 minutes. Remove from the heat. Stir in the cream, parsley, paprika, salt and pepper.
2. Butterfly shrimp, by cutting lengthwise almost in half, but leaving shrimp attached at opposite side. Spread to butterfly. Place cut side down in a greased 13x9-in. baking dish. Pour cream sauce over shrimp. Bake, uncovered, 15-18 minutes, or until shrimp turn pink. Serve with noodles or rice.
1 SERVING: *240 cal., 15g fat (9g sat. fat), 216mg chol., 410mg sod., 6g carb. (1g sugars, 0 fiber), 20g pro.*

CURRIED SQUASH SOUP

Cayenne pepper gives a little kick to this pretty golden soup, a first course that everyone seems to love. It can be made several days ahead to fit a busy schedule, then heated up whenever needed.
—Evelyn Southwell, Etters, PA

PREP: 1 hour • **COOK:** 20 min.
MAKES: 6 servings

- 1 butternut squash (about 1¾ lbs.)
- 1 large onion, chopped
- 2 garlic cloves, minced
- 2 Tbsp. canola oil
- 1 Tbsp. all-purpose flour
- 1 tsp. salt
- 1 tsp. curry powder
- ⅛ tsp. cayenne pepper
- 5 cups chicken broth
- 1 bay leaf

CILANTO CREAM TOPPING
- ½ cup sour cream
- ¼ cup heavy whipping cream
- ¼ cup minced fresh cilantro

1. Preheat oven to 400°. Cut squash in half lengthwise; discard seeds. Place squash cut side down in a greased or foil-lined baking pan. Bake, uncovered, until tender, 40-50 minutes. When cool enough to handle, scoop out pulp; set aside.
2. In a large saucepan, saute onion and garlic in oil over medium heat until tender, 2-3 minutes. Add the flour, salt, curry powder and cayenne until blended. Stir in broth; add bay leaf. Bring to a boil; cook and stir until thickened, 2 minutes. Reduce heat; simmer, uncovered, for 20 minutes. Discard the bay leaf. Cool to room temperature.
3. In a blender, combine half the broth mixture and squash; cover and process until smooth. Repeat with the remaining broth mixture and squash. Return to the saucepan; heat through. Combine the topping ingredients; place a dollop on each serving. If desired, sprinkle with additional fresh cilantro.
1 CUP: *194 cal., 12g fat (5g sat. fat), 27mg chol., 1188mg sod., 18g carb. (6g sugars, 4g fiber), 4g pro.*

SWISS & CRAB SUPPER PIE

Though some parts of Alaska are suitable for farming, we're on the Gulf, where commercial fishing is the main industry. Crab is plentiful here, and so is salmon, halibut, shrimp and sea herring. You don't need to use fresh crab for this delicious, easy-to-make supper pie, though—canned crabmeat works, too. With a handful of greens, it makes a great light meal or one elegant course in a larger feast.
—Kathy Crow, Cordova, AK

PREP: 15 min. • **BAKE:** 45 min. + standing
MAKES: 8 servings

- 1   sheet refrigerated pie crust
- 1   can (6 oz.) lump crabmeat, drained
- 1   cup shredded Swiss cheese
- 2   green onions, thinly sliced
- 3   large eggs, beaten
- 1   cup half-and-half cream
- ½   tsp. salt
- ½   tsp. grated lemon zest
- ¼   tsp. ground mustard
  Dash mace
- ¼   cup sliced almonds

1. Preheat oven to 450°. Line a 9-in. tart pan with unpricked crust; line with heavy-duty foil. Bake for 5 minutes. Remove foil; reduce oven temperature to 325°.

2. Arrange crab evenly in the baked crust; top with cheese and green onions. Combine all remaining ingredients except almonds; pour into tart shell. Sprinkle top with almonds.

3. Bake until set, 45 minutes. Let stand for 10 minutes before serving.

1 PIECE: *276 cal., 18g fat (8g sat. fat), 123mg chol., 435mg sod., 15g carb. (2g sugars, 0 fiber), 13g pro.*

HOMEMADE CRANBERRY RELISH

This baked cranberry compote couldn't be easier to prepare and tastes terrific on top of a slice of turkey or other roast bird. The recipe comes courtesy of my sister-in-law.
—Betty Johnson, Eleva, WI

PREP: 5 min. • **BAKE:** 1 hour + chilling
MAKES: 16 servings (4 cups)

- 4   cups fresh or frozen cranberries
- 2   cups sugar
- 1   cup orange marmalade
- 1   cup chopped walnuts, toasted
- 3   Tbsp. lemon juice

1. Preheat oven to 350°. In an ungreased 13x9-in. baking dish, combine cranberries and sugar. Bake, covered, for 1 hour.

2. In a large bowl, combine the orange marmalade, walnuts and lemon juice. Stir in the cranberry mixture. Refrigerate, covered, until chilled.

¼ CUP: *206 cal., 4g fat (0 sat. fat), 0 chol., 12mg sod., 42g carb. (39g sugars, 1g fiber), 2g pro.*

> ### *Holiday Helper*
> If, once you've made your relish, you find it too tart, don't add sugar—it won't dissolve unless you reheat it. Try adding a syrup, agave nectar, a sweet fruit juice or a dessert wine.

RED & GREEN HOLIDAY SIDES

Round out your serving plates with a particularly festive touch, by creating mouthwatering side dishes in celebratory shades of red and green!

CRUNCHY BACON BLUE CHEESE RED PEPPER BRUSSELS SPROUTS

This is my family's absolute favorite dish on my holiday table. What's not to love about the mixed aroma of garlic, onions, bacon and blue cheese floating through your home?
—Rozanne Gooding, Carlsbad, CA

PREP: 15 min. • **COOK:** 20 min.
MAKES: 6 servings

- ¼ cup avocado oil
- 3 cups halved fresh Brussels sprouts
- ½ cup sliced red onions
- ½ cup sliced sweet red pepper
- 2 cups fresh or frozen cranberries
- 2 Tbsp. balsamic vinegar
- 1 garlic clove, minced
- ½ cup crumbled blue cheese
- ½ cup crumbled cooked bacon
- ¾ tsp. salt
- ½ tsp. pepper
- ½ cup chopped cashews or pecans

1. In a large skillet, heat oil over medium heat. Add Brussels sprouts, onions and red pepper; cook and stir until crisp-tender, 8-10 minutes.
2. Add cranberries, vinegar and garlic. Cook just until berries are tender, about 10 minutes. Remove from the heat.
3. Stir in cheese, bacon, salt and pepper. Sprinkle with cashews. Serve warm.
⅔ **CUP:** 268 cal., 20g fat (5g sat. fat), 11mg chol., 736mg sod., 15g carb. (5g sugars, 4g fiber), 10g pro.

GARDEN-FRESH RAINBOW CHARD

Chard is a member of the beet family, prized for its green leaves and celery-like stalks. Stir up these good-for-you greens with garlic and red onion.
—Taste of Home *Test Kitchen*

TAKES: 20 min. • **MAKES:** 4 servings

- 2 Tbsp. olive oil
- 1 medium red onion, halved and sliced
- 3 garlic cloves, sliced
- ¼ cup chicken broth
- 2 bunches rainbow Swiss chard, coarsely chopped (about 16 cups)
- 2 Tbsp. lemon juice
- ¼ tsp. salt
- ¼ tsp. pepper

1. In a 6-qt. stockpot, heat oil over medium-high heat. Add onion; cook and stir until tender, 2-3 minutes. Add garlic; cook 1 minute longer.
2. Add broth and chard; cook and stir until the chard is tender, 5-6 minutes. Remove from heat; stir in lemon juice, salt and pepper.
½ **CUP:** 115 cal., 7g fat (1g sat. fat), 0 chol., 631mg sod., 11g carb. (4g sugars, 4g fiber), 4g pro.
DIABETIC EXCHANGES: 2 vegetable, 1½ fat.

MINTY SUGAR SNAP PEAS

Fresh mint adds a lively touch to cooked sugar snap peas. It's also nice on green beans or carrots.
—Alice Kaldahl, Ray, ND

TAKES: 10 min. • **MAKES:** 4 servings

- 3 cups fresh sugar snap peas, trimmed
- ¼ tsp. sugar
- 2 to 3 Tbsp. minced fresh mint
- 2 Tbsp. butter

Place 1 in. water in a large skillet. Add peas and sugar; bring to a boil. Reduce heat; simmer, covered, until peas are crisp-tender, 4-5 minutes; drain. Stir in mint and butter.
¾ **CUP:** 102 cal., 6g fat (4g sat. fat), 15mg chol., 45mg sod., 9g carb. (4g sugars, 3g fiber), 4g pro.
DIABETIC EXCHANGES: 2 vegetable, 1½ fat.

SPANAKOPITA MASHED POTATOES

I learned to cook by watching my mom in the kitchen. I created this recipe after I tried a spinach-topped baked potato. Flecks of red from the potato skins and green from the spinach make these potatoes look festive and special. By not peeling the potatoes, you not only keep some nutrients, you also save on prep time.
—Ashley Laymon, Lititz, PA

- -

PREP: 10 min. • **COOK:** 25 min. • **MAKES:** 6 servings

6 medium red potatoes, quartered
1 pkg. (6 oz.) fresh baby spinach
¼ cup 2% milk
1 Tbsp. butter
½ tsp. salt
½ tsp. pepper
¾ cup crumbled feta cheese

1. Place potatoes in a large saucepan and cover with water. Bring to a boil. Reduce heat; cover and cook for 15-20 minutes or until tender.
2. Meanwhile, in another large saucepan, bring ½ in. of water to a boil. Add spinach; boil, covered, until wilted, 3-5 minutes. Drain and coarsely chop; keep warm.
3. Drain potatoes and return to the saucepan. Add milk, butter, salt and pepper; mash until smooth. Fold in cheese and spinach.
¾ **CUP:** *145 cal., 5g fat (3g sat. fat), 13mg chol., 379mg sod., 20g carb. (2g sugars, 3g fiber), 6g pro.*
DIABETIC EXCHANGES: *1 starch, 1 fat.*

CRANBERRY-PECAN WHEAT BERRY SALAD

I love to experiment with different grains and wanted to give wheat berries a try. My whole family goes nuts for this salad, especially my mom.
—Kristen Heigl, Staten Island, NY

- -

PREP: 20 min. • **COOK:** 70 min. + cooling • **MAKES:** 8 servings

1 cup uncooked wheat berries, rinsed
2 celery ribs, finely chopped
1 medium tart apple, diced
4 green onions, sliced
1 cup dried cranberries
1 cup chopped pecans
DRESSING
3 Tbsp. walnut oil
2 Tbsp. cider vinegar
1 Tbsp. minced fresh sage or 1 tsp. rubbed sage
2 tsp. minced fresh thyme or ¾ tsp. dried thyme
2 tsp. Worcestershire sauce
1 tsp. Dijon mustard
¾ tsp. salt
½ tsp. pepper

1. Cook wheat berries according to package directions; drain and cool. Meanwhile, combine the next 5 ingredients; add wheat berries.
2. Whisk dressing ingredients. Pour over salad; toss to coat. Serve at room temperature or chilled.
¾ **CUP:** *298 cal., 15g fat (1g sat. fat), 0 chol., 261mg sod., 39g carb. (17g sugars, 6g fiber), 5g pro.*

ITALIAN SPAGHETTI SALAD

This attractive, fresh-tasting salad can conveniently be prepared the night before. It makes enough for a crowd!
—Lucia Johnson, Massena, NY

- -

PREP: 20 min. + chilling • **MAKES:** 16 servings

- 1 pkg. (16 oz.) thin spaghetti, halved
- 3 medium tomatoes, diced
- 3 small zucchini, diced
- 1 large cucumber, halved, seeded and diced
- 1 medium green pepper, diced
- 1 medium sweet red pepper, diced
- 1 bottle (8 oz.) Italian salad dressing
- 2 Tbsp. grated Parmesan cheese
- 1½ tsp. sesame seeds
- 1½ tsp. poppy seeds
- ½ tsp. paprika
- ¼ tsp. celery seed
- ⅛ tsp. garlic powder

1. Cook spaghetti according to package directions; drain and rinse in cold water. Place in a large bowl; add tomatoes, zucchini, cucumber and peppers.
2. Combine remaining ingredients; pour over salad and toss to coat. Cover and refrigerate for at least 2 hours.
1 CUP: *158 cal., 3g fat (1g sat. fat), 1mg chol., 168mg sod., 26g carb. (4g sugars, 2g fiber), 5g pro.*
DIABETIC EXCHANGES: *1½ starch, 1 vegetable, ½ fat.*

Holiday Helper

This recipe calls for chilling it at least 2 hours, but letting it sit overnight will allow more flavors to develop. It will last 3-5 days in the refrigerator.

HERBED RICE PILAF

This savory side dish has been a family favorite for years. Our daughter Jennifer became an expert on this recipe at age 12, which was always a huge help for a busy working mom like me.
—Jeri Dobrowski, Beach, ND

- -

PREP: 10 min. • **COOK:** 25 min. + standing
MAKES: 6 servings

- 1 cup uncooked long grain rice
- 1 cup chopped celery
- ¾ cup chopped onion
- ¼ cup butter, cubed
- 2½ cups water
- 1 pkg. (2 to 2½ oz.) chicken noodle soup mix
- 1 tsp. dried thyme
- ¼ tsp. rubbed sage
- ¼ tsp. pepper
- 2 Tbsp. fresh minced parsley
- 1 Tbsp. chopped pimientos, optional

1. In a large skillet, cook the rice, celery and onion in butter, stirring constantly, until rice is browned. Stir in the next 5 ingredients; bring to a boil. Reduce heat; cover and simmer for 15 minutes. Sprinkle with parsley; stir in pimientos if desired.
2. Remove from heat and let stand, covered, for 10 minutes. Fluff with a fork.
¾ CUP: *226 cal., 8g fat (5g sat. fat), 23mg chol., 426mg sod., 34g carb. (3g sugars, 2g fiber), 4g pro.*
DIABETIC EXCHANGES: *2 starch, 1½ fat.*

CRISPY SMASHED HERBED RED POTATOES

While scanning a local newspaper, I found a recipe with an intriguing title. As advertised, these potatoes are crispy, herbed and smashed.
—Althea Dye, Howard, OH

PREP: 25 min. • **BAKE:** 20 min.
MAKES: 4 servings

- 12 small red potatoes (about 1½ lbs.)
- 3 Tbsp. olive oil
- ¼ cup butter, melted
- ¾ tsp. salt
- ¼ tsp. pepper
- 3 Tbsp. minced fresh chives
- 1 Tbsp. minced fresh parsley

1. Preheat oven to 450°. Place potatoes in a large saucepan; add water to cover. Bring to a boil. Reduce heat; cook, uncovered, until potatoes are tender, 15-20 minutes. Drain.
2. Drizzle oil over the bottom of a 15x10x1-in. baking pan; arrange potatoes over oil. Using a potato masher, flatten potatoes to ½-in. thickness. Brush potatoes with butter; sprinkle with salt and pepper.
3. Roast 20-25 minutes or until golden brown. Sprinkle with chives and parsley.
3 SMASHED POTATOES: *292 cal., 22g fat (9g sat. fat), 31mg chol., 543mg sod., 22g carb. (1g sugars, 2g fiber), 3g pro.*
LEMON-ROSEMARY SMASHED POTATOES: *Boil and flatten potatoes; add 1 small halved and sliced lemon and 1½ tsp. minced fresh rosemary. Butter, season and roast. Omit herbs.*
DILL SMASHED POTATOES: *Boil, flatten and season potatoes, adding ¼ tsp. garlic powder. Butter, season and roast. Sprinkle with 2-3 tsp. snipped fresh dill instead of the chives and parsley.*
ARTICHOKE SMASHED POTATOES: *Boil, flatten and season potatoes, adding ¾ tsp. dried thyme. Butter, season and roast, adding a drained 7½-oz. jar of marinated quartered artichoke hearts during last 5 minutes. Omit herbs.*

BOHEMIAN COLLARDS

I've added unconventional ingredients to these collards that make them unique and exquisite on the palate and on the plate.
—Ally Phillips, Murrells Inlet, SC

PREP: 20 min. • **COOK:** 35 min.
MAKES: 8 servings

- 1 large bunch collard greens (about 2 lbs.)
- 6 bacon strips, chopped
- 1 Tbsp. olive oil
- ½ cup chicken broth
- 1½ cups fresh or frozen corn (about 7½ oz.)
- 1 cup chopped sweet red pepper
- ½ tsp. salt
- ¼ tsp. crushed red pepper flakes
- ¼ tsp. pepper

1. Trim thick stems from collard greens; coarsely chop leaves. In a Dutch oven, cook bacon over medium heat until crisp, stirring occasionally. Remove with a slotted spoon; drain on paper towels.
2. Cook and stir collard greens in bacon drippings and oil just until coated. Add broth; bring to a boil. Reduce heat; simmer, covered, until greens are very tender, 25-30 minutes.
3. Add corn, red pepper, salt, pepper flakes and pepper. Cook and stir until heated through. Sprinkle with bacon.
½ CUP: *168 cal., 11g fat (3g sat. fat), 14mg chol., 369mg sod., 13g carb. (2g sugars, 5g fiber), 7g pro.*
DIABETIC EXCHANGES: *2 fat, 1 starch.*

Holiday Helper

If you want to take collard greens to the next level, just before serving add chopped prosciutto in addition to the crumbled bacon. Also, don't throw out the pot liquor. That's the liquid left over from cooking the greens, and it's rich with flavor and nutrients. Serve it on the side for dunking bread, or put it aside and add it to future soup stock.

HOMEMADE PASTA

Try your hand at homemade pasta with this easy spinach dough. You don't need a pasta maker or other special equipment!
—Taste of Home *Test Kitchen*

PREP: 30 min. + standing • **COOK:** 10 min./batch • **MAKES:** 8 servings

- 1 pkg. (10 oz.) frozen chopped spinach, thawed and squeezed dry
- ¼ cup packed fresh parsley sprigs
- 3½ to 4 cups all-purpose flour
- ½ tsp. salt
- 4 large eggs
- 3 Tbsp. water
- 1 Tbsp. olive oil
  Marinara sauce

1. Place spinach and parsley in a food processor; cover and process until finely chopped. Add 3½ cups flour and the salt; process until blended. Add the eggs, water and oil. Process until dough forms a ball, 15-20 seconds.

2. Turn onto a floured surface; knead until smooth and elastic, 8-10 minutes, adding remaining flour if necessary. Cover and let rest for 30 minutes. Divide into fourths.

3. On a floured surface, roll each portion to ¹⁄₁₆-in. thickness. Dust top of dough with flour to prevent sticking; cut into ¼-in. slices. Separate the slices; allow noodles to dry on kitchen towels for at least 1 hour before cooking.

4. To cook, fill a Dutch oven three-fourths full with water. Bring to a boil. Add noodles in batches; cook, uncovered, until tender, 8-10 minutes. Drain. Serve with sauce.

NOTE: *To avoid sticky pasta, use plenty of water: at least 4 qt. for each pound of pasta. Stir the pasta after it's added to the water and maintain a boil while cooking.*

1 CUP: *259 cal., 5g fat (1g sat. fat), 106mg chol., 211mg sod., 43g carb. (1g sugars, 3g fiber), 10g pro.*

RED AND GREEN GARLAND

Decking your halls (and mantelpieces and doorways and tables) doesn't have to be complex or expensive. You can make a sweet and simple holly garland using just card stock, glue and kitchen twine.

The garland pictured above was made with a Cricut machine (available online or in craft stores), and the holly and berry shapes were found by searching in "Images" in Cricut Design Space. But you don't need special equipment to make a garland like this. You can find holly and berry templates online, or draw your own, and then just cut them out with scissors.

Once you have the cutout leaves and berries, attach them to a strand of white twine or string using fast-dry craft glue or a hot glue gun. For the garland shown here, the leaves are roughly 4½ in. long; it took 14 leaves and 26 berries to make a 6-ft.-long garland.

Once the glue is dry, hang your garland wherever you need a dose of extra joy!

PIMIENTO GREEN BEANS

Here's an easy way to turn green beans into a special side dish. Pimientos, Parmesan cheese and chicken broth add savory flavor and a dash of bright color.
—Lynn McAllister, Mount Ulla, NC

- -

PREP: 5 min. • **COOK:** 10 min.
MAKES: 10 servings

- 2   lbs. fresh green beans, cut into 2-in. pieces
- 1   can (14½ oz.) chicken broth
- ½   cup chopped onion
- 1   jar (2 oz.) chopped pimientos, drained
- ½   tsp. salt
- ⅛   to ¼ tsp. pepper
- ¼   cup shredded Parmesan cheese

In a large saucepan, bring the beans, broth and onion to a boil. Reduce heat; cover and cook until beans are crisp-tender, 10-15 minutes. Drain. Stir in pimientos, salt and pepper. Sprinkle with Parmesan cheese.

¾ CUP: *44 cal., 1g fat (0 sat. fat), 2mg chol., 336mg sod., 8g carb. (3g sugars, 3g fiber), 3g pro.*
DIABETIC EXCHANGES: *1 vegetable.*

HARVARD BEETS

This pretty side dish's bright, citrusy flavors are an ideal companion for any entree—and for people who usually shy away from beets.
—Jean Ann Perkins, Newburyport, MA

- -

TAKES: 15 min. • **MAKES:** 4 servings

- 1   can (16 oz.) sliced beets
- ¼   cup sugar
- 1½ tsp. cornstarch
- 2   Tbsp. vinegar
- 2   Tbsp. orange juice
- 1   Tbsp. grated orange zest

Drain beets, reserving 2 Tbsp. juice; set beets and juice aside. In a saucepan, combine sugar and cornstarch. Add vinegar, orange juice and beet juice; bring to a boil. Reduce heat and simmer for 3-4 minutes or until thickened. Add beets and orange zest; heat through.

½ CUP: *93 cal., 0 fat (0 sat. fat), 0 chol., 220mg sod., 23g carb. (19g sugars, 2g fiber), 1g pro.*

GERMAN RED CABBAGE

Sunday afternoons were a time for family gatherings when I was a kid. While the uncles played cards, the aunts made traditional German dishes like this.
—Jeannette Heim, Dunlap, TN

- -

PREP: 10 min. • **COOK:** 65 min.
MAKES: 10 servings

- 1   medium onion, halved and sliced
- 1   medium apple, sliced
- 1   medium head red cabbage, shredded (about 8 cups)
- ⅓   cup sugar
- ⅓   cup white vinegar
- ¾   tsp. salt, optional
- ¼   tsp. pepper

In a Dutch oven coated with cooking spray, cook and stir onion and apple over medium heat until onion is tender, about 5 minutes. Stir in remaining ingredients; cook, covered, until cabbage is tender, about 1 hour, stirring occasionally.

1 CUP: *64 cal., 0 fat (0 sat. fat), 0 chol., 23mg sod., 16g carb. (12g sugars, 2g fiber), 1g pro.*
DIABETIC EXCHANGES: *1 vegetable, ½ starch.*

Holiday Helper

To shred a red cabbage, slice off the root end, then cut the cabbage in half through the stem. Slice into quarters, diagonally cutting out the root. Finally, thinly slice cabbage in the short direction.

POTATO & CHORIZO CASSEROLE

I love the smoky flavor that chorizo gives this dish, but I've also made it with Italian sausage and substituted an Italian blend cheese for the Mexican cheese. Or you can use cream of mushroom soup and fresh mushrooms for a vegetarian option.
—*Ana Beteta, Aberdeen, MD*

- -

PREP: 25 min. • **BAKE:** 40 min.
MAKES: 12 servings

8	oz. fresh chorizo or bulk spicy pork sausage
1	pkg. (32 oz.) frozen cubed hash brown potatoes, thawed
1	can (10½ oz.) condensed cream of chicken soup, undiluted
2	cups shredded Mexican cheese blend
1	pkg. (8 oz.) cream cheese, cubed
1	medium onion, chopped
1	small sweet red pepper, chopped
1	small green pepper, chopped
½	tsp. crushed red pepper flakes
¾	cup panko bread crumbs
	Chopped fresh parsley and cilantro

1. Preheat oven to 375°. In a small skillet, cook chorizo over medium heat until cooked through, breaking into crumbles, 5-7 minutes; drain. Transfer to a large bowl. Stir in the hash browns, soup, cheeses, onion, peppers and pepper flakes. Transfer to a greased 13x9-in. baking dish. Sprinkle with panko.
2. Bake, uncovered, until golden brown and bubbly, 40-45 minutes. Sprinkle with parsley and cilantro before serving.
¾ CUP: 316 cal., 20g fat (9g sat. fat), 54mg chol., 611mg sod., 22g carb. (3g sugars, 2g fiber), 12g pro.

> ### Holiday Helper
> The 8 oz. of sausage in this casserole doesn't sound like a lot, but it adds a ton of flavor. Although it's rich enough for a side dish, it can be served as a main dish too.

SMOKY QUINOA WITH MUSHROOMS

Add quinoa cooked with smoked paprika to your list of top sides. If you want to warm the spinach before serving, quickly saute it.
—*Ellen Kanner, Miami, FL*

- -

PREP: 15 min. • **COOK:** 35 min.
MAKES: 4 servings

4	tsp. olive oil
1	lb. sliced fresh mushrooms
3	garlic cloves, minced
3	Tbsp. tomato paste
2	Tbsp. smoked paprika
2	Tbsp. lemon juice
1	tsp. ground cumin
½	tsp. salt
1	cup water or vegetable broth
¾	cup quinoa, rinsed
4	cups fresh baby spinach
	Minced fresh cilantro and lemon wedges

1. In a large saucepan, heat oil over medium-high heat. Add mushrooms; cook and stir 6-8 minutes or until tender. Add garlic; cook 1 minute longer. Reduce heat to medium-low; cook, covered, 10 minutes longer.
2. Stir in tomato paste, paprika, lemon juice, cumin and salt until blended. Add water; bring to a boil. Add quinoa. Reduce heat; simmer, covered, 15-18 minutes or until liquid is absorbed. Remove from heat; fluff with a fork.
3. Arrange spinach on a serving plate; spoon quinoa over spinach. Sprinkle with cilantro; serve with lemon wedges.
⅔ CUP QUINOA MIXTURE WITH 1 CUP SPINACH: 217 cal., 8g fat (1g sat. fat), 0 chol., 337mg sod., 31g carb. (4g sugars, 6g fiber), 10g pro.
DIABETIC EXCHANGES: 2 vegetable, 1½ starch, 1 fat.

HOLIDAY PRETZEL SALAD

I gave a classic summer salad a winter holiday twist by making green, white and red layers. The combination of salty, sweet, creamy and fruity is always a hit!
—*Renee Conneally, Northville, MI*

PREP: 35 min. + chilling • **BAKE:** 10 min.
MAKES: 15 servings

- ¾ cup butter, melted
- 3 Tbsp. sugar
- 2 cups crushed pretzels

LIME LAYER
- 1 cup boiling water
- 1 pkg. (3 oz.) lime gelatin
- 1 pkg. (8 oz.) cream cheese, softened
- 1 carton (8 oz.) frozen whipped topping, thawed
- 14 drops green food coloring, optional

CREAM CHEESE LAYER
- 1 pkg. (8 oz.) cream cheese, softened
- ½ cup sugar
- 1 carton (8 oz.) frozen whipped topping, thawed

STRAWBERRY LAYER
- 2 cups boiling water
- 2 pkg. (3 oz. each) strawberry gelatin
- 4 cups sliced fresh strawberries
  Optional: Additional whipped topping, strawberries and miniature pretzels

1. Preheat oven to 350°. Mix melted butter and sugar; stir in pretzels. Press onto bottom of an ungreased 13x9-in. baking dish. Bake 10 minutes. Cool completely on a wire rack.

2. Meanwhile, for lime layer, in a large bowl, add boiling water to lime gelatin; stir 2 minutes to completely dissolve. Refrigerate until partially set, about 1 hour. In a bowl, beat cream cheese until smooth. Add cooled lime gelatin mixture; beat until smooth. Fold in whipped topping; if desired, add green food coloring. Spread over crust. Refrigerate until set but not firm, 25-30 minutes.

3. For cream cheese layer, in a bowl, beat cream cheese and sugar until smooth. Fold in whipped topping. Spread over lime layer. Refrigerate until set.

4. For strawberry layer, in a large bowl, add boiling water to strawberry gelatin; stir 2 minutes to completely dissolve. Refrigerate until partially set, about 1 hour. Stir in strawberries. Gently spoon over cream cheese layer. Refrigerate, covered, until firm, 2-4 hours.

5. To serve, cut into squares. If desired, top with additional whipped topping, strawberries and miniature pretzels.

1 SERVING: *407 cal., 25g fat (17g sat. fat), 55mg chol., 368mg sod., 40g carb. (29g sugars, 1g fiber), 5g pro.*

CHEESY ASPARAGUS & TOMATO SALAD

This fresh and colorful side dish is delicious served warm or cold. I get lots of compliments on the homemade dressing.
—*Millie Vickery, Lena, IL*

TAKES: 25 min. • **MAKES:** 8 servings

- 1½ lbs. fresh asparagus, trimmed and cut into 2-in. pieces
- 2 small tomatoes, cut into wedges
- 3 Tbsp. cider vinegar
- ¾ tsp. Worcestershire sauce
- ⅓ cup sugar
- 1 Tbsp. grated onion
- ½ tsp. salt
- ½ tsp. paprika
- ⅓ cup canola oil
- ⅓ cup sliced almonds, toasted
- ⅓ cup crumbled blue cheese, optional

1. In a large saucepan, bring 1 cup water to a boil. Add asparagus; cook, covered, until crisp-tender, 3-5 minutes. Drain; place in a large bowl. Add tomatoes; cover and keep warm.

2. Place vinegar, Worcestershire sauce, sugar, onion, salt and paprika in a blender; cover and process until smooth. While processing, gradually add oil in a steady stream. Toss with the asparagus mixture. Top with almonds and, if desired, cheese.

NOTE: *To toast nuts, bake in a shallow pan in a 350° oven for 5-10 minutes or cook in a skillet over low heat until lightly browned, stirring occasionally.*

¾ CUP: *154 cal., 11g fat (1g sat. fat), 0 chol., 159mg sod., 12g carb. (10g sugars, 1g fiber), 2g pro.*

DIABETIC EXCHANGES: *2 fat, 1 vegetable, ½ starch.*

ROASTED FENNEL & PEPPERS

Fennel makes for a tasty change of pace in this versatile side that goes nicely with grilled meats. Best of all, it's full of flavor and easy to do—and it doesn't seem light at all!
—*Taste of Home Test Kitchen*

TAKES: 30 min. • **MAKES:** 6 servings

- 2 fennel bulbs, halved and sliced
- 2 medium sweet red peppers, cut into 1-in. pieces
- 1 medium onion, cut into 1-in. pieces
- 3 garlic cloves, minced
- 1 Tbsp. olive oil
- ½ tsp. salt
- ½ tsp. pepper
- ½ tsp. rubbed sage
  Fresh sage leaves, thinly sliced, optional

1. Preheat oven to 425°. Place the fennel, peppers, onion and garlic in a 15x10x1-in. baking pan coated with cooking spray. Drizzle with oil; sprinkle with salt, pepper and rubbed sage. Toss to coat.

2. Bake, uncovered, until tender, 20-25 minutes, stirring twice. Garnish with fresh sage if desired.

⅔ CUP: *67 cal., 3g fat (0 sat. fat), 0 chol., 240mg sod., 10g carb. (5g sugars, 4g fiber), 2g pro.*

DIABETIC EXCHANGES: *1 vegetable, ½ fat.*

STOCKINGS ARE HUNG...

Stretchy, colorful and festive, holiday-themed socks make a clever ingredient for an easy homemade wreath.

WHAT YOU'LL NEED

- Foam wreath form
- Colorful Christmas socks (these can be found in online stores or department stores around the holidays)
- Scissors
- Craft knife
- Hot glue

INSTRUCTIONS

1. Slice the wreath in 1 place so that you can slide the socks onto the form.
2. Cut the toes off the socks. Slide the socks, 1 by 1, onto the wreath, scrunching them together until the form is full. Slide a sock over the opening so that the cut is hidden.
3. Use dabs of hot glue to secure loose socks to the wreath form as needed.
4. Cut a rectangle of fabric from 1 sock, tie it into a bow, then add it to the top of the wreath.

SAVORY RICE-STUFFED APPLES

My family loves apples. Since we have several trees, I am constantly challenged to create new recipes. This side dish is wonderful with pork roast and is practically effortless thanks to the slow cooker.
—Roxanne Chan, Albany, CA

PREP: 15 min. • **COOK:** 1½ hours
MAKES: 6 servings

- 6 medium apples
- ½ cup cooked brown rice
- 1 Tbsp. thinly sliced green onions
- 1 Tbsp. chopped sweet red pepper
- 1 Tbsp. minced fresh parsley
- 1 Tbsp. finely chopped celery
- 1 Tbsp. chopped carrot
- 1 Tbsp. chopped walnuts
- ½ tsp. ground cinnamon
- 2 Tbsp. shredded cheddar cheese
- 1 cup unsweetened apple juice
- 1 Tbsp. chili sauce

1. Core apples, leaving bottoms intact. Combine the brown rice and the next 8 ingredients; mix well. Fill each apple with about 2 Tbsp. filling, packing it well.
2. Place the stuffed apples in a greased 4-qt. slow cooker. Pour in the apple juice and chili sauce. Cover and cook on high until the apples are soft, 1½-2 hours. Spoon liquid over each apple serving.
1 STUFFED APPLE: *139 cal., 2g fat (1g sat. fat), 2mg chol., 60mg sod., 31g carb. (20g sugars, 4g fiber), 2g pro.*
DIABETIC EXCHANGES: *1 starch, 1 fruit.*

WILTED SPINACH SALAD WITH BUTTERNUT SQUASH

This warm winter salad is packed with good-for-you spinach, squash and almonds. It feels so festive served at the holidays.
—Margee Berry, White Salmon, WA

- -

PREP: 20 min. • **COOK:** 25 min.
MAKES: 4 servings

1	cup cubed peeled butternut squash
½	tsp. chili powder
½	tsp. salt, divided
4	tsp. olive oil, divided
⅓	cup balsamic vinegar
2	Tbsp. dry red wine or chicken broth
2	Tbsp. whole-berry cranberry sauce
5	cups fresh baby spinach
4	slices red onion
½	cup dried cranberries
⅓	cup slivered almonds, toasted
⅓	cup crumbled goat cheese
	Coarsely ground pepper, optional

1. In a small skillet, saute the squash, chili powder and ¼ tsp. salt in 2 tsp. oil until tender, 11-13 minutes. Set aside; keep warm.

2. In a small saucepan, bring vinegar to a boil. Reduce heat; simmer for 4-6 minutes or until reduced to ¼ cup. Stir in the wine, cranberry sauce, remaining 2 tsp. oil and remaining ¼ tsp. salt. Bring to a boil; cook 1 minute longer.

3. Place spinach on a serving platter; top with onion, cranberries and the squash mixture. Drizzle with warm dressing. Sprinkle with almonds, goat cheese and, if desired, pepper. Serve immediately.

1 SERVING: *228 cal., 12g fat (3g sat. fat), 12mg chol., 382mg sod., 28g carb. (17g sugars, 4g fiber), 5g pro.*
DIABETIC EXCHANGES: *2 fat, 1½ starch, 1 vegetable.*

5-STAR DESSERTS

For a truly showstopping finale to your holiday meal, look no further than the recipes in this chapter. These are some of our most impressive and highly rated desserts ever.

UPSIDE-DOWN PEAR GINGERBREAD CAKE

The aroma of baking gingerbread stirs up such warm memories. This cake looks festive and is even on the lighter side.
—Nancy Beckman, Helena, MT

PREP: 25 min. • **BAKE:** 25 min. + cooling
MAKES: 8 servings

- 3 Tbsp. butter
- ⅓ cup packed dark brown sugar
- 2 medium Bosc pears, peeled and thinly sliced

CAKE
- ½ cup 2% milk
- 1 Tbsp. cider vinegar
- 1 large egg
- ½ cup packed dark brown sugar
- ⅓ cup molasses
- ¼ cup butter, melted
- 1¼ cups all-purpose flour
- 2 tsp. ground cinnamon
- 1 tsp. baking soda
- 1 tsp. ground ginger
- ¼ tsp. salt
- ¼ tsp. ground cloves
  Whipped cream, optional

1. Preheat the oven to 350°. In a small saucepan, melt butter over medium heat; stir in brown sugar. Spread over bottom of a greased 9-in. round baking pan. Arrange pear slices over top.
2. For cake, mix milk and vinegar; let stand for 5 minutes. In a large bowl, beat egg, brown sugar, molasses, melted butter and milk mixture until well blended. In another bowl, whisk flour, cinnamon, baking soda, ginger, salt and cloves; gradually beat into the molasses mixture. Spoon carefully over pear slices.
3. Bake until a toothpick inserted in the center comes out clean, 25-30 minutes. Cool for 10 minutes before inverting onto a serving plate. Serve warm or at room temperature; top with whipped cream if desired.
1 PIECE: *331 cal., 11g fat (7g sat. fat), 51mg chol., 348mg sod., 56g carb. (37g sugars, 2g fiber), 4g pro.*

LINZER TART

This lovely versatile tart shows up regularly at family gatherings. I can customize it for any holiday occasion by using different-shaped cookie cutouts or different fruit fillings. And even my picky children gobble it up!
—Karen Ehatt, Chester, MD

PREP: 25 min. + freezing
BAKE: 20 min. + cooling
MAKES: 12 servings

- ½ cup butter, softened
- ¾ cup sugar
- 1 large egg, room temperature
- ½ tsp. grated lemon zest
- ½ cup slivered almonds, toasted
- 1½ cups all-purpose flour
- 1 tsp. ground cinnamon
- ¼ tsp. salt
- 1 jar (18 oz.) raspberry preserves
  Confectioners' sugar, optional

1. In a large bowl, cream butter and sugar until light and fluffy, 5-7 minutes. Add egg and lemon zest; mix well. Place almonds in a blender or food processor; cover and process until ground. Combine almonds, flour, cinnamon and salt; gradually add to creamed mixture until well blended. Remove ⅓ cup of dough; roll between 2 sheets of waxed paper to ⅛-in. thickness. Freeze until firm, 8-10 minutes.
2. Press remaining dough evenly onto the bottom and up the side of an ungreased 11-in. fluted tart pan with a removable bottom. Spread raspberry preserves over the crust. Remove remaining dough from freezer; using small cookie cutters, cut out desired shapes. Place over preserves.
3. Bake at 375° for 20-25 minutes or until crust is golden brown and filling is bubbly. Cool for 10 minutes. Loosen side of pan. Cool completely on a wire rack. Remove side of pan. If desired, sprinkle top with confectioners' sugar.
1 PIECE: *311 cal., 10g fat (5g sat. fat), 38mg chol., 132mg sod., 53g carb. (38g sugars, 1g fiber), 3g pro.*

THREE-LAYER CHOCOLATE GANACHE CAKE

This decadent triple-layer beauty is pure chocolate indulgence. The cake layers can be frozen prior to final assembly; in fact, they're easier to work with when frozen.
—Kathleen Smith, Overland, MO

- -

PREP: 30 min. • **BAKE:** 30 min. + chilling
MAKES: 16 servings

- 4 cups all-purpose flour
- 2¼ cups sugar
- ¾ cup baking cocoa
- 4 tsp. baking soda
- 2¼ cups mayonnaise
- 2¼ cups brewed coffee, cold
- 1½ tsp. vanilla extract

FILLING
- 1 cup sugar
- 2 Tbsp. cornstarch
- 1 cup 2% milk
- 2 tsp. vanilla extract
- 1 cup butter, softened
- ¾ cup miniature semisweet chocolate chips

GANACHE
- 8 oz. semisweet chocolate, chopped
- 2 cups heavy whipping cream
- 1 tsp. vanilla extract

GLAZE
- 8 oz. semisweet chocolate, chopped
- ¾ cup heavy whipping cream
- ¼ cup butter, cubed
- Finely chopped semisweet chocolate, optional

1. Preheat oven to 350°. Line bottoms of 3 greased 9-in. round baking pans with parchment; grease parchment. In a large bowl, whisk flour, sugar, cocoa and baking soda. Beat in mayonnaise, coffee and vanilla. Transfer batter to prepared pans. Bake 30-35 minutes or until a toothpick inserted in the center comes out clean. Cool in pans 10 minutes before removing to wire racks; remove parchment. Let cool completely.

2. For filling, in a small heavy saucepan, mix sugar and cornstarch. Whisk in milk. Cook and stir over medium heat until thickened and bubbly. Reduce heat to low; cook and stir 2 minutes longer. Remove from heat; stir in vanilla. Cool completely. In a large bowl, cream butter. Gradually beat in the cooled mixture. Stir in the chocolate chips.

3. For ganache, place chocolate in a large bowl. In a small saucepan, bring cream just to a boil. Pour over chocolate; let stand for 5 minutes. Whisk until smooth. Stir in vanilla. Cool to room temperature, stirring occasionally. Refrigerate, covered, until cold. Beat just until soft peaks form, 15-30 seconds (do not overbeat).

4. Place 1 cake layer on a serving plate; spread with half the filling. Repeat layers. Top with the remaining cake layer. Frost the top and side of cake with ganache.

5. For glaze, in a microwave-safe bowl, combine chocolate, cream and cubed butter. Microwave at 50% power for 1-2 minutes or until smooth, stirring twice. Cool slightly, stirring occasionally. Drizzle glaze over cake, allowing some to flow over the edge. Scatter finely chopped semisweet chocolate over top of cake if desired. Refrigerate for at least 2 hours before serving.

1 PIECE: *970 cal., 65g fat (30g sat. fat), 88mg chol., 607mg sod., 81g carb. (53g sugars, 3g fiber), 8g pro.*

GET THE LOOK

To get the distinctive "naked cake" look, spread a layer of ganache on the outside of the cake that's thin enough to leave the layers exposed. Start pouring the glaze in the center of the cake, and work your way outward to where you want it to drip down. The glaze should be thin enough to pour but still thick enough to cling.

AMARETTO RICOTTA CHEESECAKE

There's a good reason why a relative handed this cherished recipe down to me. It's a keeper! The amaretto and ricotta make for a truly impressive dessert.
—Isabel Neuman, Surprise, AZ

PREP: 35 min. + chilling
BAKE: 1 hour + chilling
MAKES: 16 servings

- 2¾ cups whole-milk ricotta cheese
- ⅓ cup cornstarch
- ¼ cup amaretto
- 2 pkg. (8 oz. each) cream cheese, softened
- 1½ cups sugar
- 1 cup sour cream
- 5 large eggs, room temperature, lightly beaten

TOPPING
- 1 cup sour cream
- 2 Tbsp. sugar
- 2 Tbsp. amaretto

GARNISH
- 1 Tbsp. light corn syrup
- 1 cup fresh cranberries
- ⅓ cup sugar
- ½ cup sliced almonds, toasted

1. Line a strainer or colander with 4 layers of cheesecloth or 1 coffee filter; place over a bowl. Place ricotta in prepared strainer; cover ricotta with sides of cheesecloth. Refrigerate at least 8 hours or overnight. Remove ricotta from cheesecloth; discard liquid in bowl.

2. Preheat oven to 350°. In a small bowl, mix cornstarch and amaretto. In a large bowl, beat cream cheese, sugar, sour cream and drained ricotta until smooth. Beat in amaretto mixture. Add eggs; beat on low speed just until blended.

3. Pour into a greased 10-in. springform pan. Place on a baking sheet. Bake until center is almost set, 1-1¼ hours. Let stand 5 minutes on a wire rack.

4. In a small bowl, mix topping ingredients; spread over the top of the cheesecake. Bake 5 minutes longer.

5. Cool on a wire rack 10 minutes. Loosen sides from pan with a knife. Cool 1 hour longer. Refrigerate overnight, covering when completely cooled. Remove rim from pan.

6. For garnish, place corn syrup in a small microwave-safe bowl. Microwave, uncovered, until warm, about 10 seconds. Add cranberries; toss to coat. Place sugar in a small bowl; add cranberries and toss to coat. Place on waxed paper and let stand until set, about 1 hour.

7. Top cheesecake with almonds and sugared cranberries.

NOTE: *To toast nuts, bake in a shallow pan in a 350° oven for 5-10 minutes or cook in a skillet over low heat until lightly browned, stirring occasionally.*

1 PIECE: *351 cal., 21g fat (13g sat. fat), 134mg chol., 168mg sod., 29g carb. (26g sugars, 0 fiber), 10g pro.*

ELEGANT WHITE CHOCOLATE MOUSSE

Simply elegant is a fitting description for this smooth treat. Whipped cream teams up with white chocolate to make this easy recipe extra special.
—Laurinda Johnston, Belchertown, MA

- -

PREP: 20 min. + chilling • **MAKES:** 8 servings

- 12 oz. white baking chocolate, coarsely chopped
- 2 cups heavy whipping cream, divided
- 1 Tbsp. confectioners' sugar
- 1 tsp. vanilla extract
  Mixed fresh berries, optional

1. In a small heavy saucepan, combine chocolate and ⅔ cup cream; cook and stir over medium-low heat until smooth. Transfer mixture to a large bowl; let cool to room temperature.
2. In a small bowl, beat the remaining 1⅓ cup cream until it begins to thicken. Add confectioners' sugar and vanilla; beat until soft peaks form. Fold ¼ cup whipped cream into chocolate mixture, then fold in remaining whipped cream.
3. Spoon into dessert dishes. Refrigerate, covered, for at least 2 hours. If desired, garnish with fresh berries.
½ CUP: 422 cal., 34g fat (23g sat. fat), 68mg chol., 47mg sod., 30g carb. (30g sugars, 0 fiber), 5g pro.

WHITE CHOCOLATE CRANBERRY ALMOND TART

This tart of white chocolate and cranberries is my signature holiday dessert. I also make it for local coffeehouses and restaurants— it's always highly requested.
—Trisha Kruse, Eagle, ID

- -

PREP: 55 min. • **BAKE:** 20 min. + chilling
MAKES: 12 servings

- ½ cup slivered almonds, toasted
- 3 Tbsp. sugar
- 1⅔ cups all-purpose flour
- ¼ tsp. salt
- ¼ cup butter, melted
- ¼ cup heavy whipping cream
- ⅔ cup white baking chips

FILLING
- 2 cups fresh or frozen cranberries
- 1 cup sugar
- ½ cup dried cranberries
- ⅓ cup orange juice
- 2 Tbsp. butter

TOPPING
- ⅔ cup white baking chips
- 2 tsp. shortening
- ⅓ cup slivered almonds, toasted

1. Place almonds and sugar in a food processor; pulse until almonds are ground. Add flour and salt; pulse until blended. Transfer to a small bowl; stir in melted butter and cream. Press onto bottom and up sides of an ungreased 9-in. fluted tart pan with a removable bottom.
2. Bake at 375° for 15-18 minutes or until lightly browned. Remove from oven; sprinkle baking chips evenly over bottom. Cool on a wire rack.
3. In a saucepan, combine the filling ingredients; bring to a boil. Reduce heat; simmer, uncovered, for 10-15 minutes or until slightly thickened, stirring occasionally. Pour over baking chips.
4. Bake 20-25 minutes or until filling is bubbly and crust is golden brown. Cool on a wire rack. Refrigerate for 2 hours or until cold.
5. For topping, in a microwave, melt baking chips and shortening; stir until smooth. Drizzle over tart. Sprinkle with toasted almonds.
NOTE: *To toast nuts, bake in a shallow pan in a 350° oven for 5-10 minutes or cook in a skillet over low heat until lightly browned, stirring occasionally.*
1 PIECE: *393 cal., 18g fat (9g sat. fat), 25mg chol., 115mg sod., 56g carb. (38g sugars, 3g fiber), 5g pro.*

ORANGE GINGERBREAD TASSIES

I make big Christmas cookie plates every year, and it's fun to have something with a different shape to include. These have a delicious flavor with the gingerbread and orange, and they are really easy! The tassies are also yummy made with lemon zest if you prefer that to orange.
—Elisabeth Larsen, Pleasant Grove, UT

- -

PREP: 20 min. + chilling • **BAKE:** 15 min. + cooling • **MAKES:** 2 dozen

- ½   cup butter, softened
- 4   oz. cream cheese, softened
- ¼   cup molasses
- 1   tsp. ground ginger
- ½   tsp. ground cinnamon
- ½   tsp. ground allspice
- ¼   tsp. ground cloves
- 1   cup all-purpose flour
- ½   cup white baking chips
- ¼   cup heavy whipping cream
- 2   Tbsp. butter
- 4   tsp. grated orange zest
    Candied orange peel, optional

1. Beat the first 7 ingredients until light and fluffy. Gradually beat in the flour. Refrigerate, covered, until firm enough to shape, about 1 hour. Preheat oven to 350°.

2. Shape dough into twenty-four 1-in. balls; press evenly onto bottoms and up sides of ungreased mini-muffin cups. Bake until golden brown, 15-18 minutes. Press centers with the handle of a wooden spoon to reshape as necessary. Cool completely in pan before removing to wire rack.

3. In a microwave-safe bowl, heat baking chips, cream and butter until blended, stirring occasionally. Stir in orange zest; cool completely. Spoon into crusts. Refrigerate until filling is soft-set. If desired, garnish with orange peel.

1 COOKIE: *91 cal., 6g fat (4g sat. fat), 13mg chol., 43mg sod., 9g carb. (5g sugars, 0 fiber), 1g pro.*

WALNUT BLITZ TORTE

This pretty torte is very popular at family gatherings. The cake layers are baked with the "frosting"—crunchy, sweet meringue—already in place, and then assembled with a layer of luscious custard in the center. Everyone always asks for the recipe.
—Suzan Stacey, Parsonsfield, ME

- -

PREP: 30 min. + chilling • **BAKE:** 35 min. + cooling
MAKES: 16 servings

- 2   Tbsp. sugar
- 4½   tsp. cornstarch
- 1   cup whole milk
- 1   large egg yolk, room temperature, lightly beaten
- 1   tsp. vanilla extract

CAKE BATTER
- ½   cup butter, softened
- ½   cup sugar
- 4   large egg yolks, room temperature
- 1   tsp. vanilla extract
- 1   cup all-purpose flour
- 1   tsp. baking powder
- ¼   tsp. salt
- 5   Tbsp. whole milk

MERINGUE
- 5   large egg whites, room temperature
- 1   cup sugar
- 2   cups chopped walnuts, divided

1. Preheat oven to 325°. In a small saucepan, combine sugar and cornstarch. Stir in milk until smooth. Cook and stir over medium-high heat until thickened and bubbly. Reduce heat to low; cook and stir 2 minutes longer. Remove from the heat. Stir a small amount of hot filling into beaten egg yolk; return all to the pan, stirring constantly. Bring to a gentle boil; cook and stir for 2 minutes. Remove from the heat; stir in vanilla. Cover and refrigerate.

2. Meanwhile, in a large bowl, cream the butter and sugar until light and fluffy, 5-7 minutes. Beat in the egg yolks and vanilla. Combine the flour, baking powder and salt; gradually add to creamed mixture alternately with milk and mix well. Spread into 2 greased and floured 9-in. round baking pans; set aside.

3. In a small bowl, beat egg whites on medium speed until foamy. Gradually beat in sugar, a tablespoon at a time, on high until stiff glossy peaks form and sugar is dissolved. Fold in 1 cup nuts. Spread meringue evenly over batter. Sprinkle with the remaining 1 cup nuts.

4. Bake for 35-40 minutes or until meringue is browned and crisp. Cool on wire racks for 10 minutes (meringue will crack).

5. Carefully run a knife around edge of pans to loosen. Remove to wire racks; cool with meringue side up. To assemble, place 1 cake with meringue side up on a serving plate; carefully spread with custard. Top with remaining cake. Refrigerate until serving.

1 PIECE: *292 cal., 17g fat (5g sat. fat), 85mg chol., 149mg sod., 30g carb. (21g sugars, 1g fiber), 7g pro.*

CHOCOLATE VELVET DESSERT

This extra-special creation is the result of several attempts to duplicate a dessert I enjoyed on vacation. It looks so beautiful on a buffet table that many folks are tempted to forgo the main course in favor of it.
—Molly Seidel, Edgewood, NM

PREP: 20 min. • **BAKE:** 45 min. + chilling
MAKES: 16 servings

1½ cups chocolate wafer crumbs
2 Tbsp. sugar
¼ cup butter, melted
2 cups semisweet chocolate chips
6 large egg yolks
1¾ cups heavy whipping cream
1 tsp. vanilla extract

CHOCOLATE BUTTERCREAM FROSTING
½ cup butter, softened
3 cups confectioners' sugar
3 Tbsp. baking cocoa
3 to 4 Tbsp. 2% milk

1. Preheat oven to 350°. In a small bowl, combine wafer crumbs and sugar; stir in butter. Press onto the bottom and 1½ in. up the inside of a greased 9-in. springform pan. Place on a baking sheet. Bake for 10 minutes. Cool on a wire rack.
2. In a large microwave-safe bowl, melt chocolate chips; stir until smooth. Cool. In a small bowl, combine the egg yolks, cream and vanilla. Gradually stir a small amount of egg mixture into the melted chocolate until blended; gradually stir in remaining egg mixture. Pour into crust.
3. Place pan on a baking sheet. Bake for 45-50 minutes or until center is almost set. Cool on a wire rack for 10 minutes. Carefully run a knife around edge of pan to loosen; cool 1 hour longer. Refrigerate overnight.
4. For frosting, in a large bowl, combine the butter, confectioners' sugar, cocoa and enough milk to achieve a piping consistency. Using a large star tip, pipe onto dessert.

1 PIECE: 432 cal., 28g fat (16g sat. fat), 139mg chol., 164mg sod., 46g carb. (35g sugars, 2g fiber), 4g pro.

HOLIDAY STAR COOKIES

These lovely treats are both a cookie and a candy. The melted hard-candy center looks like stained glass surrounded by a frosted cutout cookie.
—Taste of Home *Test Kitchen*

PREP: 45 min.
BAKE: 10 min./batch + cooling
MAKES: 22 cookies

1½ cups butter, softened
1½ cups sugar
2 large eggs, room temperature
3 tsp. vanilla extract
4½ cups all-purpose flour
1 tsp. baking soda
1 tsp. cream of tartar
1 tsp. salt
   Assorted colors of
   Jolly Rancher hard candies
1 Tbsp. meringue powder
3 Tbsp. plus ½ tsp. water
2⅔ cups confectioners' sugar
   Colored sugar

1. Cream butter and sugar until light and fluffy, 5-7 minutes. Add eggs, 1 at a time, beating well after each addition. Beat in vanilla. Combine flour, baking soda, cream of tartar and salt; gradually add to creamed mixture. Divide into 3 portions; cover and refrigerate until easy to handle, about 30 minutes.
2. Preheat oven to 350°. Roll out 1 portion of dough between 2 pieces of parchment to ¼-in. thickness. Cut with a floured 5-in. star-shaped cookie cutter. Cut out centers with a floured 2½-in. star-shaped cookie cutter. Place larger cutouts 2 in. apart on parchment-lined baking sheets. Repeat with remaining dough; reroll small cutouts if desired.
3. Bake until just lightly browned, 8-10 minutes. Let cool completely.
4. Separate candies by color. Place each color of candy in a small resealable plastic bag; crush candies. Sprinkle in center of each cookie. Bake cookies until candy is melted, 2 minutes more. While candy is still hot and melted, use a toothpick to carefully spread candy into the corners. Cool until candies are set, 2-3 minutes; remove to wire racks to cool completely.
5. For icing, in a small bowl, beat meringue powder and water until soft peaks form. Gradually add the confectioners' sugar. Decorate cookies with icing; sprinkle with colored sugar.

NOTE: *Meringue powder is available from Wilton Industries. Call 800-794-5866 or visit* wilton.com.

1 COOKIE: 323 cal., 13g fat (8g sat. fat), 50mg chol., 275mg sod., 48g carb. (28g sugars, 1g fiber), 4g pro.

MAPLE-ORANGE PEAR CRISP

My family loves to kick back after dinner and dig into big bowls of this spiced crisp. It isn't too sweet, but it still satisfies a sweet tooth.
—Noreen McCormick Danek, Cromwell, CT

PREP: 15 min. • **BAKE:** 30 min.
MAKES: 8 servings

- ½ cup chopped pecans
- ¼ cup butter, cubed
- 3 Tbsp. brown sugar
- 3 Tbsp. all-purpose flour
- 1 tsp. grated orange zest
- ½ tsp. ground cinnamon
- ¼ tsp. salt
- ¼ tsp. ground ginger
- ⅛ tsp. ground cloves
- 1 tsp. butter, softened

FILLING
- 6 medium ripe Bosc pears
- 2 Tbsp. lemon juice
- ⅓ cup maple syrup
- 1 Tbsp. butter
- 2 tsp. grated orange zest
- 1 tsp. ground cinnamon
  Ice cream or whipped cream

1. Preheat oven to 375°. Place the first 9 ingredients in a food processor; pulse until crumbly. Grease an 8-in. square baking dish with the softened butter.
2. Peel, core and cut each pear lengthwise into 8 wedges; toss with lemon juice. Place in prepared baking dish.
3. In a small saucepan, combine syrup, butter, orange zest and cinnamon; bring to a boil, stirring constantly. Pour over pears. Sprinkle with crumb mixture. Bake until golden brown and pears are tender, 30-40 minutes. Serve with ice cream.
1 SERVING: *254 cal., 12g fat (5g sat. fat), 19mg chol., 135mg sod., 38g carb. (26g sugars, 5g fiber), 2g pro.*

Holiday Helper

If you can't get Bosc pears, opt for Anjou pears instead; they both hold their shape well when baked. Pears are picked before they've ripened, so plan on buying your pears several days before you plan to use them.

PEPPERMINT CHEESECAKE

People are thrilled when they see me coming with this rich, smooth cheesecake—it's always a crowd-pleaser. Not only does it look sensational, it is so scrumptious.
—Carrie Price, Ottawa, IL

PREP: 40 min. • **BAKE:** 1¼ hours + chilling
MAKES: 16 servings

- 2½ cups cream-filled chocolate sandwich cookie crumbs
- ⅓ cup butter, melted
- 5 pkg. (8 oz. each) cream cheese, softened
- 1 cup sugar
- 1 cup sour cream
- 3 Tbsp. all-purpose flour
- 3 tsp. vanilla extract
- 1 tsp. peppermint extract
- 3 large eggs, lightly beaten
- 1 pkg. (10 oz.) Andes creme de menthe baking chips or 2 pkg. (4.67 oz. each) mint Andes candies, chopped

TOPPING
- 1 pkg. (8 oz.) cream cheese, softened
- ⅓ cup sugar
- 1 carton (12 oz.) frozen whipped topping, thawed
  Optional: Crushed candy canes and chocolate shavings

1. Preheat oven to 325°. Place a greased 9-in. springform pan on a double thickness of heavy-duty foil (about 18 in. square). Securely wrap foil around pan.
2. In a small bowl, combine cookie crumbs and butter. Press onto the bottom and 1 in. up inside of the prepared pan. Place pan on a baking sheet. Bake until set, 12-14 minutes. Cool on a wire rack.
3. In a large bowl, beat cream cheese and sugar until smooth. Beat in the sour cream, flour and extracts. Add eggs; beat on low speed just until combined. Fold in chips. Pour into crust. (Pan will be full.) Place springform pan in a large baking pan; add 1 in. hot water to larger pan.
4. Bake until center is just set and top appears dull, 1¼-1½ hours. Remove springform pan from water bath. Cool on a wire rack 10 minutes. Carefully run a knife around edge of pan to loosen; cool 1 hour longer. Refrigerate overnight. Remove side of pan.
5. For topping, in a large bowl, beat cream cheese and sugar until smooth. Stir one-fourth of the whipped topping into mixture; fold in remaining whipped topping. Spread or pipe onto cheesecake. Garnish with crushed candy canes and shaved chocolate if desired.
1 PIECE: *711 cal., 51g fat (33g sat. fat), 153mg chol., 424mg sod., 52g carb. (38g sugars, 2g fiber), 10g pro.*

BAKLAVA CHEESECAKE

With sugared cranberries and rosemary sprigs, my unique baklava cheesecake makes a grand display for office parties and other special events.
—*Aryanna Gamble, New Orleans, LA*

- -

PREP: 1¼ hours • **BAKE:** 50 min. + chilling
MAKES: 16 servings

- 12 sheets phyllo dough (14x9-in.)
- ⅓ cup butter, melted
- 1 cup finely chopped walnuts
- ¼ cup sugar
- ½ tsp. ground cinnamon
- ¼ tsp. ground nutmeg
- ⅛ tsp. ground allspice
- 2 pkg. (8 oz. each) cream cheese, softened
- 1 carton (8 oz.) mascarpone cheese
- ⅔ cup honey
- ¼ cup 2% milk
- 3 Tbsp. all-purpose flour
- 3 large eggs, room temperature, lightly beaten

GARNISH
- 3 Tbsp. light corn syrup
- 3 fresh rosemary sprigs
- ¼ cup sugar, divided
- ½ cup fresh or frozen cranberries, thawed and patted dry

1. Preheat oven to 425°. Place 1 sheet of phyllo dough in a greased 9-in. springform pan, pressing phyllo onto bottom and up side of pan; brush with butter. Layer with the remaining phyllo sheets, brushing each layer and rotating sheets slightly to stagger the corners. (While working, keep unused phyllo covered with a damp towel to prevent it from drying out.) Place the springform on a 15x10x1-in. baking pan.

2. In a small bowl, mix walnuts, sugar and spices; sprinkle over bottom of phyllo. Bake 5-7 minutes or until the edge is lightly browned (side will puff). Cool in springform pan on a wire rack. Reduce oven setting to 325°.

3. In a large bowl, beat cream cheese and mascarpone cheese on low speed until smooth. Beat in honey, milk and flour. Add eggs; beat on low speed just until blended. Pour into crust.

4. Return springform pan to baking pan. Bake 50-60 minutes or until center is almost set. Cool on wire rack 1 hour. Refrigerate overnight, covering when completely cooled. Remove rim from pan.

5. For garnish, place corn syrup in a small microwave-safe bowl. Microwave, uncovered, 10 seconds or until warm. Brush corn syrup lightly over both sides of rosemary. Place on waxed paper; sprinkle with 1 Tbsp. sugar.

6. If needed, reheat remaining corn syrup until warm; gently toss cranberries in syrup. Place remaining 3 Tbsp. sugar in a small bowl; add cranberries and toss to coat. Place on waxed paper and let stand until set, about 1 hour.

7. Just before serving, top cheesecake with sugared rosemary and cranberries.
1 PIECE: *351 cal., 26g fat (13g sat. fat), 92mg chol., 178mg sod., 26g carb. (19g sugars, 1g fiber), 6g pro.*

COCONUT CREAM ANGEL PIE

Mom would whip up this wonderful dessert on an impulse, using an ancient whisk and an old skillet. I am still amazed that the pie turned out perfect every time!
—Ginny Werkmeister, Tilden, NE

PREP: 30 min. + chilling • **BAKE:** 20 min. + cooling • **MAKES:** 8 servings

       Dough for single-crust pie
½   cup sugar
¼   cup cornstarch
¼   tsp. salt
2   cups whole milk
3   large egg yolks, lightly beaten
½   cup sweetened shredded coconut
1   Tbsp. butter
1½ tsp. vanilla extract
MERINGUE
3   large egg whites, room temperature
¼   tsp. cream of tartar
¼   tsp. vanilla extract
6   Tbsp. sugar
¼   cup sweetened shredded coconut

1. On a lightly floured surface, roll dough to a ⅛-in.-thick circle; transfer to a 9-in. pie plate. Trim to ½ in. beyond rim of plate; flute edge. Refrigerate 30 minutes. Preheat oven to 425°.
2. Line unpricked crust with a double thickness of foil. Fill with pie weights, dried beans or uncooked rice. Bake on a lower oven rack until edges are light golden brown, 15-20 minutes. Remove foil and weights; bake until bottom is golden brown, 3-6 minutes longer. Cool on a wire rack. Reduce oven setting to 350°.
3. In a small heavy saucepan, combine the sugar, cornstarch and salt. Add milk; stir until smooth. Cook and stir over medium-high heat until thickened and bubbly. Reduce heat to low; cook and stir 2 minutes longer.
4. Remove from the heat. Stir a small amount of hot filling into egg yolks; return all to the pan, stirring constantly. Bring to a gentle boil; cook and stir 2 minutes longer. Remove from the heat; stir in the coconut, butter and vanilla. Pour into crust.
5. In a small bowl, beat the egg whites, cream of tartar and vanilla on medium speed until soft peaks form. Gradually beat in sugar, 1 Tbsp. at a time, on high until stiff peaks form. Spread meringue over hot filling, sealing edges to crust. Sprinkle with coconut.
6. Bake until golden brown, 17-20 minutes. Cool on a wire rack for 1 hour. Refrigerate for at least 3 hours before serving. Store leftovers in the refrigerator.
NOTE: *Let pie weights cool before storing. Beans and rice may be reused for pie weights, but not for cooking.*
DOUGH FOR SINGLE-CRUST PIE: *Combine 1¼ cups all-purpose flour and ¼ tsp. salt; cut in ½ cup cold butter until crumbly. Gradually add 3-5 Tbsp. ice water, tossing with a fork until dough holds together when pressed. Shape into a disk; wrap and refrigerate for 1 hour.*
1 PIECE: *342 cal., 15g fat (8g sat. fat), 92mg chol., 255mg sod., 46g carb. (29g sugars, 0 fiber), 6g pro.*

MIXED NUT BARS

One pan of these bars goes a long way. They get a nice flavor from butterscotch chips.
—Bobbi Brown, Waupaca, WI

PREP: 10 min. • **BAKE:** 20 min. + cooling • **MAKES:** 2½ dozen

1½ cups all-purpose flour
¾   cup packed brown sugar
¼   tsp. salt
½   cup plus 2 Tbsp. cold butter, divided
1   cup butterscotch chips
½   cup light corn syrup
1   can (11½ oz.) mixed nuts

1. Preheat oven to 350°. In a small bowl, combine the flour, brown sugar and salt. Cut in ½ cup butter until the mixture resembles coarse crumbs. Press into a greased 13x9-in. baking pan. Bake for 10 minutes.
2. Meanwhile, in a microwave, melt butterscotch chips and remaining 2 Tbsp. butter; stir until smooth. Stir in corn syrup.
3. Sprinkle nuts over crust; top with butterscotch mixture. Bake until set, about 10 minutes. Cool on a wire rack. Cut into bars.
1 BAR: *201 cal., 12g fat (5g sat. fat), 10mg chol., 98mg sod., 22g carb. (15g sugars, 1g fiber), 3g pro.*

CHOCOLATE-RASPBERRY CREME BRULEE

Just when I thought nothing could beat classic creme brulee, I created this decadent version that stars rich chocolate and sweet raspberries. Cracking through the top reveals a smooth and rich custard everyone enjoys.
—Jan Valdez, Chicago, IL

PREP: 25 min. • **BAKE:** 40 min. + chilling
MAKES: 10 servings

- 8 oz. semisweet chocolate, chopped
- 4 cups heavy whipping cream
- ½ cup plus 2 Tbsp. sugar, divided
- 8 large egg yolks, beaten
- 1 Tbsp. vanilla extract
- 30 fresh raspberries
- 2 Tbsp. brown sugar
  Additional fresh raspberries, optional

1. Preheat oven to 325°. Place chocolate in a large bowl. In a large saucepan, bring cream and ½ cup sugar just to a boil. Pour over chocolate; whisk until smooth. Slowly stir hot cream mixture into egg yolks; stir in vanilla.
2. Place 3 raspberries in each of 10 ungreased 6-oz. ramekins or custard cups. Evenly divide custard among ramekins. Place in a baking pan; add 1 in. of boiling water to pan. Bake, uncovered, for 40-50 minutes or until centers are just set (custard will jiggle). Remove ramekins from water bath; cool for 10 minutes. Refrigerate, covered, at least 4 hours.
3. Combine brown sugar and remaining sugar. Sprinkle custards with sugar mixture. Heat sugar with a culinary torch until caramelized. Serve immediately.
BROIL OPTION: *If broiling the custards, place chilled ramekins on a baking sheet and let stand at room temperature 15 minutes. Sprinkle with sugar mixture. Broil 8 in. from the heat until sugar is caramelized, 4-7 minutes. Refrigerate again until firm, 1-2 hours. If desired, top with additional fresh raspberries.*
1 SERVING: *549 cal., 46g fat (27g sat. fat), 294mg chol., 44mg sod., 32g carb. (27g sugars, 2g fiber), 6g pro.*

SALTED CARAMEL CUPCAKES

To help balance the sweetness of this brown sugar cupcake, our Test Kitchen cooks created a unique salty frosting. It's the best of both worlds!
—Taste of Home *Test Kitchen*

PREP: 25 min. + chilling
BAKE: 20 min. + cooling
MAKES: 10 cupcakes

- ½ cup butter, softened
- ½ cup packed brown sugar
- ¼ cup sugar
- 2 large eggs, room temperature
- 1 tsp. vanilla extract
- 1¼ cups all-purpose flour
- ¾ tsp. baking powder
- ¼ tsp. salt
- ½ cup 2% milk

FROSTING
- ⅓ cup sugar
- 4 tsp. water
- ⅛ tsp. salt
- 1⅓ cups heavy whipping cream
  Optional: Caramel ice cream topping and flaky sea salt

1. Preheat oven to 350°. In a large bowl, cream butter and sugars until light and fluffy, 5-7 minutes. Add eggs, 1 at a time, beating well after each addition. Beat in vanilla. Combine flour, baking powder and salt; add to creamed mixture alternately with milk, beating well after each addition.
2. Fill 10 paper-lined muffin cups three-fourths full. Bake 18-22 minutes or until a toothpick inserted in the center of a cupcake comes out clean. Cool for 10 minutes before removing from pan to a wire rack to cool completely.
3. In a large, heavy saucepan, combine sugar, water and salt. Cook over medium-low heat until sugar begins to melt. Gently pull melted sugar to center of pan until sugar melts evenly. Cook, without stirring, until mixture turns an amber color.
4. Remove from heat; gradually stir in cream until smooth. Transfer to a small bowl; cover and refrigerate for 4 hours. Beat until stiff peaks form. Frost cupcakes. If desired, top with caramel and sea salt.
1 CUPCAKE: *416 cal., 22g fat (14g sat. fat), 111mg chol., 224mg sod., 52g carb. (39g sugars, 0 fiber), 4g pro*

LEMON-ROSEMARY LAYER CAKE

Tall and impressive, this unique dessert is a treat for the senses with flecks of lemon zest and fresh rosemary. Just wait till you taste it!
—Mary Fraser, Surprise, AZ

PREP: 20 min. • **BAKE:** 25 min. + cooling
MAKES: 16 servings

1	cup plus 2 Tbsp. butter, softened
2½	cups sugar
4	large eggs, room temperature
1	large egg yolk, room temperature
4	cups all-purpose flour
3	tsp. baking powder
1½	tsp. salt
¼	tsp. plus ⅛ tsp. baking soda
1½	cups sour cream
6	Tbsp. lemon juice
3	tsp. grated lemon zest
3	tsp. minced fresh rosemary

FROSTING

2	pkg. (8 oz. each) cream cheese, softened
8¼	cups confectioners' sugar
3	tsp. grated lemon zest
2¼	tsp. lemon juice
	Optional: Candied lemon and rosemary sprigs

1. Preheat oven to 350°. In a large bowl, cream butter and sugar until light and fluffy, 5-7 minutes. Add eggs and yolk, 1 at a time; beat well after each addition. Combine flour, baking powder, salt and baking soda; add to the creamed mixture alternately with sour cream, beating well after each addition. Beat in the lemon juice, zest and rosemary.

2. Transfer to 3 greased and floured 9-in. round baking pans. Bake until the edges begin to brown, 25-30 minutes. Cool for 10 minutes before removing from pans to wire racks to cool completely.

3. For frosting, in a large bowl, beat cream cheese until fluffy. Add the confectioners' sugar, lemon zest and lemon juice; beat until smooth.

4. Spread frosting between layers and over top and side of cake. If desired, decorate with candied lemon and rosemary. Refrigerate leftovers.
1 PIECE: *756 cal., 28g fat (17g sat. fat), 146mg chol., 527mg sod., 119g carb. (90g sugars, 1g fiber), 8g pro*

Holiday Helper

For the perfectly frosted cake, start with a "crumb coat," which is a fancy term for the first layer of frosting. This thin layer helps seal the cake layers and will trap any cake crumbs. Refrigerate until cake is chilled, then complete the second coat of frosting.

SWEET POTATO COCONUT PIE WITH MARSHMALLOW MERINGUE

My grandmother's sweet potato casserole contains coconut and marshmallows. I translated her beloved side dish into a pie, and it's even better!
—Simone Bazos, Baltimore, MD

PREP: 1 hour • **BAKE:** 40 minutes + chilling
MAKES: 8 servings

1½ cups all-purpose flour
¼ tsp. salt
¼ tsp. ground ginger
6 Tbsp. cold butter
2 Tbsp. shortening
3 to 4 Tbsp. cold water
FILLING
1 cup coconut milk
¾ cup packed brown sugar
¼ cup cream cheese, softened
2 cups mashed sweet potatoes
3 large eggs, lightly beaten
2 tsp. lemon juice
1½ tsp. vanilla extract
¼ tsp. salt
¼ tsp. ground cinnamon
MERINGUE
¾ cup sugar
⅓ cup water
4 large egg whites, room temperature
¼ tsp. cream of tartar
1 jar (7 oz.) marshmallow creme
Optional: Miniature marshmallows and sweetened shredded coconut

1. In a food processor, combine flour, salt and ginger; cover and pulse to blend. Add butter and shortening; cover and pulse until mixture resembles coarse crumbs.
2. While processing, gradually add cold water just until moist crumbs form. Shape into a disk; wrap and refrigerate for 30 minutes or until easy to handle.

3. Preheat oven to 425°. Roll out dough to fit a 9-in. deep-dish pie plate. Transfer to pie plate. Trim to ½ in. beyond rim of plate; flute or press edge. Refrigerate until ready to fill.
4. For the filling, in a small saucepan, combine the coconut milk, brown sugar and cream cheese. Cook and stir until smooth. Transfer to a large bowl; cool 5 minutes. Whisk in the sweet potatoes, eggs, lemon juice, vanilla, salt and cinnamon. Pour into the prepared crust.
5. Bake on lower oven rack 10-15 minutes. Reduce oven setting to 325°; bake until set, 40-50 minutes. Cover edge with foil if necessary during the last 15 minutes to prevent overbrowning. Cool on a wire rack. Refrigerate at least 3 hours before topping with meringue.
6. For meringue, combine sugar and water in a small saucepan over medium-high heat; using a pastry brush dipped in water, wash down the sides of the pan to eliminate sugar crystals. When the mixture comes to a boil, stop brushing. Cook without stirring until a thermometer reads 240° (soft-ball stage).
7. As the sugar mixture cooks, preheat broiler. Beat egg whites and cream of tartar on medium speed until soft peaks form. While beating, gradually drizzle hot sugar mixture over egg whites; continue beating until stiff glossy peaks form.
8. Place marshmallow creme in a separate large bowl; fold in a third of the egg white mixture, then fold in the remaining mixture. If necessary, beat again until stiff glossy peaks form.
9. Spread the meringue over the cool pie; broil 4-6 in. from heat until slightly browned, 1-2 minutes. Cool on a wire rack. Store leftovers in the refrigerator.
1 PIECE: *598 cal., 21g fat (13g sat. fat), 100mg chol., 348mg sod., 88g carb. (60g sugars, 3g fiber), 9g pro.*

> ### Holiday Helper
> This meringue will be softer than a baked meringue because of the marshmallow in it. You can also use a culinary torch to toast the meringue instead of the broiler.

STICKY TOFFEE RICE PUDDING WITH CARAMEL CREAM

Simple rice pudding gets a makeover with this upscale recipe. It has just the right thickness to soak up a hot caramel topping.
—*Janice Elder, Charlotte, NC*

PREP: 45 min. • **BAKE:** 35 min. + cooling • **MAKES:** 16 servings

- 3 cups water
- 1 cup uncooked medium-grain rice
- ¼ tsp. salt
- 3 cups pitted dates, chopped
- 3 cups 2% milk
- 2 tsp. vanilla extract
- 1 cup packed brown sugar
- 1½ cups heavy whipping cream, divided
- ¼ cup butter, cubed
- ½ cup sour cream
- ¼ cup hot caramel ice cream topping

1. Preheat oven to 350°. In a large saucepan, bring water, rice and salt to a boil. Reduce heat; cover and simmer 12-15 minutes or until the rice is tender. Add dates and milk; cook and stir for 10 minutes. Remove from the heat; stir in vanilla. Set aside.
2. In a small saucepan, combine brown sugar, 1 cup cream and the butter. Bring to a boil. Reduce heat; simmer, uncovered, for 2 minutes, stirring constantly. Stir into the rice mixture. Transfer to a greased 13x9-in. baking dish. Bake, uncovered, until bubbly, 35-40 minutes. Cool for 15 minutes.
3. Meanwhile, in a small bowl, beat the sour cream, caramel topping and remaining ½ cup cream until slightly thickened. Serve with warm rice pudding. Refrigerate leftovers.
½ CUP RICE PUDDING WITH 1 TBSP. TOPPING: *329 cal., 14g fat (8g sat. fat), 38mg chol., 112mg sod., 50g carb. (37g sugars, 2g fiber), 4g pro.*

HAZELNUT PECAN PIE

With a blend of chocolate, pecans and hazelnuts, this pie is top-level tasty. But because so it's easy to make, you can enjoy it often. Your family and friends will think you worked for hours in the kitchen. It's incredible plain, but a dollop of whipped cream takes it over the top.
—*Brenda Melancon, McComb, MS*

PREP: 25 min. • **BAKE:** 50 min. + cooling • **MAKES:** 8 servings

- 1 sheet refrigerated pie crust
- 3 large eggs
- 1 cup sugar
- ½ cup hazelnut flavoring syrup
- ½ cup dark corn syrup
- 3 Tbsp. all-purpose flour
- 2 Tbsp. butter, softened
- 1 tsp. vanilla extract
- 1½ cups coarsely chopped pecans
- ½ cup chopped hazelnuts
- ½ cup semisweet chocolate chips
  Whipped cream, optional

1. Preheat oven to 350°. Unroll crust into a 9-in. pie plate; flute edge. In a large bowl, whisk the eggs, sugar, syrups, flour, butter and vanilla. Stir in the pecans, hazelnuts and chocolate chips. Transfer to crust.
2. Bake for 50-55 minutes or until set. Cool on a wire rack. Serve with whipped cream if desired. Refrigerate leftovers.
1 PIECE: *629 cal., 35g fat (9g sat. fat), 92mg chol., 179mg sod., 77g carb. (48g sugars, 4g fiber), 7g pro.*

SUGARPLUMS

When our kids read about sugarplums in a holiday tale, they were intrigued...and so was I! In short order, I figured out a no-bake way to make the sweets from dried fruits and nuts.
—*Suzanne McKinley, Lyons, GA*

TAKES: 15 min. + standing • **MAKES:** about 8 dozen

- 1 pkg. (15 oz.) raisins
- 2 cups pitted dried plums (prunes)
- 1 pkg. (8 oz.) dried mixed fruit
- 1½ cups chopped pecans
  Sugar

1. In a food processor, combine the raisins, plums, mixed fruit and pecans. Cover and process until chopped. Transfer to a large bowl.
2. Roll into 1-in. balls, then roll balls in sugar. Place on waxed paper and let stand at room temperature for 4 hours. Store in an airtight container. Roll in additional sugar before serving if desired.
1 SUGARPLUM: *42 cal., 1g fat (0 sat. fat), 0 chol., 4mg sod., 8g carb. (5g sugars, 1g fiber), 0 pro.*

BREAKFAST IN BED

*Before the guests arrive and the rush of the holiday
begins, take time to enjoy a quiet morning together.
These indulgent breakfast and brunch recipes
are perfectly portioned for two.*

OVERNIGHT OATMEAL

Start this breakfast the night before so you can get some extra sleep in the morning. My husband adds coconut to his, and I stir in dried fruit.
—June Thomas, Chesterton, IN

PREP: 10 min. + chilling • **MAKES:** 1 serving

- ⅓ cup old-fashioned oats
- 3 Tbsp. fat-free milk
- 3 Tbsp. reduced-fat plain yogurt
- 1 Tbsp. honey
- ½ cup assorted fresh fruit
- 2 Tbsp. chopped walnuts, toasted

In a small container or Mason jar, combine oats, milk, yogurt and honey. Top with fruit and nuts. Seal; refrigerate overnight.

NOTE: *To toast nuts, bake in a shallow pan in a 350° oven for 5-10 minutes or cook in a skillet over low heat until lightly browned, stirring occasionally.*

1 SERVING: *345 cal., 13g fat (2g sat. fat), 4mg chol., 53mg sod., 53g carb. (31g sugars, 5g fiber), 10g pro.*

CHOCOLATE-CHERRY OATS: *Use cherry-flavored yogurt and add 1 Tbsp. cocoa powder; top with fresh or frozen pitted cherries.*

BANANA BREAD OATS: *Replace honey with maple syrup; stir in half a mashed banana and ½ tsp. cinnamon. Top with toasted pecans.*

CARROT CAKE OATS: *Add 2 Tbsp. grated carrots, and substitute spreadable cream cheese for the yogurt.*

PINA COLADA OATS: *Add half a mashed banana, 2 Tbsp. crushed pineapple and 1 Tbsp. shredded coconut to the oat mixture.*

> ### Holiday Helper
> Make this dairy-free by using ½ cup soy or coconut milk instead of milk and yogurt.

PECAN FRENCH TOAST

Make-ahead convenience is a bonus with this yummy brunch dish. It couldn't be easier but tastes like you really fussed!
—Cindy Fish, Summerfield, NC

PREP: 10 min. + standing • **BAKE:** 30 min. • **MAKES:** 2 servings

- 2 large eggs
- ⅔ cup 2% milk
- ½ tsp. vanilla extract
- ⅛ tsp. salt
- 4 slices French bread (1 in. thick)
- ¼ cup packed brown sugar
- 2 Tbsp. butter, cubed
- 1 Tbsp. corn syrup
- ¼ cup chopped pecans

Preheat oven to 350°. In a bowl, whisk the eggs, milk, vanilla and salt; pour over bread. Let stand for 10 minutes, turning once. Meanwhile, in a small saucepan, combine brown sugar, butter and corn syrup; cook over medium heat until thickened, 1-2 minutes. Pour into a greased 8-in. square baking dish; sprinkle with pecans. Top with bread. Bake, uncovered, until a thermometer reads 160°, 30-35 minutes. Invert onto a serving platter. Serve immediately.

2 PIECES: *577 cal., 30g fat (11g sat. fat), 249mg chol., 666mg sod., 65g carb. (37g sugars, 3g fiber), 14g pro.*

HAM & EGG POCKETS

Refrigerated crescent roll dough make these savory breakfast pockets a snap to prepare.
—Taste of Home *Test Kitchen*

TAKES: 20 min. • **MAKES:** 2 servings

- 1 large egg
- 2 tsp. 2% milk
- 2 tsp. butter
- 1 oz. thinly sliced deli ham, chopped
- 2 Tbsp. shredded cheddar cheese
- 1 tube (4 oz.) refrigerated crescent rolls

1. Preheat oven to 375°. In a small bowl, combine egg and milk. In a small skillet heat butter until hot. Add egg mixture; cook and stir over medium heat until egg is completely set. Remove from the heat. Fold in ham and cheese.
2. On a greased baking sheet, separate crescent dough into 2 rectangles. Seal perforations; spoon half the filling down the center of each rectangle. Fold in ends and sides; pinch to seal. Bake until golden brown, 10-14 minutes.
1 POCKET: *345 cal., 22g fat (8g sat. fat), 132mg chol., 756mg sod., 23g carb. (5g sugars, 0 fiber), 12g pro.*

RUBY ROSE PALOMA

Rose water adds a delicate touch to citrusy grapefruit and lime. If you can't find rose water in your area, it is available online.
—Gina Nistico, Denver, CO

TAKES: 10 min. • **MAKES:** 2 servings

- 1 cup ruby red grapefruit juice
- 4 oz. mezcal or tequila
- 1 Tbsp. fresh lime juice
- 1½ tsp. rosewater
- 1 Tbsp. kosher salt
- 1 tsp. coarse sugar
- ½ cup grapefruit soda
  Grapefruit slices

1. In a small pitcher, combine the first 4 ingredients.
2. Mix salt and sugar on a plate. Moisten the rims of 2 cocktail glasses with water. Hold each glass upside down and dip moistened rim into salt mixture. Discard remaining salt mixture.
3. To serve, fill glasses with ice. Add half the grapefruit juice mixture to each; top with grapefruit soda and grapefruit slices.
1 SERVING: *214 cal., 0 fat (0 sat. fat), 0 chol., 324mg sod., 19g carb. (7g sugars, 0 fiber), 1g pro.*

WHAT'S THE DEAL WITH WHITE POINSETTIAS?

All poinsettias stem from a single species, a Mexican native shrub that produces bright scarlet leaves (yes, those are leaves, not flowers) in the winter. Newer varieties of poinsettias on the market—in shades of pink, cream and bright white—are the result of careful cross breeding between the original Mexican poinsettia and a summer-blooming dogwood poinsettia.

In addition to their use in holiday displays, making a dramatic contrast with the traditional deep red plants, white poinsettias have also become a symbol of December birthdays.

CHAI TEA LATTE

My family loves to sip this comforting spiced tea instead of cocoa. I simplified the recipe by using the filter basket of our coffeepot.
—Julie Plummer, Sykesville, MD

TAKES: 15 min. • **MAKES:** 2 servings

- 2 tea bags
- 1 tsp. ground cinnamon
- ½ tsp. ground ginger
- ¼ tsp. ground allspice
- 1 cup water
- 1 cup whole milk
- ¼ cup packed brown sugar
- 2 Tbsp. refrigerated French vanilla nondairy creamer
  Optional: Whipped topping and ground nutmeg

1. Place the tea bags, cinnamon, ginger and allspice in the coffee filter of a drip coffeemaker. Add water; brew according to manufacturer's directions.
2. Meanwhile, in a small saucepan, combine the milk, brown sugar and creamer. Cook and stir over medium heat until heated through and sugar is dissolved. Pour milk mixture into mugs; stir in tea. If desired, dollop with whipped topping and sprinkle with nutmeg.
1 CUP: *223 cal., 6g fat (2g sat. fat), 12mg chol., 65mg sod., 39g carb. (37g sugars, 1g fiber), 4g pro.*

> ## Holiday Helper
>
> Chai tea is a black tea blend from India and literally translates to "tea" in Hindi. The tea is full of flavor because of its many spices, like ginger, cardamom, cinnamon, fennel, black pepper and cloves. Star anise, coriander seeds and peppercorns are other well-liked options; you can add the spices you like to this recipe. Chai tea lattes are a newer adaptation that typically contain frothed hot milk and added sugar. If you like, you can use a whisk or a frother to give your latte a bit of foam.

FRUIT & CREAM CREPES

This creamy crepes recipe is fresh and indulgent without being too sweet.
—Ruth Kaercher, Hudsonville, MI

PREP: 20 min. + chilling • **COOK:** 15 min.
MAKES: 2 servings

- ⅓ cup 2% milk
- 2 Tbsp. beaten egg
- ¼ tsp. vanilla extract
- ¼ cup all-purpose flour
- 1½ tsp. confectioners' sugar
- ¼ tsp. baking powder
  Dash salt
- 2 tsp. butter, divided

FILLING

- 2 oz. cream cheese, softened
- 3 Tbsp. plus ½ tsp. confectioners' sugar, divided
- 4 tsp. 2% milk
- ⅛ tsp. vanilla extract
- ⅓ cup each fresh blueberries, strawberries and raspberries

1. In a small bowl, combine the first 7 ingredients. Cover and refrigerate for 1 hour.
2. In an 8-in. nonstick skillet, melt 1 tsp. butter. Stir batter; pour about 2 Tbsp. into the center of skillet. Lift and tilt pan to evenly coat bottom. Cook until top appears dry; turn and cook 15-20 seconds longer. Remove to a wire rack. Make 3 more crepes, adding the remaining 1 tsp. butter to the skillet as needed.
3. For filling, in a small bowl, beat the cream cheese, 3 Tbsp. confectioners' sugar, milk and vanilla until smooth. Spread 1 rounded Tbsp. of filling on each crepe; top with ¼ cup berries and roll up. Sprinkle with the remaining ½ tsp. confectioners' sugar.
2 CREPES: *329 cal., 17g fat (10g sat. fat), 110mg chol., 273mg sod., 38g carb. (0 sugars, 2g fiber), 8g pro.*

PUFFY APPLE OMELET

With all the eggs our chickens produce, I could make this omelet every day! It's a pretty festive-looking dish, but you could fix it anytime.
—Melissa Davenport, Campbell, MN

- -

TAKES: 30 min. • **MAKES:** 2 servings

  3   Tbsp. all-purpose flour
  ¼   tsp. baking powder
  ⅛   tsp. salt, optional
  2   large eggs, separated,
       room temperature
  3   Tbsp. 2% milk
  1   Tbsp. lemon juice
  3   Tbsp. sugar
TOPPING
  1   large apple, peeled if desired,
       and thinly sliced
  1   tsp. sugar
  ¼   tsp. ground cinnamon

1. Preheat oven to 375°. Mix flour, baking powder and, if desired, salt. In a small bowl, whisk together egg yolks, milk and lemon juice; stir into flour mixture.
2. In another bowl, beat egg whites on medium speed until foamy. Gradually add sugar, 1 Tbsp. at a time, beating on high after each addition until stiff peaks form. Fold into the flour mixture.
3. Pour into a 9-in. deep-dish pie plate coated with cooking spray. Arrange apple slices over top. Mix sugar and cinnamon; sprinkle over apple.
4. Bake, uncovered, until a knife inserted in center comes out clean, 18-20 minutes. Serve immediately.
1 PIECE: *253 cal., 5g fat (2g sat. fat), 188mg chol., 142mg sod., 44g carb. (32g sugars, 2g fiber), 9g pro.*

Holiday Helper
Most puff pancakes are pretty lean, but satisfying for breakfast or dinner. The filling often makes them unhealthy, but this recipe uses just a touch of sugar for sweetness.

BACON-BROCCOLI QUICHE CUPS

Filled with veggies and melted cheese, this comforting and colorful egg bake has become a holiday brunch classic at my home. For a tasty variation, try using asparagus instead of broccoli and Swiss in place of the cheddar cheese.
—Irene Steinmeyer, Denver, CO

- -

PREP: 10 min. • **BAKE:** 25 min.
MAKES: 2 servings

  4   bacon strips, chopped
  ¼   cup small fresh broccoli florets
  ¼   cup chopped onion
  1   garlic clove, minced
  3   large eggs
  1   Tbsp. dried parsley flakes
  ⅛   tsp. seasoned salt
       Dash pepper
  ¼   cup shredded cheddar cheese
  2   Tbsp. chopped tomato

1. Preheat oven to 400°. In a skillet, cook bacon over medium heat until crisp, stirring occasionally. Remove bacon with a slotted spoon; drain on paper towels. Pour off drippings, reserving 2 tsp. in pan.
2. Add broccoli and onion to the drippings in pan; cook and stir 2-3 minutes or until tender. Add garlic; cook 1 minute longer.
3. In a small bowl, whisk eggs, parsley, seasoned salt and pepper until blended. Stir in cheese, tomato, bacon and the broccoli mixture.
4. Divide mixture evenly between 2 greased 10-oz. ramekins or custard cups. Bake until a knife inserted in the center comes out clean, 22-25 minutes.
1 SERVING: *302 cal., 23g fat (9g sat. fat), 314mg chol., 597mg sod., 5g carb. (2g sugars, 1g fiber), 19g pro.*

SPICED BLUEBERRY QUINOA

I took up eating quinoa when I found out how much protein it has. This is a really easy dish to experiment with; my first version of the recipe was made with shredded apples instead of blueberries. It's delicious either way!
—Shannon Copley, Upper Arlington, OH

PREP: 10 min. • **COOK:** 30 min.
MAKES: 2 servings

- ½ cup quinoa, rinsed and well drained
- 2 cups unsweetened almond milk
- 2 Tbsp. honey
- ½ tsp. ground cinnamon
- ¼ tsp. salt
- 1 cup fresh or frozen blueberries, thawed
- ¼ tsp. vanilla extract
- 2 Tbsp. chopped almonds, toasted

1. In a small saucepan, cook and stir quinoa over medium heat until lightly toasted, 5-7 minutes. Stir in almond milk, honey, cinnamon and salt; bring to a boil. Reduce heat and simmer, uncovered, until quinoa is tender and liquid is almost absorbed, 20-25 minutes, stirring occasionally.
2. Remove from heat; stir in blueberries and vanilla. Sprinkle with almonds.
1 CUP: *352 cal., 10g fat (1g sat. fat), 0 chol., 479mg sod., 59g carb. (25g sugars, 7g fiber), 9g pro.*

BREAKFAST BANANA SPLITS

I can't brag enough about this recipe. It's elegant enough for a formal brunch, yet simple and nutritious. With different fruits and cereals, the variations are endless.
—Renee Lloyd, Pearl, MS

TAKES: 10 min. • **MAKES:** 2 servings

- 1 medium banana
- ⅓ cup each fresh blueberries, halved seedless grapes, sliced peeled kiwifruit and halved fresh strawberries
- 1 cup vanilla yogurt
- ½ cup granola with fruit and nuts
- 2 maraschino cherries with stems

Cut banana crosswise in half. For each serving, split each banana half in half lengthwise and place in a serving dish; top with half of each remaining ingredient.
1 SERVING: *337 cal., 6g fat (1g sat. fat), 6mg chol., 96mg sod., 66g carb. (42g sugars, 8g fiber), 12g pro.*

CRANBERRY CHIP PANCAKES

A few simple ingredients—orange juice, cranberries and white chips—make for pancakes so luscious you may not reach for the syrup.
—Aris Gonzalez, Deltona, FL

TAKES: 25 min. • **MAKES:** 6 pancakes

- ½ cup fresh or frozen cranberries
- 1 cup water, divided
- 1 cup complete pancake mix
- 1 tsp. grated orange zest
- ¼ cup orange juice
- ¼ cup white baking chips

1. In a small saucepan over medium heat, cook the cranberries and ½ cup water until berries pop, about 10 minutes. Meanwhile, in a large bowl, combine the pancake mix, orange zest, orange juice and the remaining ½ cup water just until moistened. Fold in chips. Drain cranberries; fold into batter.
2. Pour by ¼ cupfuls onto a greased hot griddle; turn when bubbles form on top. Cook until second side is golden brown.
3 PANCAKES: *368 cal., 9g fat (4g sat. fat), 4mg chol., 853mg sod., 66g carb. (24g sugars, 3g fiber), 8g pro.*

PORTOBELLO MUSHROOMS FLORENTINE

A fun and surprisingly hearty breakfast dish packed with flavor and richness.
—Sara Morris, Laguna Beach, CA

TAKES: 25 min. • **MAKES:** 2 servings

- 2 large portobello mushrooms, stems removed
  Cooking spray
- ⅛ tsp. garlic salt
- ⅛ tsp. pepper
- ½ tsp. olive oil
- 1 small onion, chopped
- 1 cup fresh baby spinach
- 2 large eggs
- ⅛ tsp. salt
- ¼ cup crumbled goat cheese or feta cheese
  Minced fresh basil, optional

1. Preheat oven to 425°. Spritz the mushrooms with cooking spray; place in a 15x10x1-in. pan, stem side up. Sprinkle with garlic salt and pepper. Bake, uncovered, until tender, about 10 minutes.

2. Meanwhile, in a nonstick skillet, heat oil over medium-high heat; saute onion until tender. Stir in spinach until wilted.

3. Whisk together eggs and salt; add to skillet. Cook and stir until eggs are thickened and no liquid egg remains; spoon onto mushrooms. Sprinkle with cheese and, if desired, basil.

1 STUFFED MUSHROOM: *126 cal., 5g fat (2g sat. fat), 18mg chol., 472mg sod., 10g carb. (4g sugars, 3g fiber), 11g pro.* **DIABETIC EXCHANGES:** *2 vegetable, 1 lean meat, ½ fat.*

Holiday Helper

Try filling your mushroom caps with other combinations like cooked sausage, sauce and mozzarella; feta, fresh basil and tomatoes; quinoa, garbanzos and goat cheese.

APPLE FRITTERS

This is an old Southern recipe. When we got home from a trip through the South years ago, I found the recipe among the brochures I brought back. I've been making these fritters ever since.
—John Robbins, Springdale, PA

TAKES: 20 min. • **MAKES:** 2 servings

1 cup cake flour
1 Tbsp. sugar
¾ tsp. baking powder
¼ tsp. salt
1 large egg, room temperature
⅓ cup whole milk
4 tsp. butter, melted
1 Tbsp. orange juice
2 tsp. grated orange zest
¼ tsp. vanilla extract
¾ cup chopped peeled tart apple
  Oil for frying
  Confectioners' sugar

1. In a large bowl, combine flour, sugar, baking powder and salt. In another bowl, combine the egg, milk, butter, orange juice, zest and vanilla. Add to the dry ingredients just until moistened. Fold in apples.
2. In an electric skillet or deep-fat fryer, heat ¼ in. of oil to 375°. Drop batter by rounded Tbsp. into oil. Fry until golden brown on both sides. Drain on paper towels. Dust with confectioners' sugar. Serve warm.

1 SERVING: *533 cal., 24g fat (3g sat. fat), 97mg chol., 530mg sod., 69g carb. (13g sugars, 2g fiber), 10g pro.*

Holiday Helper

For the best apple fritters, be sure not to overcrowd the frying pan. This will keep the temperature of the oil consistent for all of the batches. A dash of cinnamon goes a long way if you want to add extra flavor. You can also leave out the orange zest or replace the orange juice with an equal amount of milk or maple syrup.

PUMPKIN CREAM OF WHEAT

This dessert-inspired breakfast tastes like pumpkin pie—without the guilt! Double the recipe to make a morning meal perfect for sharing.
—Amy Bashtovoi, Sidney, NE

TAKES: 10 min. • **MAKES:** 1 serving

½ cup 2% milk
¼ cup half-and-half cream
3 Tbsp. Cream of Wheat
¼ cup canned pumpkin
2 tsp. sugar
⅛ tsp. ground cinnamon
  Additional 2% milk

In a small microwave-safe bowl, combine the milk, cream and Cream of Wheat. Microwave, uncovered, on high 1 minute; stir until blended. Cook, covered, for 1-2 minutes or until thickened; stir every 30 seconds. Stir in pumpkin, sugar and cinnamon. Serve with additional milk.
1 CUP: *314 cal., 9g fat (6g sat. fat), 39mg chol., 96mg sod., 46g carb. (18g sugars, 4g fiber), 10g pro.*

WARM GRAPEFRUIT WITH GINGER SUGAR

Sweetly broiled grapefruit is a specialty at my bed-and-breakfast. In addition to serving it at breakfast or brunch, try it as a light snack or dessert.
—Stephanie Levy, Lansing, NY

TAKES: 15 min. • **MAKES:** 2 servings

1 large red grapefruit
2 to 3 tsp. chopped crystallized ginger
2 tsp. sugar

1. Preheat broiler. Cut grapefruit crosswise in half. With a small knife, cut around the membrane in the center of each half and discard. Cut around each section to loosen fruit. Place grapefruit halves on a baking sheet, cut side up.
2. Mix ginger and sugar; sprinkle over fruit. Broil 4 in. from heat until sugar is melted, about 4 minutes.
½ GRAPEFRUIT: *85 cal., 0 fat (0 sat. fat), 0 chol., 3mg sod., 22g carb. (17g sugars, 2g fiber), 1g pro.*
DIABETIC EXCHANGES: *1 fruit, ½ starch.*

TASTE OF HOME CHRISTMAS

AIR-FRYER RASPBERRY FRENCH TOAST CUPS

A delightful twist on French toast, these individual treats make any morning special.
—Sandi Tuttle, Hayward, WI

PREP: 20 min. + chilling • **COOK:** 20 min.
MAKES: 2 servings

- 2 slices Italian bread, cut into ½-in. cubes
- ½ cup fresh or frozen raspberries
- 2 oz. cream cheese, cut into ½-in. cubes
- 2 large eggs
- ½ cup 2% milk
- 1 Tbsp. maple syrup

RASPBERRY SYRUP
- 2 tsp. cornstarch
- ⅓ cup water
- 2 cups fresh or frozen raspberries, divided
- 1 Tbsp. lemon juice
- 1 Tbsp. maple syrup
- ½ tsp. grated lemon zest
  Ground cinnamon, optional

1. Divide half the bread cubes between 2 greased 8-oz. custard cups. Sprinkle with raspberries and cream cheese. Top with the remaining bread cubes. In a small bowl, whisk eggs, milk and syrup; pour over bread. Cover and refrigerate for at least 1 hour.

2. Preheat air fryer to 325°. Place custard cups on tray in air-fryer basket. Cook until golden brown and puffed, 12-15 minutes.

3. Meanwhile, in a small saucepan, combine cornstarch and water until smooth. Add 1½ cups raspberries, lemon juice, syrup and lemon zest. Bring to a boil; reduce heat. Cook and stir until thickened, about 2 minutes. Strain and discard seeds; cool slightly.

4. Gently stir remaining ½ cup berries into the syrup. If desired, sprinkle French toast cups with cinnamon; serve with syrup.

NOTE: *If you don't have an air fryer, you can make this recipe in an oven.*

1 SERVING: *406 cal., 18g fat (8g sat. fat), 221mg chol., 301mg sod., 50g carb. (24g sugars, 11g fiber), 14g pro.*

FETA ASPARAGUS FRITTATA

Asparagus and feta cheese come together to make this frittata extra special. Perfect for a lazy morning or to serve with a tossed salad for a light lunch.
—Mildred Sherrer, Fort Worth, TX

TAKES: 30 min. • **MAKES:** 2 servings

- 12 fresh asparagus spears, trimmed
- 6 large eggs
- 2 Tbsp. heavy whipping cream
  Dash salt
  Dash pepper
- 1 Tbsp. olive oil
- 2 green onions, chopped
- 1 garlic clove, minced
- ½ cup crumbled feta cheese

1. Preheat oven to 350°. Place ½ in. of water and the asparagus in a large skillet; bring to a boil. Cook, covered, until asparagus is crisp-tender, 3-5 minutes; drain. Cool slightly.

2. In a bowl, whisk together the eggs, cream, salt and pepper. Chop 2 of the cooled asparagus spears. In an 8-in. cast-iron or other ovenproof skillet, heat oil over medium heat until hot. Saute green onions, garlic and chopped asparagus 1 minute. Stir in egg mixture; cook, covered, over medium heat until eggs are nearly set, 3-5 minutes. Top with whole asparagus spears and cheese.

3. Bake until the eggs are completely set, 7-9 minutes.

½ FRITTATA: *425 cal., 31g fat (12g sat. fat), 590mg chol., 1231mg sod., 8g carb. (3g sugars, 3g fiber), 27g pro.*

SALMON CROQUETTE BREAKFAST SANDWICHES

I simply love smoked salmon on bagels with all the accouterments! I could eat it every day for breakfast! But smoked salmon can get pricey, so I found a cheaper alternative without losing the flavor.
—Jessi Hampton, Richmond Hill, GA

- -

PREP: 25 min. • **COOK:** 10 min. • **MAKES:** 2 servings

- 1   **large egg, lightly beaten**
- ¼   **cup dry bread crumbs**
- 1   **tsp. garlic powder**
- 1   **tsp. smoked paprika**
- 1   **pouch (6 oz.) boneless skinless pink salmon**
- 1   **Tbsp. olive oil**
- 2   **everything bagels, split and toasted**
- 4   **Tbsp. cream cheese, softened**
- 1   **Tbsp. capers, drained**
- 1   **medium tomato, sliced**
- ½   **medium red onion, thinly sliced into rings**
     Snipped fresh dill, optional

1. In a small bowl, combine egg, bread crumbs, garlic powder and smoked paprika. Add salmon and mix lightly but thoroughly. Shape into 2 patties.

2. In a large skillet, cook patties in oil over medium heat until browned, 5-6 minutes on each side. Spread cut sides of bagels with cream cheese; sprinkle with capers. Serve patties on bagels with tomato, red onion and, if desired, dill.

1 SANDWICH: *656 cal., 25g fat (10g sat. fat), 152mg chol., 1205mg sod., 75g carb. (14g sugars, 4g fiber), 34g pro.*

VEGETABLE SCRAMBLED EGGS

These colorful eggs go perfectly with sausage, toasted English muffins and fresh fruit. If you like, you can use a mix of red and green bell peppers to make the dish even more festive.
—Marilyn Ipson, Rogers, AR

- -

TAKES: 10 min. • **MAKES:** 2 servings

- 4   **large eggs, lightly beaten**
- ¼   **cup fat-free milk**
- ½   **cup chopped green pepper**
- ¼   **cup sliced green onions**
- ¼   **tsp. salt**
- ⅛   **tsp. pepper**
- 1   **small tomato, chopped and seeded**

In a small bowl, combine the eggs and milk. Add green pepper, onions, salt and pepper. Pour into a lightly greased skillet. Cook and stir over medium heat until eggs are nearly set, 2-3 minutes. Add tomato; cook and stir until eggs are completely set.

¾ CUP: *173 cal., 10g fat (3g sat. fat), 373mg chol., 455mg sod., 7g carb. (4g sugars, 2g fiber), 15g pro.*
DIABETIC EXCHANGES: *2 medium-fat meat, 1 vegetable.*

> ### *Holiday Helper*
> To save time in the morning, chop up the vegetables the night before; they'll keep well in the fridge overnight.

BLUEBERRY OAT WAFFLES

I truly enjoy recipes that make just enough for the two of us, like this one for yummy waffles. Instead of blueberries, you can slice ripe strawberries on top—or use the batter to make pancakes.
—Ruth Andrewson, Leavenworth, WA

- -

TAKES: 25 min. • **MAKES:** 4 waffles

⅔   cup all-purpose flour
½   cup quick-cooking oats
1   Tbsp. brown sugar
1   tsp. baking powder
½   tsp. salt
1   large egg, room temperature
⅔   cup 2% milk
¼   cup canola oil
½   tsp. lemon juice
¼   cup ground pecans
½   cup fresh or frozen blueberries
     Optional: Additional blueberries, chopped pecans, maple syrup and butter

1. In a bowl, combine flour, oats, brown sugar, baking powder and salt. In another bowl, combine egg, milk, oil and lemon juice; stir into dry ingredients just until combined. Fold in ground pecans and blueberries. Let stand for 5 minutes.
2. Bake mixture in a preheated waffle iron according to the manufacturer's directions until golden brown. If desired, top with additional blueberries and chopped pecans, and serve with maple syrup and butter.
2 WAFFLES: *691 cal., 44g fat (5g sat. fat), 100mg chol., 907mg sod., 64g carb. (15g sugars, 5g fiber), 14g pro.*

FREEZE YOUR FRESH FRUIT

1. Prep fruits as usual. Rinse fruits; leave small berries whole; core, peel, slice and prep other fruits as you normally would before serving.

2. Place fruit in a parchment or waxed paper-lined shallow pan and freeze. Avoid overcrowding so the fruits can freeze quickly.

3. Place the frozen fruit in freezer containers, and label with the contents and date. Freeze for up to 3 months.

SEASONAL GET-TOGETHERS

Here are three great ways to host a change-of-pace holiday gathering—a casual pasta night for family and friends, a meal designed just for kids, and a small-scale dinner party for a select guest list.

Casual Pasta Bar

For a fun, low-pressure get-together with friends during the holiday week, why not serve up a pasta buffet? Fresh pasta and a variety of homemade sauces make it not just delicious, but convenient as well!

ITALIAN PASTA SAUCE

When my daughter Kris got married, her new husband made something special for their wedding buffet—a big batch of this thick, flavorful pasta sauce. His grandmother brought the recipe from Italy nearly 100 years ago.
—Judy Braun, Juneau, WI

PREP: 25 min. • **COOK:** 2½ hours
MAKES: 20 servings

- 4 lbs. ground beef
- 1 lb. bulk Italian sausage
- 1 large onion, finely chopped
- 3 celery ribs, finely chopped
- 4 garlic cloves, minced
- 2 Tbsp. olive oil
- 3 cans (28 oz. each) crushed tomatoes in puree
- 3 cans (6 oz. each) tomato paste
- 3 cups chicken or beef broth
- 1 lb. fresh mushrooms, sliced
- ¾ cup minced fresh parsley
- 1 Tbsp. sugar
- 2 to 3 tsp. salt
- ½ tsp. pepper
- ½ tsp. ground allspice, optional
  Hot cooked pasta

1. In a Dutch oven or soup kettle, cook beef in 2 batches over medium heat until no longer pink; drain and set aside. Cook sausage over medium heat until no longer pink; drain and set aside. In the same pan, saute onion, celery and garlic in oil until vegetables are tender.

2. Return beef and sausage to the pan. Add the next 9 ingredients, including allspice if desired, and bring to a boil. Reduce heat; cover and simmer until sauce reaches desired thickness, stirring occasionally, 2-3 hours. Serve over pasta.

1 CUP: *284 cal., 15g fat (5g sat. fat), 57mg chol., 821mg sod., 16g carb. (9g sugars, 3g fiber), 23g pro.*

MAKE HOMEMADE PASTA

INGREDIENTS

- 2 large eggs
- 1 large egg yolk
- ¼ cup water
- 1 Tbsp. olive oil
- ½ tsp. coarsely ground pepper
- ¼ tsp. salt
- 1½ cups all-purpose flour
- ½ cup semolina flour

1. In a small bowl, whisk first 6 ingredients. On a clean work surface, mix the all-purpose and semolina flours, forming a mound. Make a large well in the center. Pour the egg mixture into the well.

2. Using a fork or your fingers, gradually mix the flour mixture into the egg mixture, forming a soft, slightly sticky dough.

3. Lightly dust work surface with flour; knead dough until smooth, 8-10 minutes. Divide dough into 6 portions; cover. Let rest for 30 minutes.

4. Roll each portion of dough into a 10×8-in. rectangle—the thinner the better.

5. Dust work surface lightly with flour; roll up the dough.

6. Cut into ¼-inch-wide strips for fettuccine, broader strips for lasagna, or thinner for spaghetti.

NOTE: *To store pasta, dust lightly with flour to keep it from sticking, and place it in an airtight container in the freezer. It is best cooked within 18-24 hours.*

CAESAR DRESSING

Looking for a new salad dressing you can whisk up in minutes for special occasions? You can't miss with this light and savory variation on a traditional Caesar. It really dresses up fresh greens!
—Taste of Home *Test Kitchen*

PREP: 15 min. + chilling • **MAKES:** 1⅔ cups

- ⅔ cup reduced-fat mayonnaise
- ½ cup reduced-fat sour cream
- ½ cup buttermilk
- 1 Tbsp. red wine vinegar
- 1 Tbsp. stone-ground mustard
- 1½ tsp. lemon juice
- 1½ tsp. Worcestershire sauce
- ⅓ cup grated Parmigiano-Reggiano cheese
- 2 anchovy fillets, minced
- 2 garlic cloves, minced
- ½ tsp. coarsely ground pepper

Whisk the mayonnaise, sour cream, buttermilk, vinegar, mustard, lemon juice and Worcestershire sauce. Stir in the cheese, anchovies, garlic and pepper. Cover and refrigerate at least 1 hour.
2 TBSP.: *71 cal., 6g fat (2g sat. fat), 10mg chol., 205mg sod., 3g carb. (2g sugars, 0 fiber), 2g pro.*
DIABETIC EXCHANGES: *1 fat.*

Holiday Helper
Go for freshly squeezed lemon juice when preparing this dressing. Bottled lemon juice, which is from concentrate, won't provide the same bright, fresh flavor.

SAGE FONTINA FOCACCIA
These rustic loaves have plenty of sage flavor—a tasty addition to any feast.
—Beth Dauenhauer, Pueblo, CO

PREP: 30 min. + rising • **BAKE:** 10 min.
MAKES: 1 loaf (8 wedges)

- 1¼ tsp. active dry yeast
- ½ cup warm water (110° to 115°)
- ½ tsp. honey
- ¾ to 1 cup all-purpose flour
- ¼ cup whole wheat flour
- 2 Tbsp. olive oil, divided
- 2 tsp. minced fresh sage
- ¼ tsp. salt

TOPPING
- 1½ tsp. olive oil, divided
- 8 fresh sage leaves
- ½ cup shredded fontina cheese

1. In a large bowl, dissolve the yeast in warm water. Stir in honey; let stand for 5 minutes. Add ¾ cup all-purpose flour, the whole wheat flour, oil, minced sage and salt. Beat on medium speed for 3 minutes or until smooth. Stir in enough of the remaining flour to form a soft dough (dough will be sticky).

2. Turn the dough onto a lightly floured surface; knead until smooth and elastic, 6-8 minutes. Place in a greased bowl, turning once to grease the top. Cover and let rise in a warm place until doubled, about 1 hour.

3. Punch dough down. Cover and let rest for 5 minutes. Place remaining 1 Tbsp. olive oil in a 10-in. cast-iron or other ovenproof skillet; tilt pan to evenly coat. Add dough; shape to fit pan. Cover and let rise until doubled, about 30 minutes.

4. With fingertips, make several dimples over the top of the dough. For topping, brush dough with 1 tsp. oil. Top with sage leaves; brush leaves with remaining ½ tsp. oil. Sprinkle with cheese. Bake at 400° until golden brown, 10-15 minutes. Remove to a wire rack. Serve warm.
1 WEDGE: *112 cal., 5g fat (2g sat. fat), 8mg chol., 131mg sod., 12g carb. (1g sugars, 1g fiber), 4g pro.*

ANTIPASTO PLATTER

We entertain often, and antipasto is one of our favorite crowd-pleasers. Guests love having their choice of so many delicious nibbles, including pepperoni and cubes of provolone. This platter is best assembled ahead of time—the flavor gets better as it sits!
—Teri Lindquist, Gurnee, IL

PREP: 10 min. + chilling • **MAKES:** 16 servings (4 qt.)

- 1   jar (24 oz.) pepperoncini, drained
- 1   can (15 oz.) garbanzo beans or chickpeas, rinsed and drained
- 2   cups halved fresh mushrooms
- 2   cups halved cherry tomatoes
- ½   lb. provolone cheese, cubed
- 1   can (6 oz.) pitted ripe olives, drained
- 1   pkg. (3½ oz.) sliced pepperoni
- 1   bottle (8 oz.) Italian vinaigrette dressing
      Lettuce leaves

1. In a large bowl, combine pepperoncini, beans, mushrooms, tomatoes, cheese, olives and pepperoni. Pour vinaigrette over mixture; toss to coat.
2. Refrigerate at least 30 minutes or overnight. Arrange on a lettuce-lined platter. Serve with toothpicks.
1 CUP: *178 cal., 13g fat (4g sat. fat), 15mg chol., 852mg sod., 8g carb. (2g sugars, 2g fiber), 6g pro.*

ASPARAGUS BRUSCHETTA

I really like asparagus, so I'm always trying it in different things. This is a delicious twist on traditional bruschetta.
—Elaine Sweet, Dallas, TX

TAKES: 30 min. • **MAKES:** 1 dozen

- ½   lb. fresh asparagus, trimmed and cut into ½-in. pieces
- 2   cups grape tomatoes, halved
- ¼   cup minced fresh basil
- 3   green onions, chopped
- 3   Tbsp. lime juice
- 1   Tbsp. olive oil
- 3   garlic cloves, minced
- 1½ tsp. grated lime zest
- ¼   tsp. salt
- ¼   tsp. pepper
- 12 slices French bread baguette (½ in. thick), toasted
- ½   cup crumbled blue cheese

1. In a large saucepan, bring 3 cups of water to a boil. Add the asparagus; cover and boil for 2-4 minutes. Drain and immediately place the asparagus in ice water. Drain and pat dry.
2. Combine asparagus, tomatoes, basil, onions, lime juice, oil, garlic, lime zest, salt and pepper. Using a slotted spoon, spoon mixture onto toasted bread slices. Sprinkle with blue cheese.
1 PIECE: *88 cal., 3g fat (1g sat. fat), 4mg chol., 237mg sod., 13g carb. (1g sugars, 1g fiber), 3g pro.*
DIABETIC EXCHANGES: *1 starch, ½ fat.*

A CHOICE OF SAUCES

HOMEMADE ALFREDO SAUCE

In a large saucepan, heat 3 Tbsp. butter over medium heat. Add ½ cup finely chopped shallots; cook and stir until tender, 2-3 minutes. Add 5 garlic cloves, minced; cook 1 minute longer. Add 2 cups heavy whipping cream; cook and stir until heated through. Stir in 1¼ cups shredded Asiago cheese, ½ cup Parmesan, ¾ cup grated Romano cheese, ¼ tsp. salt and ¼ tsp. pepper; bring to a boil, stirring constantly. Reduce heat; simmer, uncovered, until thickened, about 10 minutes, whisking occasionally.

—*Jackie Charlesworth Stiff, Frederick, CO*

CLASSIC PESTO

Place 4 cups loosely packed basil leaves, ½ cup grated Parmesan cheese, 2 garlic cloves, halved, and ¼ tsp. salt in a food processor; cover and pulse until chopped. Add ½ cup toasted pine nuts; cover and process until blended. While processing, gradually add ½ cup olive oil in a steady stream. Store in an airtight container in the freezer up to 1 year.

—*Iola Egle, Bella Vista, AR*

HOMEMADE MARINARA SAUCE

In a large saucepan, heat 1 Tbsp. olive oil over medium heat. Add 1 small onion, chopped; cook and stir until softened, 3-4 minutes. Add 2 garlic cloves, minced; cook 1 minute longer. Add 2 cans (28 oz. each) Italian crushed tomatoes, 1 Tbsp. Italian seasoning, ½ tsp. salt, ½ tsp. pepper and 1 to 2 Tbsp. sugar; bring to a boil. Reduce heat; simmer, covered, for 10 minutes.

—*Cara Bjornlie, Detroit Lakes, MN*

TIRAMISU CHEESECAKE DESSERT

Tiramisu didn't do it for me until I tried this recipe with its luscious layers of cheesecake. It's one of my favorite desserts to make this time of year.
—Christie Nelson, Taylorville, IL

PREP: 20 min. • **BAKE:** 40 min. + chilling
MAKES: 12 servings

- 1   pkg. (12 oz.) vanilla wafers
- 5   tsp. instant coffee granules, divided
- 3   Tbsp. hot water, divided
- 4   pkg. (8 oz. each) cream cheese, softened
- 1   cup sugar
- 1   cup sour cream
- 4   large eggs, room temperature, lightly beaten
- 1   cup whipped topping
- 1   Tbsp. baking cocoa

1. Preheat oven to 325°. Layer half the wafers in a greased 13x9-in. baking dish. In a small bowl, dissolve 2 tsp. coffee granules in 2 Tbsp. hot water; brush 1 Tbsp. mixture over wafers. Set the remaining mixture aside.
2. In a large bowl, beat cream cheese and sugar until smooth. Beat in sour cream. Add eggs; beat on low speed just until blended. Remove half of the filling to another bowl. Dissolve the remaining 3 tsp. coffee granules in the remaining 1 Tbsp. hot water; stir into 1 portion of filling. Spread over wafers.
3. Layer remaining wafers over top; brush with reserved coffee mixture. Spread with remaining filling.
4. Bake for 40-45 minutes or until the center is almost set. Cool on a wire rack 10 minutes. Loosen sides from dish with a knife. Cool 1 hour longer. Refrigerate overnight, covering when completely cooled.
5. To serve, spread with whipped topping. Dust with cocoa.
1 PIECE: *536 cal., 37g fat (21g sat. fat), 171mg chol., 343mg sod., 43g carb. (29g sugars, 1g fiber), 10g pro.*

BRUSCHETTA WITH PROSCIUTTO

A crowd-pleaser any time of year, this savory-tasting appetizer is perfect for get-togethers.
—Debbie Manno, Fort Mill, SC

TAKES: 25 min. • **MAKES:** about 6½ dozen

- 8   plum tomatoes, seeded and chopped
- 1   cup chopped sweet onion
- ¼   cup grated Romano cheese
- ¼   cup minced fresh basil
- 2   oz. thinly sliced prosciutto, finely chopped
- 1   shallot, finely chopped
- 3   garlic cloves, minced
- ⅓   cup olive oil
- ⅓   cup balsamic vinegar
- 1   tsp. minced fresh rosemary
- ¼   tsp. pepper
- ⅛   tsp. hot pepper sauce, optional
- 2   French bread baguettes (10½ oz. each), cut into ¼-in. slices

1. In a large bowl, combine the first 7 ingredients. In another bowl, whisk the oil, vinegar, rosemary, pepper and, if desired, pepper sauce. Pour over the tomato mixture; toss to coat.
2. Place bread slices on ungreased baking sheets. Broil 3-4 in. from the heat or until golden brown, 1-2 minutes. With a slotted spoon, top each slice with tomato mixture.
1 APPETIZER: *33 cal., 1g fat (0 sat. fat), 1mg chol., 67mg sod., 5g carb. (1g sugars, 0 fiber), 1g pro.*

Merry Little Christmas

You can still have a full-fledged Christmas feast even if you're not feeding a crowd! Here are some fabulous menu options that top out at 6 servings.

TURKEY BREAST WITH CRANBERRY BROWN RICE

As a single retiree, I roast a turkey breast half instead of making a whole turkey dinner. This is a perfect meal for anyone cooking for just a few people, and if you're cooking for one, it also leaves enough leftovers for sandwiches and tacos.
—Nancy Heishman, Las Vegas, NV

PREP: 20 min. • **BAKE:** 45 min. + standing • **MAKES:** 6 servings

- 2 Tbsp. jellied cranberry sauce
- 2 Tbsp. chopped celery
- 2 Tbsp. minced red onion
- 1 Tbsp. olive oil
- 1½ tsp. minced fresh parsley
- ½ tsp. grated orange zest
- ⅛ tsp. garlic powder
- ½ tsp. poultry seasoning, divided
- 1 boneless skinless turkey breast half (2 lbs.)
- ½ tsp. kosher salt
- ¼ tsp. pepper
- ¼ cup orange juice

RICE
- 1⅓ cups uncooked long grain brown rice
- 2⅔ cups water
- ¼ cup chopped celery
- 3 Tbsp. minced red onion
- ¾ tsp. salt
- ¼ tsp. pepper
- ⅔ cup dried cranberries
- ⅔ cup sliced almonds, toasted
- 1 Tbsp. minced fresh parsley
- ½ tsp. grated orange zest

1. Preheat oven to 350°. Mix the first 7 ingredients and ¼ tsp. of the poultry seasoning.

2. Place turkey in a greased foil-lined 13x9-in. baking pan; rub with salt, pepper and remaining ¼ tsp. poultry seasoning. Spread with cranberry mixture. Roast until a thermometer reads 165°, 45-55 minutes, drizzling with orange juice halfway.

3. Meanwhile, in a saucepan, combine the first 6 rice ingredients; bring to a boil. Reduce heat; simmer, covered, until rice is tender and the liquid is absorbed, 40-45 minutes. Stir in the remaining ingredients.

4. Remove turkey from oven; tent with foil. Let stand 10 minutes before slicing. Serve with rice.

NOTE: *To toast nuts, bake in a shallow pan in a 350° oven for 5-10 minutes or cook in a skillet over low heat until lightly browned, stirring occasionally.*

5 OZ. COOKED TURKEY WITH ⅔ CUP RICE: *465 cal., 11g fat (1g sat. fat), 86mg chol., 642mg sod., 50g carb. (13g sugars, 5g fiber), 42g pro.*
DIABETIC EXCHANGES: *5 lean meat, 3 starch, 1½ fat.*

FRENCH ONION SOUP

Our daughter and I enjoy spending time together cooking, but our days are busy, so we appreciate quick and tasty recipes like this one. This classic soup hits the spot for lunch or dinner or as an elegant early course as part of a larger meal.
—Sandra Chambers, Carthage, MS

PREP: 30 min. • **COOK:** 30 min. • **MAKES:** 6 servings

- 4 cups thinly sliced onions
- 1 garlic clove, minced
- ¼ cup butter
- 6 cups water
- 8 beef bouillon cubes
- 1 tsp. Worcestershire sauce
- 6 slices French bread (¾ in. thick), buttered and toasted
- 6 slices Swiss cheese

1. In a large covered saucepan, cook the onions and garlic in butter over medium-low heat for 8-10 minutes or until tender and golden, stirring occasionally. Add water, bouillon and Worcestershire sauce; bring to a boil. Reduce heat; cover and simmer for 30 minutes.

2. Ladle hot soup into 6 ovenproof bowls. Top each with a piece of French bread. Cut each slice of cheese in half and place over the bread. Broil until cheese melts. Serve immediately.

1 SERVING: *244 cal., 15g fat (10g sat. fat), 46mg chol., 1387mg sod., 17g carb. (5g sugars, 2g fiber), 9g pro.*

WINTER SQUASH WITH MAPLE GLAZE

You can use any type of winter squash in this simple vegetable bake, but I like to use at least two varieties. It can be assembled a day ahead, then baked just before serving.
—Teri Kreyche, Tustin, CA

- -

PREP: 20 min. • **BAKE:** 50 min. • **MAKES:** 6 servings

- 2 cups chopped peeled parsnips
- 2 cups cubed peeled kabocha squash
- 2 cups cubed peeled butternut squash
- ⅓ cup butter, cubed
- ½ cup maple syrup
- 1 Tbsp. minced fresh rosemary or
  1 tsp. dried rosemary, crushed
- 1 garlic clove, minced
- ½ tsp. salt
- ¼ tsp. pepper
- ¾ cup coarsely chopped almonds

1. Preheat oven to 375°. In a large bowl, combine parsnips and squashes. In a small saucepan, melt butter over medium heat; whisk in maple syrup, rosemary, garlic, salt and pepper. Pour over vegetables and toss to coat.

2. Transfer to a greased 11x7-in. baking dish. Bake, covered, 40 minutes. Uncover; sprinkle with almonds. Bake until the vegetables are tender, 10-15 minutes longer.

¾ **CUP:** 339 cal., 19g fat (7g sat. fat), 27mg chol., 290mg sod., 43g carb. (22g sugars, 7g fiber), 5g pro.

CRANBERRY-KISSED CHOCOLATE SILK

I combined fresh cranberry salad with the rich custard known as pots de creme, and the result is ever so elegant compared to the usual desserts!
—Carmell Childs, Orangeville, UT

- -

PREP: 25 min. + chilling • **MAKES:** 6 servings

- 1 cup cranberry juice
- ⅛ tsp. salt
- 4 large eggs, beaten
- 1 cup milk chocolate chips
- 1 cup semisweet chocolate chips
- 1 tsp. vanilla extract
- 1 cup fresh or frozen cranberries, thawed
- ⅓ cup sugar
- ¾ cup sweetened whipped cream
- 3 Tbsp. sliced almonds, toasted

1. Place cranberry juice and salt in a small heavy saucepan; bring just to a boil. Remove from heat. In a small bowl, slowly whisk hot juice into eggs; return all to pan. Cook over low heat 2-3 minutes or until mixture thickens and a thermometer reads 170°, stirring constantly.

2. Place egg mixture, chocolate chips and vanilla in a blender; let stand 2 minutes. Cover and process until smooth. Pour into 6 dessert dishes. Refrigerate at least 4 hours, covering when completely cooled.

3. Place cranberries in a small food processor; pulse until finely chopped. Transfer to a small bowl; toss with sugar. Top each serving with cranberries, whipped cream and almonds.

NOTE: *To toast nuts, bake in a shallow pan in a 350° oven for 5-10 minutes or cook in a skillet over low heat until lightly browned, stirring occasionally.*

1 SERVING: 473 cal., 27g fat (15g sat. fat), 151mg chol., 129mg sod., 54g carb. (47g sugars, 4g fiber), 9g pro.

HERB CANDLES

A few natural elements can turn an ordinary candle into something truly festive.

WHAT YOU'LL NEED

- Fresh rosemary or sage
- ½ lb. soy wax flakes
- ½ lb. beeswax pellets
- Double boiler
- Essential oils
- 8-oz. jars
- Paintbrush
- Glue dots
- 6-in. candle wick
- Clothespins

INSTRUCTIONS

1. Press herbs between sheets of waxed paper for a few days until flat and dry.
2. In a double boiler, melt soy wax flakes and beeswax pellets. Add your choice of essential oils for scent.
3. Dip herbs into wax and push them against the sides of the jar. Paint wax over them; let dry.
4. Use a glue dot to attach candle wick to the bottom of the jar; use a clothespin to secure it at the mouth.
5. Pour wax into jar and let sit for 48 hours. Trim wick.

BACON PARMESAN POPOVERS

This recipe proves simple ingredients often result in the best-tasting dishes. These popovers are a nice change from ordinary rolls.
—Donna Gaston, Coplay, PA

PREP: 10 min. • **BAKE:** 30 min.
MAKES: 6 popovers

- 2 large eggs, room temperature
- 1 cup 2% milk
- 1 cup all-purpose flour
- 2 Tbsp. grated Parmesan cheese
- ¼ tsp. salt
- 3 bacon strips, diced

1. In a large bowl, beat the eggs and milk. Combine flour, cheese and salt; add to egg mixture and mix well. Cover and let stand at room temperature for 45 minutes.

2. Preheat oven to 450°. In a large skillet, cook bacon over medium heat until crisp. Using a slotted spoon, remove to paper towels to drain. Grease cups of a nonstick popover pan with some of the bacon drippings; set aside. Stir bacon into batter; fill the prepared cups two-thirds full.

3. Bake for 15 minutes. Reduce heat to 350° (do not open oven door). Bake until deep golden brown, about 15 minutes longer (do not underbake).

4. Run a table knife or small metal spatula around the edges of the cups to loosen if necessary. Immediately remove from pan; prick with a small sharp knife to allow steam to escape. Serve immediately.

1 POPOVER: *167 cal., 7g fat (3g sat. fat), 73mg chol., 248mg sod., 18g carb. (2g sugars, 1g fiber), 7g pro.*

Holiday Helper

You may use greased muffin tins instead of a popover pan. Fill every other cup two-thirds full with batter to avoid crowding; fill the remaining cups with water. Bake at 450° for 15 minutes, then bake at 350° for 10 minutes. Makes: 9 popovers.

ROASTED BRUSSELS SPROUTS & GRAPES

I've been introducing people to roasted grapes in balsamic glaze served as crostini or on flatbread with seasoned ricotta. Here, I combined them with Brussels sprouts as a side dish. The juices from the grapes combined with balsamic glaze and maple syrup is a sophisticated flavor combination for a rustic dish.
—Lisa Benoit, Cookeville, TN

PREP: 30 min. • **BAKE:** 30 min.
MAKES: 6 servings

- 4   bacon strips, chopped
- 1   lb. fresh Brussels sprouts, trimmed and halved
- 1   tsp. dried rosemary, crushed
- 1   tsp. dried thyme
- ½   tsp. salt
- ¼   tsp. pepper
- 2   Tbsp. maple syrup
- 1   Tbsp. balsamic glaze
- 1   lb. seedless black or red grapes, halved
- 2   tsp. grated lemon zest
- ⅓   cup chopped almonds

1. Preheat oven to 425°. In a small skillet, cook bacon over medium heat until crisp, stirring occasionally. Remove with a slotted spoon; drain on paper towels. Reserve drippings.
2. Place Brussels sprouts in a 15x10x1-in. baking pan; toss with reserved bacon drippings, rosemary, thyme, salt and pepper. In a small bowl, combine syrup and balsamic glaze. Drizzle over mixture; toss to coat. Roast 15 minutes; add the grapes to the pan. Roast until Brussels sprouts are lightly charred and tender, 15-20 minutes longer.
3. In a large serving bowl, combine Brussels sprouts mixture, cooked bacon and lemon zest; toss to combine. Sprinkle with almonds.

⅔ CUP: 228 cal., 11g fat (3g sat. fat), 12mg chol., 348mg sod., 28g carb. (19g sugars, 4g fiber), 6g pro.
DIABETIC EXCHANGES: *2 starch, 2 fat.*

WARM ROASTED BEET SALAD

Beets shine in this hearty salad. It's beautiful on the plate, too. I prefer to use hazelnut oil in this salad when I can find it.
—Jill Anderson, Sleepy Eye, MN

PREP: 30 min. • **BAKE:** 40 min.
MAKES: 6 servings

- 8   fresh beets
    Cooking spray
- 1½ cups orange juice
- 1   shallot, chopped
- 2   Tbsp. olive oil
- 2   Tbsp. balsamic vinegar
- 1   tsp. minced fresh thyme or ¼ tsp. dried thyme
- ½   tsp. grated orange zest
- ⅛   tsp. salt
- ⅛   tsp. pepper
- 6   cups fresh arugula or baby spinach
- 3   Tbsp. crumbled blue cheese
- 3   Tbsp. chopped hazelnuts, toasted

1. Preheat oven to 350°. Scrub and peel beets. Cut into wedges; place on a baking sheet coated with cooking spray. Spritz beets with additional cooking spray until coated. Bake for 40-50 minutes or until tender, turning occasionally.
2. Meanwhile, for dressing, heat orange juice in a small saucepan over medium heat. Bring to a boil. Reduce heat; simmer, uncovered, until liquid is syrupy and reduced to about ⅓ cup. Remove from heat. Whisk in next 7 ingredients. Set aside to cool.
3. Just before serving, place arugula in a large bowl. Drizzle with ¼ cup dressing; toss to coat. Divide mixture among 6 salad plates. Place beets in the same bowl; add the remaining dressing and toss to coat. Arrange on plates. Sprinkle salads with blue cheese and hazelnuts.
1 SERVING: *147 cal., 8g fat (2g sat. fat), 3mg chol., 167mg sod., 17g carb. (12g sugars, 2g fiber), 4g pro.*
DIABETIC EXCHANGES: *2 vegetable, 1½ fat, ½ fruit.*

Santa's Little Helpers

Christmas is a time for giving, and kids love getting involved! Find a way for the kids to give back to the community (we have some suggestions!), then throw them a party while they do it!

SPINACH PIZZA QUESADILLAS

This simple five-ingredient dinner is special to me because my daughter and I created it together. You can make variations with other veggies, too. It's a smart way to get kids to eat healthier.
—Tanna Mancini, Gulfport, FL

- -

TAKES: 20 min. • **MAKES:** 6 servings

- 6 **whole wheat tortillas (8 in.)**
- 3 **cups shredded part-skim mozzarella cheese**
- 3 **cups chopped fresh spinach**
- 1 **can (8 oz.) pizza sauce**

1. Preheat oven to 400°. On half of each tortilla, layer ½ cup cheese, ½ cup spinach and about 2 Tbsp. sauce. Fold the other half over the filling. Place on baking sheets coated with cooking spray.
2. Bake 10-12 minutes or until cheese is melted. If desired, serve with additional pizza sauce.

1 QUESADILLA: *301 cal., 13g fat (7g sat. fat), 36mg chol., 650mg sod., 29g carb. (3g sugars, 4g fiber), 19g pro.*
DIABETIC EXCHANGES: *2 starch, 2 medium-fat meat.*

HOW KIDS CAN HELP

- Collect and help sort food at a local food pantry. *www.feedingamerica.org*
- Write holiday cards to local senior care facilities or deployed soldiers.
- Make thank-you cards for health-care workers, firefighters and teachers. To search for volunteer opportunities in your community, go to *volunteermatch.org.*

MINI MAC & CHEESE BITES

Some young relatives were coming for a Christmas party, and I created these so they'd have something fun to eat. Instead, the adults devoured my mini mac and cheese bites! You can customize them by adding chopped jalapenos, crumbled bacon or minced garlic.
—Kate Mainiero, Elizaville, NY

- -

PREP: 35 min. • **BAKE:** 10 min.
MAKES: 3 dozen

- 2 **cups uncooked elbow macaroni**
- 1 **cup seasoned bread crumbs, divided**
- 2 **Tbsp. butter**
- 2 **Tbsp. all-purpose flour**
- ½ **tsp. onion powder**
- ½ **tsp. garlic powder**
- ½ **tsp. seasoned salt**
- 1¾ **cups 2% milk**
- 2 **cups shredded sharp cheddar cheese, divided**
- 1 **cup shredded Swiss cheese**
- ¾ **cup biscuit/baking mix**
- 2 **large eggs, room temperature, lightly beaten**

1. Preheat oven to 425°. Cook macaroni according to package directions; drain.
2. Meanwhile, sprinkle ¼ cup bread crumbs into 36 greased mini-muffin cups. In a large saucepan, melt the butter over medium heat. Stir in flour and seasonings until smooth; gradually whisk in milk. Bring to a boil, stirring constantly; cook and stir until thickened, 1-2 minutes. Stir in 1 cup cheddar cheese and Swiss cheese until melted.
3. Remove from heat; stir in biscuit mix, eggs and ½ cup bread crumbs. Add the macaroni; toss to coat. Spoon about 2 Tbsp. macaroni mixture into prepared mini-muffin cups; sprinkle with remaining 1 cup cheddar cheese and ¼ cup bread crumbs.
4. Bake until golden brown, 8-10 minutes. Cool in pans 5 minutes before serving.

1 APPETIZER: *91 cal., 5g fat (3g sat. fat), 22mg chol., 162mg sod., 8g carb. (1g sugars, 0 fiber), 4g pro.*

ITALIAN MEAT STROMBOLI

As a mother of two, I feel as if the only time I have for creativity in my day is when I'm in the kitchen! I received a similar recipe from a co-worker but added veggies and spices to give it my own spin.
—Denise Tutton, Ridgway, PA

PREP: 25 min. + rising • **BAKE:** 25 min.
MAKES: 10 servings

- 1   loaf (1 lb.) frozen bread dough, thawed
- 1   can (8 oz.) pizza sauce
- ¼   tsp. garlic powder, divided
- ¼   tsp. dried oregano, divided
- 8   oz. brick cheese, sliced
- 1   cup shredded part-skim mozzarella cheese
- ½   cup chopped green pepper
- ¼   cup chopped onion
- 1   cup sliced fresh mushrooms
- ½   cup shredded Parmesan cheese
- 1   pkg. (3 oz.) sliced pepperoni
- 5   oz. sliced deli ham

1. Place dough in a greased bowl, turning once to grease the top. Cover and let rise in a warm place until doubled, about 1 hour.

2. Preheat oven to 350°. Mix pizza sauce and ⅛ tsp. each of the garlic powder and oregano.

3. Punch down dough. On a lightly floured surface, roll the dough into a 15x10-in. rectangle. Top with brick cheese, sauce mixture and remaining ingredients to within 1 in. of edges.

4. Roll up, jelly-roll style, starting with a long side. Pinch seam to seal and tuck ends under; transfer to a greased baking sheet. Sprinkle with the remaining garlic powder and oregano. Bake until golden brown, 25-30 minutes.

1 PIECE: 335 cal., 16g fat (8g sat. fat), 46mg chol., 871mg sod., 27g carb. (4g sugars, 3g fiber), 19g pro.

> ### Holiday Helper
> You can make whatever adjustments you'd like to the filling of this recipe—practically anything you'd put on top of a pizza would work here. Also look to Italian subs for inspiration!

CARAMEL GINGERBREAD CUPCAKES

One night, my niece and I put our heads together to come up with this fabulous cupcake. We combined our favorite gingerbread cookie and cupcake recipes, then added caramel frosting and a drizzle of caramel ice cream topping. Our guests reached for seconds and thirds until nothing was left but a delicious memory and a stellar recipe to share.
—Delaine Smith, Barrie, ON

PREP: 25 min. • **BAKE:** 15 min. + cooling
MAKES: 1 dozen

- 1½   cups all-purpose flour
- ¾   cup sugar
- ¼   cup packed brown sugar
- 2   tsp. baking powder
- 1   tsp. ground ginger
- ½   tsp. ground cinnamon
- ½   tsp. ground nutmeg
- ¼   tsp. ground cloves
- ¼   tsp. salt
- 1   large egg, room temperature
- ½   cup 2% milk
- ⅓   cup canola oil
- ¼   cup molasses
- 1   tsp. vanilla extract
- ½   tsp. caramel extract

FROSTING
- 3   cups confectioners' sugar
- 6   Tbsp. butter, softened
- 1   tsp. caramel extract
- 3   to 4 Tbsp. 2% milk
  Caramel sundae syrup

1. Preheat oven to 350°. Line 12 muffin cups with paper liners.

2. Whisk together first 9 ingredients. In another bowl, whisk together egg, milk, oil, molasses and extracts. Add to the flour mixture; stir just until moistened.

3. Fill prepared cups two-thirds full. Bake until a toothpick inserted in center comes out clean, 15-18 minutes. Cool in pans for 10 minutes before removing to wire racks; cool completely.

4. For frosting, beat confectioners' sugar, butter, extract and enough milk to reach desired consistency. Spread over the cupcakes. Drizzle with caramel syrup before serving.

1 CUPCAKE: 382 cal., 13g fat (4g sat. fat), 32mg chol., 192mg sod., 65g carb. (52g sugars, 1g fiber), 3g pro.

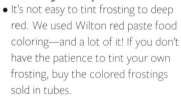

COOKIES & CREAM STUFFED SANTA BELLIES

All hands will be reaching for these cute cookies, and you know kids love 'em! If your kitchen is warm from baking all day, chill your dough for a bit before rolling it out.
—Crystal Schlueter, Northglenn, CO

PREP: 55 min. + chilling
BAKE: 10 min./batch + cooling
MAKES: about 2 dozen

1   cup unsalted butter, softened
1   cup sugar
2   large eggs, room temperature
1   Tbsp. vanilla extract
3½ cups all-purpose flour
1   Tbsp. baking powder
½   tsp. salt
6   to 7 Hershey's Cookies 'n' Creme
    candy bars (1.55 oz. each), broken into
    3-section pieces
2½ cups vanilla frosting
    Red, black and yellow
    paste food coloring

1. Cream butter and sugar until light and fluffy, 5-7 minutes. Beat in the eggs and vanilla. In another bowl, whisk the flour, baking powder and salt; gradually beat into creamed mixture. Divide dough in half; shape each into a disk. Wrap and refrigerate until firm enough to roll, at least 1 hour.
2. On a lightly floured surface, roll each portion of dough to ⅛-in. thickness. Cut with a floured 3-in. round cutter.
3. Place half of the circles 1 in. apart on ungreased baking sheets; top with candy bar pieces. Top with remaining circles, pinching edges to seal.
4. Bake at 350° until bottoms are light brown, 10-12 minutes. Remove from pans to wire racks; cool completely.
5. Tint 1⅔ cups frosting red; spread over cookies. Tint ⅔ cup frosting black; pipe belts and buttons over top. Tint remaining frosting yellow; pipe buckles on belts.

1 FILLED COOKIE: *350 cal., 16g fat (8g sat. fat), 37mg chol., 202mg sod., 49g carb. (30g sugars, 0 fiber), 3g pro.*

Holiday Helper

● It's not easy to tint frosting to deep red. We used Wilton red paste food coloring—and a lot of it! If you don't have the patience to tint your own frosting, buy the colored frostings sold in tubes.

● If you find yourself getting heavy-handed with flour while rolling out your dough, gently flip over each cutout piece of dough and brush away the flour with a pastry brush before placing on the baking sheet.

FARMHOUSE BARBEQUE MUFFINS

This is an interesting take on barbeques—you just bake it right in its own bun. The hardest part is waiting those 5 minutes to cool before you get to remove from the pan and start eating!
—Val Lundby, Fergus Falls, MN

PREP: 30 min. • **BAKE:** 20 min.
MAKES: 5 servings

- 1 lb. ground beef
- 1 garlic clove, minced
- ½ cup ketchup
- 3 Tbsp. brown sugar
- 1 Tbsp. cider vinegar
- 2 tsp. chili powder
- ¼ tsp. salt
- ¼ tsp. pepper
- 2 tubes (6 oz. each) refrigerated buttermilk biscuits
- ¾ cup shredded cheddar cheese

1. Preheat oven to 375°. In a large skillet, cook beef over medium heat until no longer pink, 6-8 minutes, breaking up into crumbles; drain. Add garlic; cook for 1 minute longer. Stir in the ketchup, brown sugar, vinegar, chili powder, salt and pepper; set aside.
2. Press 1 biscuit dough onto the bottom and up the sides of each of 10 greased muffin cups. Fill with beef mixture.
3. Bake 15 minutes on a lower oven rack; sprinkle with cheese. Bake until cheese is melted and the biscuits are dark golden, 2-4 minutes longer. Let stand 5 minutes before removing from pan.
2 MUFFINS: *493 cal., 24g fat (10g sat. fat), 73mg chol., 1177mg sod., 46g carb. (19g sugars, 0 fiber), 24g pro.*

CHICKEN ALPHABET SOUP

I'm a teenager and love to make this fun chicken soup for my family. It makes me so happy when they tell me how much they like it!
—Sarah Mackey, New Smyrna Beach, FL

TAKES: 25 min.
MAKES: 10 servings (2½ qt.)

- 3 medium carrots, chopped
- 2 celery ribs, chopped
- ¾ cup chopped sweet onion
- 1 Tbsp. olive oil
- 2 qt. chicken broth
- 3 cups shredded cooked chicken breast
- ¼ tsp. dried thyme
- 1½ cups uncooked alphabet pasta
- 3 Tbsp. minced fresh parsley

In a Dutch oven, saute the carrots, celery and onion in oil until tender, 3-5 minutes. Stir in the broth, chicken and thyme. Bring to a boil. Stir in the pasta. Reduce heat; simmer, uncovered, until pasta is tender, about 10 minutes. Stir in parsley.
1 CUP: *163 cal., 4g fat (1g sat. fat), 26mg chol., 828mg sod., 20g carb. (3g sugars, 2g fiber), 12g pro.*

SPICED APPLE-GRAPE JUICE

For some outdoor fun, we pour this spiced juice into a Thermos and take it with us. But it's also nice to cuddle up indoors while sipping on a cup of this warm cider.
—Claire Beattie, Toronto, ON

PREP: 10 min. • **COOK:** 1 hour
MAKES: 8 servings

- 4 cups white grape juice
- 3 cups unsweetened apple juice
- 1 cup water
- 2 cinnamon sticks (3 in.)
- 12 whole cloves
- 8 whole allspice

1. In a large saucepan, combine the grape juice, apple juice and water. Place the cinnamon, cloves and allspice on a double thickness of cheesecloth; bring up corners of cloth and tie with string to form a bag. Add to the pan.
2. Bring to a boil. Reduce heat; simmer, uncovered, for 1-1½ hours or until flavors are blended. Discard spice bag. Serve warm in mugs.
¾ CUP: *121 cal., 0 fat (0 sat. fat), 0 chol., 10mg sod., 29g carb. (27g sugars, 0 fiber), 1g pro.*

ALL THINGS EGGNOG

Creamy, indulgent eggnog is the ultimate holiday beverage, but who says it's just for drinking? Sweets, breads, cakes, rolls—even a side dish!—are elevated from simply delicious to fabulously festive with the addition of eggnog.

EGGNOG FUDGE

I experimented with many recipes featuring eggnog before coming up with this winning combination.
—Richell Welch, Buffalo, TX

PREP: 1 hour + cooling
MAKES: about 3¼ lbs.

- 1 Tbsp. plus ¾ cup butter, softened, divided
- 3 cups sugar
- ⅔ cup eggnog
- 2 Tbsp. heavy whipping cream
- 1 pkg. (10 to 12 oz.) white baking chips
- 1 cup marshmallow creme
- 1 cup finely chopped walnuts
- 2 tsp. vanilla extract

1. Line a 13x9-in. pan with foil and grease the foil with 1 Tbsp. butter; set aside. In a large saucepan, combine sugar, eggnog, cream and the remaining ¾ cup butter. Bring to a boil over medium heat, stirring constantly. Reduce heat; cook until a candy thermometer reads 238° (soft-ball stage), stirring occasionally.
2. Remove from the heat. Stir in baking chips until melted. Stir in marshmallow creme, walnuts and vanilla.
3. Spread into prepared pan. Let cool to room temperature. Using foil, lift fudge out of pan. Discard foil; cut fudge into 1-in. squares. Store in an airtight container in the refrigerator.

NOTE: *We recommend that you test your candy thermometer before each use by bringing water to a boil; the thermometer should read 212°. Adjust your recipe temperature based on your test.*

1 PIECE: *56 cal., 3g fat (1g sat. fat), 5mg chol., 14mg sod., 8g carb. (7g sugars, 0 fiber), 0 pro.*

EGGNOG CREAM PUFFS

If you want to receive rave reviews and recipe requests, combine two Christmas classics: eggnog and cream puffs. When it comes to Santa, this recipe goes on the nice list!
—Kristen Heigl, Staten Island, NY

PREP: 40 min. • **BAKE:** 30 min. + cooling
MAKES: about 2 dozen

- 1 cup water
- ½ cup butter, cubed
- ⅛ tsp. salt
- 1 cup all-purpose flour
- ¾ tsp. ground nutmeg
- 4 large eggs, room temperature

WHIPPED CREAM
- 1½ cups heavy whipping cream
- 1½ cups confectioners' sugar
- ¼ cup eggnog
- 1 tsp. vanilla extract
- ⅛ tsp. ground nutmeg
  Additional confectioners' sugar

1. Preheat oven to 400°. In a large saucepan, bring water, butter and salt to a rolling boil. Add flour all at once and nutmeg and stir until blended. Cook over medium heat, stirring vigorously until mixture pulls away from side of pan. Remove from heat; let stand 5 minutes.
2. Add eggs, 1 at a time, beating well after each addition until smooth. Continue beating until mixture is smooth and shiny. Drop dough by rounded tablespoonfuls 1 in. apart onto greased baking sheets. Bake 30-35 minutes or until puffed, very firm and golden brown.
3. Pierce sides of puffs with tip of a knife. Cool on wire racks. Cut top third off each puff.
4. In a large bowl, beat cream until it begins to thicken. Add confectioners' sugar, eggnog, vanilla and nutmeg; beat until soft peaks form. Just before serving, fill cream puffs with whipped cream; replace tops. Dust with additional confectioners' sugar. Serve immediately.

1 CREAM PUFF: *127 cal., 9g fat (5g sat. fat), 51mg chol., 52mg sod., 10g carb. (7g sugars, 0 fiber), 2g pro.*

EGGNOG

Store-bought eggnog just can't compete with my homemade version. Apricot brandy is my secret ingredient!
—Shelia Weimer, Bluefield, WV

PREP: 15 min. • **COOK:** 25 min. + chilling
MAKES: 20 servings

- 1¾ cups sugar
- ¼ cup all-purpose flour
- ½ tsp. salt
- 2 qt. 2% milk
- 6 large eggs, beaten
- 1 cup apricot brandy or brandy
- ½ cup rum
- 2 Tbsp. bourbon
- 2 Tbsp. vanilla extract
- 1 qt. half-and-half cream
- ½ tsp. ground nutmeg
  Optional: Turbinado (washed raw) sugar, ground cinnamon and pirouette cookies

1. In a Dutch oven, combine the sugar, flour and salt. Gradually whisk in milk until smooth. Cook and stir over medium-high heat until thickened and bubbly, 15 minutes. Reduce heat; cook and stir 2 minutes longer. Remove from the heat.
2. Stir a small amount of the hot mixture into the eggs; return all to the pan, stirring constantly. Cook and stir over medium heat until mixture is slightly thickened and coats the back of a spoon, 5 minutes.
3. Transfer to a large bowl; cool quickly by placing bowl in ice water and stirring for 2 minutes. Stir in brandy, rum, bourbon and vanilla. Let cool completely. Cover and refrigerate for at least 3 hours.
4. Just before serving, stir in cream and nutmeg. If desired, mix turbinado sugar and cinnamon in a small bowl; dip rims of glasses into a shallow dish of water then into the sugar mixture, pressing lightly to adhere. Fill glasses with eggnog. If desired, serve with pirouette cookies.
¾ **CUP:** *252 cal., 8g fat (5g sat. fat), 95mg chol., 153mg sod., 25g carb. (24g sugars, 0 fiber), 7g pro.*

A BOOZY HISTORY

Eggnog as we know it has its roots in a drink from medieval Britain called a *posset*—a mixture of egg and cream spiked with ale or wine.

In the New World, colonists made changes that have stuck. In the North, rum was the added liquor of choice; in the South, it was bourbon. And yes, eggnog was by definition an alcoholic drink—sometimes extremely so. George Washington's eggnog recipe included not only rum *and* rye whiskey, but also brandy and sherry.

In fact, eggnog's notorious alcohol content made the drink the catalyst for the infamous West Point Eggnog Riot of 1826. Alcohol was banned from the academy's grounds; students—being students—set about sneaking in liquor so they could celebrate Christmas in their customary manner.

When officers attempted to break up the carousing, the party turned violent as students took up arms (luckily with impaired aim). When the smoke cleared (and hangovers receded), 19 cadets were expelled for their bad behavior.

Today, of course, you're welcome to enjoy your nog with or without booze—no riots needed!

CRANBERRY PISTACHIO EGGNOG DOUGHNUTS

As a doughnut lover, I wanted to create a holiday variation. I came up with these festive baked doughnuts full of pistachios and cranberries with a wonderful glaze. Fresh nutmeg makes them even better.
—Mark Banick, Turner, OR

- -

PREP: 30 min.
BAKE: 15 min./batch + cooling
MAKES: 2 dozen

2 cups all-purpose flour, sifted
½ cup packed brown sugar
2½ tsp. baking powder
1 tsp. baking soda
½ tsp. salt
½ tsp. ground allspice

2½ cups eggnog
4 tsp. canola oil
1 tsp. rum extract
¼ cup dried cranberries, finely chopped
½ cup pistachios, finely chopped, divided

GLAZE
1½ cups confectioners' sugar
1 to 2 Tbsp. unsweetened cranberry juice
Whole nutmeg, optional

1. Preheat oven to 350°. Combine first 6 ingredients. In a second bowl, whisk eggnog, oil and extract. Add to dry ingredients; stir until blended. Stir in cranberries just until blended.
2. Cut a small hole in the corner of a food-safe piping bag; fill with batter.

Pipe batter into a 6-cavity doughnut pan coated with cooking spray, filling the cavities three-fourths full. Sprinkle with 5 Tbsp. pistachios.
3. Bake until golden brown, 12-15 minutes. Cool for 5 minutes before removing from pan to a wire rack. Repeat with the remaining batter.
4. For glaze, in a small bowl whisk together confectioners' sugar and cranberry juice until smooth and desired thickness is reached. Drizzle doughnuts with glaze; immediately sprinkle with remaining pistachios. If desired, grate whole nutmeg over tops. Place on wire rack; let stand until set.

1 DOUGHNUT: *135 cal., 3g fat (1g sat. fat), 16mg chol., 179mg sod., 24g carb. (15g sugars, 1g fiber), 3g pro.*
DIABETIC EXCHANGES: *1½ starch, ½ fat.*

EGGNOG SWEET POTATO BAKE

I love eggnog so I am always looking for new ways to use it. Why not in a side dish? When I added it to mashed sweet potatoes, I knew I had a winner. You can make this the night before and refrigerate it unbaked; the next day, let it stand at room temperature for 30 minutes before baking.
—Katherine Wollgast, Troy, MO

- -

PREP: 1¼ hours + cooling • **BAKE:** 30 min.
MAKES: 8 servings

- 3½ lbs. sweet potatoes (about 5 large)
- ⅔ cup eggnog
- ½ cup golden raisins
- 2 Tbsp. sugar
- 1 tsp. salt

TOPPING
- ¼ cup all-purpose flour
- ¼ cup quick-cooking oats
- ¼ cup packed brown sugar
- ¼ cup chopped pecans
- ½ tsp. ground cinnamon
- ¼ tsp. ground nutmeg
- 2 Tbsp. butter, melted

1. Preheat oven to 400°. Scrub sweet potatoes; pierce several times with a fork. Place on a foil-lined 15x10x1-in. baking pan; bake until tender, 1 hour. Remove from oven. Reduce oven setting to 350°.
2. When potatoes are cool enough to handle, remove and discard skins. Mash potatoes in a large bowl (you should have about 6 cups mashed). Stir in eggnog, raisins, sugar and salt. Transfer to a greased 11x7-in. baking dish.
3. For topping, in a small bowl, mix flour, oats, brown sugar, pecans and spices; stir in butter. Sprinkle over the sweet potatoes. Bake, uncovered, until heated through and topping is lightly browned, 30-35 minutes.
1 CUP: *362 cal., 7g fat (3g sat. fat), 20mg chol., 352mg sod., 72g carb. (37g sugars, 7g fiber), 6g pro.*

Holiday Helper
We tested the recipes in this chapter using commercially prepared eggnog, but you can use your own homemade nog instead!

EGGNOG FUDGE BRULEE BROWNIES

These fudge brownies boast a holiday twist that lifts the treats far beyond basic. The flavors of eggnog, spices and rum will surely get you into a spirit of celebration. The recipe does require that you whisk the ingredients constantly while they are on the stovetop, so don't be tempted to walk away from the stove!
—Colleen Delawder, Herndon, VA

- -

PREP: 20 min. • **BAKE:** 30 min.
MAKES: 16 servings

- 1½ cups sugar
- ½ cup butter
- ⅓ cup eggnog
- ¼ cup baking cocoa
- 1 milk chocolate candy bar with caramel and sea salt (4.4 oz.)
- 1 tsp. vanilla extract
- 1 tsp. rum or rum extract
- 1 large egg
- 1 large egg yolk
- 1 cup all-purpose flour
- ¼ tsp. salt

GLAZE
- 1 milk chocolate candy bar with caramel and sea salt (4.4 oz.)
- 3 Tbsp. eggnog
- ¼ tsp. vanilla extract

1. Preheat oven to 350°. Line an 8x8-in. square baking dish with nonstick foil, letting the ends extend up sides. Lightly spray with cooking spray; set aside.
2. In a large heavy saucepan, combine sugar, butter, eggnog and baking cocoa. Bring to a boil, stirring constantly. Remove from heat; add milk chocolate bar, vanilla and rum, stirring until the chocolate has melted. Cool slightly. In a large bowl, whisk egg and egg yolk until foamy, about 3 minutes. Gradually whisk in chocolate mixture. In another bowl, whisk in flour and salt; stir into chocolate mixture. Pour into prepared pan.
3. Bake until a toothpick inserted in the center comes out with moist crumbs, 30-35 minutes (do not overbake). Cool completely on a wire rack.
4. For glaze, in a small saucepan melt the chocolate bar, eggnog and vanilla over medium heat, stirring constantly until smooth. Spread over cooled brownies. Let stand at room temperature until glaze has cooled, 1-2 hours. Lifting with foil, remove brownies from pan. Cut into squares. Store in refrigerator.
1 BROWNIE: *256 cal., 12g fat (7g sat. fat), 47mg chol., 105mg sod., 36g carb. (28g sugars, 1g fiber), 3g pro.*

CHRISTMAS MORNING SWEET ROLLS

These make-ahead rolls have been a holiday tradition in our house for years. The eggnog in the frosting makes them extra special on Christmas morning.
—*Kimberly Williams, Brownsburg, IN*

PREP: 45 min. + chilling • **BAKE:** 20 min. • **MAKES:** 1 dozen

- 1   pkg. (¼ oz.) active dry yeast
- 1   cup warm water (110° to 115°)
- ½   cup sugar
- 1   tsp. salt
- 4   to 4½ cups all-purpose flour
- ¼   cup canola oil
- 1   large egg, room temperature

FILLING
- ⅓   cup sugar
- 1½   tsp. ground cinnamon
- ¼   tsp. ground nutmeg
- 3   Tbsp. butter, softened

FROSTING
- 2½   cups confectioners' sugar
- 5   Tbsp. butter, softened
- ½   tsp. ground cinnamon
- ½   tsp. vanilla extract
- 2   to 3 Tbsp. eggnog

1. In a small bowl, dissolve yeast in warm water. In a large bowl, combine sugar, salt, 1 cup flour, oil, egg and the yeast mixture; beat on medium speed until smooth. Stir in enough remaining flour to form a soft dough (dough will be sticky).
2. Do not knead. Place in a greased bowl, turning once to grease the top. Cover and refrigerate overnight.
3. For filling, in a small bowl, mix sugar, cinnamon and nutmeg. Punch down dough; turn onto a lightly floured surface. Roll into a 18x8-in. rectangle. Spread with butter to within ½ in. of edges; sprinkle with sugar mixture. Roll up jelly-roll style, starting with a long side; pinch seam to seal. Cut into 12 slices.
4. Place slices in a greased 13x9-in. baking pan, cut side down. Cover with a kitchen towel; let rise in a warm place until doubled, about 45 minutes.
5. Preheat oven to 350°. Bake until golden brown, 20-25 minutes. Place on a wire rack to cool slightly. For frosting, beat confectioners' sugar, butter, cinnamon, vanilla and enough eggnog to reach desired consistency; spread over warm rolls.
NOTE: *The dough can be held in the refrigerator 8 to 24 hours before assembling. You can even prepare the rolls and store them in the refrigerator overnight before baking. In the morning, let them sit at room temperature for 30 minutes before baking.*
1 ROLL: *424 cal., 13g fat (5g sat. fat), 37mg chol., 267mg sod., 72g carb. (39g sugars, 2g fiber), 5g pro.*

> ## Holiday Helper
> Give the frosting holiday cheer by adding ½ tsp. rum extract.

BANANA EGGNOG BREAD

The easy and delicious quick bread combines two of my favorite winter treats, banana bread and eggnog. Fresh from the oven, a big slice will warm you from head to toe.
—*Kristin Stone, Little Elm, TX*

PREP: 20 min. • **BAKE:** 50 min. + cooling • **MAKES:** 1 loaf (16 pieces)

- ½   cup butter, softened
- 1½   cups sugar
- 2   large eggs, room temperature
- 1   cup mashed ripe bananas (about 2 medium)
- ¼   cup eggnog
- 1   tsp. vanilla extract
- 1¾   cups all-purpose flour
- 1   tsp. baking powder
- ½   tsp. ground nutmeg, divided
- ¼   tsp. salt
- ⅛   tsp. baking soda

1. Preheat oven to 350°. In a large bowl, cream butter and sugar until light and fluffy, 5-7 minutes. Add eggs, 1 at a time, beating well after each addition. Beat in bananas, eggnog and vanilla. In another bowl, whisk flour, baking powder, ¼ tsp. nutmeg, salt and the baking soda; gradually beat into the banana mixture.
2. Transfer batter to a greased 9x5-in. loaf pan; sprinkle with remaining ¼ tsp. nutmeg. Bake 50-60 minutes or until a toothpick inserted in center comes out clean. Cool in pan 10 minutes before removing to a wire rack to cool.
1 PIECE: *200 cal., 7g fat (4g sat. fat), 41mg chol., 134mg sod., 33g carb. (21g sugars, 1g fiber), 3g pro.*

EGGLESS SKINNY NOG

If you love eggnog but not the calories, then this seems-naughty-but-it's-really-nice version is for you.
—*Peg Manderscheid, Maquoketa, IA*

TAKES: 10 min. • **MAKES:** 8 servings

- 4   cups fat-free milk
- 1   pkg. (1 oz.) sugar-free instant vanilla pudding mix
- ½   tsp. rum extract
- ¼   tsp. ground nutmeg
      Frozen fat-free whipped topping, thawed, optional

In a large bowl, whisk milk and pudding mix until smooth. Whisk in rum extract and nutmeg. Serve immediately. If desired, top with whipped topping.

½ CUP: *55 cal., 0 fat (0 sat. fat), 2mg chol., 105mg sod., 9g carb. (6g sugars, 0 fiber), 4g pro.*
DIABETIC EXCHANGES: *½ fat-free milk.*

BAUBLE DECOR

Ball ornaments don't belong only on the tree—a collection of balls of different sizes and colors can be displayed in a tray as an easy and accessible centerpiece for your holiday table.

EGGNOG PUMPKIN PIE

My mom's is the absolute best pumpkin pie I've ever tasted. Eggnog is her signature ingredient in the creamy custard filling.
—*Terri Gonzalez, Roswell, NM*

PREP: 10 min. • **BAKE:** 1 hour + cooling • **MAKES:** 8 servings

      Dough for single-crust pie
- 1   can (15 oz.) solid-pack pumpkin
- 1¼ cups eggnog
- ⅔   cup sugar
- 3   large eggs
- 1½ tsp. pumpkin pie spice
- ¼   tsp. salt
      Whipped cream, optional

1. Preheat oven to 375°. On a lightly floured surface, roll dough to a ⅛-in.-thick circle; transfer to a 9-in. pie plate. Trim crust to ½ in. beyond rim of plate; flute edge. In a large bowl, combine pumpkin, eggnog, sugar, eggs, pumpkin pie spice and salt. Pour into crust.

2. Bake until a knife inserted in the center comes out clean, 60-65 minutes. Cool on a wire rack. Refrigerate until serving. If desired, top with whipped cream.

1 PIECE: *317 cal., 15g fat (9g sat. fat), 123mg chol., 280mg sod., 40g carb. (22g sugars, 2g fiber), 7g pro.*
DOUGH FOR SINGLE-CRUST PIE: *Combine 1¼ cups all-purpose flour and ¼ tsp. salt; cut in ½ cup cold butter until crumbly. Gradually add 3-5 Tbsp. ice water, tossing with a fork until dough holds together when pressed. Shape into a disk; wrap and refrigerate 1 hour.*

CRANBERRY EGGNOG CHEESECAKE BARS

My family loves everything cheesecake. These bars combine tart cranberries and rich cream cheese, and taste even better when chilled overnight!
—Carmell Childs, Orangeville, UT

- -

PREP: 20 min. • **BAKE:** 50 min. + chilling
MAKES: 2 dozen

- 1 pkg. spice cake mix (regular size)
- 2½ cups old-fashioned oats
- ¾ cup butter, melted
- 2 pkg. (8 oz. each) cream cheese, softened
- ½ cup sugar
- ⅛ tsp. ground nutmeg
- ½ cup eggnog
- 2 Tbsp. all-purpose flour
- 3 large eggs, room temperature
- 1 can (14 oz.) whole-berry cranberry sauce
- 2 Tbsp. cornstarch

1. Preheat oven to 350°. Line a 13x9-in. baking pan with parchment, letting ends extend up sides; grease paper.
2. In a large bowl, combine cake mix and oats; stir in melted butter. Reserve 1⅓ cups crumb mixture for topping; press the remaining mixture onto bottom of prepared pan.
3. In a large bowl, beat cream cheese, sugar and nutmeg until smooth. Gradually beat in eggnog and flour. Add eggs; beat on low speed just until blended. Pour over crust.
4. In a small bowl, mix cranberry sauce and cornstarch until blended; spoon over cheesecake layer. Sprinkle with the reserved crumb mixture. Bake until edges are brown and center is almost set, 50-55 minutes.
5. Cool for 1 hour on a wire rack. Refrigerate at least 2 hours. Lifting with parchment, remove cheesecake from pan. Cut into bars.
1 BAR: *282 cal., 15g fat (8g sat. fat), 62mg chol., 254mg sod., 34g carb. (18g sugars, 1g fiber), 4g pro.*

CONTEST-WINNING EGGNOG CAKE

This wonderful cake is full of eggnog flavor. It's a beloved favorite around Christmastime.
—Debra Frappolli, Wayne, NJ

- -

PREP: 30 min. + cooling
BAKE: 30 min. + cooling
MAKES: 16 servings

- ½ cup butter, softened
- 1¼ cups sugar
- 3 large eggs, room temperature
- ½ tsp. vanilla extract
- ½ tsp. rum extract
- 2 cups all-purpose flour
- 2 tsp. baking powder
- 1 tsp. salt
- 1 cup eggnog

FROSTING
- ¼ cup all-purpose flour
- ¼ tsp. salt
- 1½ cups eggnog
- 1 cup butter, softened
- 1½ cups confectioners' sugar
- 1½ tsp. vanilla extract
- Pearlized nonpareils, optional

1. Preheat oven to 350°. In a large bowl, cream butter and sugar until light and fluffy, 5-7 minutes. Add eggs, 1 at a time, beating well after each addition. Add extracts. Combine flour, baking powder and salt; gradually add to the creamed mixture alternately with eggnog, beating well after each addition. Pour batter into 2 greased 9-in. round baking pans.
2. Bake until a toothpick inserted in the center comes out clean, 25-30 minutes. Cool in pans for 10 minutes before removing to wire racks to cool completely.
3. For frosting, in a small saucepan, combine flour and salt. Gradually stir in eggnog until smooth. Bring to a boil over medium heat whisking constantly; cook and stir until thickened, about 2 minutes. Cool to room temperature.
4. In a large bowl, cream butter and confectioners' sugar until light and fluffy, 5-7 minutes. Gradually beat in eggnog mixture and vanilla until smooth. Spread between layers and over top and side of cake. If desired, pipe additional frosting for decoration and top with nonpareils. Store in the refrigerator.
1 PIECE: *372 cal., 20g fat (12g sat. fat), 104mg chol., 417mg sod., 44g carb. (30g sugars, 0 fiber), 5g pro.*

SPICED EGGNOG RUM COOKIES

One year, when I had a lot of eggnog on hand, I created this new holiday cookie recipe. The flavor is subtle, but somehow the eggnog transforms regular cookies into something exceptional for the holidays.
—*Mark Banick, Turner, OR*

- -

PREP: 25 min. + chilling
BAKE: 10 min./batch + cooling
MAKES: 4 dozen

- ¾ cup butter, softened
- 1¼ cups sugar
- 1 large egg, room temperature
- 1 cup eggnog, divided
- 1¾ tsp. rum extract, divided
- 3½ cups all-purpose flour
- 1 tsp. baking powder
- ½ tsp. ground cinnamon
- ½ tsp. ground nutmeg
- ¼ tsp. salt
- ¼ tsp. ground ginger
- ¼ tsp. ground allspice
- 3 cups confectioners' sugar
  Colored sugar or sprinkles

1. In a large bowl, cream butter and sugar until light and fluffy, 5-7 minutes. Beat in egg, ⅓ cup eggnog and 1 tsp. extract. In another bowl, whisk the flour, baking powder, cinnamon, nutmeg, salt, ginger and allspice; gradually beat into the creamed mixture.
2. Divide dough in half and shape each portion into a disk; cover and refrigerate disks until firm enough to roll, about 30 minutes.
3. Preheat oven to 375°. On a lightly floured surface, roll each portion of dough to ¼-in. thickness. Cut with a floured 3¼-in. star-shaped cookie cutter. Place stars 1 in. apart on parchment-lined baking sheets.
4. Bake until edges begin to brown, 8-10 minutes. Cool on pans 1 minute. Remove to wire racks to cool completely. For glaze, mix confectioners' sugar, remaining ¾ tsp. extract and enough of the remaining eggnog to achieve a drizzling consistency; drizzle over cookies. Decorate as desired.
1 COOKIE: *114 cal., 3g fat (2g sat. fat), 14mg chol., 50mg sod., 20g carb. (13g sugars, 0 fiber), 1g pro.*

EGGNOG MINI LOAVES

The seasonal flavors of eggnog, rum and nutmeg shine through in these moist, golden loaves. Tender slices are just right with a cup of coffee.
—*Beverly Elmore, Spokane, MI*

- -

PREP: 15 min. • **BAKE:** 30 min. + cooling
MAKES: 3 loaves (6 pieces each)

- 2¼ cups all-purpose flour
- 2½ tsp. baking powder
- ½ tsp. salt
- ½ tsp. ground cinnamon
- ½ tsp. ground nutmeg
- 2 large eggs, room temperature
- 1 cup eggnog
- ¾ cup sugar
- ½ cup butter, melted
- 2 tsp. vanilla extract
- 2 tsp. rum extract

1. Preheat oven to 350°. In a large bowl, combine the flour, baking powder, salt, cinnamon and nutmeg. In another bowl, beat the eggs, eggnog, sugar, melted butter and extracts; stir into the dry ingredients just until moistened.

2. Pour into 3 greased 5¾x3x2-in. loaf pans. Bake until a toothpick inserted in the center comes out clean, 30-35 minutes. Cool for 10 minutes before removing from pans to wire racks.
1 PIECE: *158 cal., 6g fat (4g sat. fat), 43mg chol., 189mg sod., 22g carb. (10g sugars, 0 fiber), 3g pro.*

Holiday Helper
- That's the spirit! Rum, brandy or whiskey can be swapped in for the rum extract if you prefer. Pay homage to another holiday cocktail, the Tom and Jerry, by adding a bit more spice to your batter. Try ⅛ tsp. each cloves and allspice.
- For a festive tray (and an added gift!), get 5x7-in. picture frames from a craft store and place holiday wrapping paper under the glass. Wrap the loaves in waxed paper and place on the frames. Tie everything together with colorful ribbon.

EGGNOG BISCOTTI

You may substitute additional eggnog if rum isn't your thing. For a variation, try using one of the flavored eggnogs available around the holidays.
—Shannon Dobos, Calgary, AB

- -

PREP: 25 min. • **BAKE:** 40 min. + cooling
MAKES: about 3 dozen

- ½ cup butter, softened
- 1 cup sugar
- 2 large eggs, room temperature
- ¼ cup eggnog
- ½ tsp. vanilla extract
- 2⅓ cups all-purpose flour
- 2 tsp. baking powder
- ½ tsp. ground nutmeg
  Dash salt

GLAZE
- ¾ cup confectioners' sugar
- 3 to 5 tsp. eggnog
- 1 tsp. dark rum, optional

1. Preheat oven to 375°. Beat butter and sugar until blended. Beat in eggs, 1 at a time. Beat in eggnog and vanilla. In another bowl, whisk together flour, baking powder, nutmeg and salt; gradually beat into butter mixture (dough will be sticky).
2. Divide dough in half. On a greased baking sheet, shape each portion into a 12x3-in. rectangle. Bake until a toothpick inserted in center comes out clean, 16-19 minutes. Reduce oven setting to 300°. Remove rectangles from pans to wire racks; cool 10 minutes.
3. Place rectangles on a cutting board. Using a serrated knife, trim ends of rectangles and cut diagonally into ½-in. slices. Return slices to baking sheets, cut side down. Bake until firm, about 10 minutes per side. Remove from pans to wire racks; cool completely.
4. Mix all the glaze ingredients. Drizzle over biscotti with a spoon.

1 COOKIE: *90 cal., 3g fat (2g sat. fat), 18mg chol., 56mg sod., 15g carb. (8g sugars, 0 fiber), 1g pro.*

Holiday Helper

Since the dough is on the sticky side, use a gentle touch or, if necessary, lightly floured hands when shaping it.

EGGNOG CHEESECAKE

I make good use of extra eggnog by baking this luscious cheesecake. A bit of rum extract adds a distinctive flavor.
—Kristen Grula, Hazelton, PA

- -

PREP: 15 min. • **BAKE:** 45 min. + chilling
MAKES: 16 servings

- 1 cup graham cracker crumbs
- 2 Tbsp. sugar
- 3 Tbsp. butter, melted

FILLING
- 3 pkg. (8 oz. each) cream cheese, softened
- 1 cup sugar
- 3 Tbsp. all-purpose flour
- 2 large eggs, room temperature, lightly beaten
- ¾ cup eggnog
- ½ tsp. rum extract
  Dash ground nutmeg
  Optional: Whipped cream and additional ground nutmeg

1. Preheat oven to 325°. Place a greased 9-in. springform pan on a double thickness of heavy-duty foil (about 18 in. square). Securely wrap foil around pan.
2. In a small bowl, combine the cracker crumbs, sugar and butter. Press onto the bottom of pan. Place on a baking sheet. Bake for 10 minutes. Cool on a wire rack.
3. In a large bowl, beat the cream cheese, sugar and flour until smooth. Add eggs; beat on low speed just until combined. Gradually stir in the eggnog, extract and nutmeg. Pour filling over crust.
4. Place springform pan in a larger baking pan; add 1 in. hot water to larger pan.
5. Bake until center is just set and top appears dull, 45-50 minutes. Remove springform pan from water bath. Cool on a wire rack for 10 minutes. Loosen side from pan with a knife; cool 1 hour longer.
6. Refrigerate overnight, covering when completely cooled. If desired, top with whipped cream, then sprinkle with ground nutmeg.

1 PIECE: *275 cal., 19g fat (11g sat. fat), 79mg chol., 195mg sod., 24g carb. (18g sugars, 0 fiber), 5g pro.*

NO-CHURN EGGNOG ICE CREAM

As a fanatical lover of all things eggnog, I like to say that this soft-serve eggnog ice cream stole my heart. Served with gingerbread or holiday cookies, it's bound to find a place in your heart as well.
—Colleen Delawder, Herndon, VA

- -

PREP: 10 min. + freezing • **MAKES:** 8 servings

2 cups eggnog
1 cup heavy whipping cream
½ cup sugar
¼ cup spiced rum
½ tsp. ground cinnamon
½ tsp. ground nutmeg

Place all ingredients in a blender; process until thickened, 1-2 minutes. Transfer to freezer containers, allowing headspace for expansion. Freeze until firm, several hours or overnight.
½ **CUP:** 222 cal., 14g fat (9g sat. fat), 71mg chol., 43mg sod., 19g carb. (19g sugars, 0 fiber), 4g pro.

Holiday Helper
You can omit the rum, but your ice cream may be a touch firmer, as the alcohol helps to keep it soft and creamy. To keep it soft, substitute a few tablespoons of vanilla or rum extract, or add a bit more heavy whipping cream—the butterfat in the cream does not freeze too hard.

CREAMY PUMPKIN EGGNOG

My family loves eggnog and pumpkin, and this recipe combines both! I love using fresh eggs from our own hens to create the delicious seasonal treat.
—Patricia Prescott, Manchester, NH

- -

PREP: 15 min. + chilling. • **COOK:** 15 min.
MAKES: 10 servings

5 large eggs, separated
3½ cups whole milk
1 cup heavy whipping cream
2 tsp. pumpkin pie spice
1 tsp. vanilla extract
1 cup sugar, divided
1 cup canned pumpkin
Ground nutmeg, optional

1. Place egg whites in a large heat-proof bowl; cover and refrigerate.
2. In a large saucepan, heat milk and cream over medium heat, stirring frequently, until bubbles form around sides of pan, 3-4 minutes; remove from heat. Meanwhile, in a large bowl, whisk egg yolks and ½ cup sugar until thickened; whisk in pumpkin. Slowly add hot milk mixture to egg yolk mixture, whisking constantly; return all to saucepan.
3. Cook over medium-low heat, whisking constantly until slightly thickened and a thermometer reads 160°, 3-4 minutes (do not allow to boil). Immediately strain mixture into a large bowl; add pumpkin pie spice and vanilla, and whisk to combine. Press plastic wrap onto the surface of the eggnog; refrigerate until cold, several hours or overnight.
4. Remove egg whites from refrigerator and let stand at room temperature for 30 minutes. Add remaining ½ cup sugar to egg whites and stir to combine; place bowl over a saucepan with simmering water. Heat, stirring constantly until sugar has dissolved and a thermometer reads 160°, 4-5 minutes. Remove from heat; beat on high until stiff glossy peaks forms and mixture is cooled slightly, 5-7 minutes. Fold into custard mixture. (Mixture may separate; stir before serving.) If desired, top with additional nutmeg.
1 **CUP:** 258 cal., 14g fat (8g sat. fat), 129mg chol., 80mg sod., 27g carb. (26g sugars, 1g fiber), 7g pro.

DOUBLE WHAMMY EGGNOG COOKIES

I often make these cookies to use up leftover eggnog, but they're so good it's worth it to buy a new supply! They've become a new family classic.
—*Teresa Morris, Laurel, DE*

PREP: 30 min. + chilling • **BAKE:** 15 min./batch + cooling
MAKES: 4 dozen

- 1⅓ cups butter, softened
- 1 cup packed brown sugar
- 4 large egg yolks, room temperature
- 2 Tbsp. eggnog
- ½ tsp. rum extract
- 3 cups all-purpose flour

EGGNOG FROSTING
- 4½ cups confectioners' sugar
- ¾ cup butter, softened
- 1½ tsp. rum extract
- ½ tsp. ground nutmeg
- ¼ tsp. ground cinnamon
- 2 to 3 Tbsp. eggnog
  Additional ground nutmeg

1. In a large bowl, cream butter and brown sugar until light and fluffy, 5-7 minutes. Beat in egg yolks, eggnog and extract. Gradually beat in flour. Refrigerate, covered, for at least 2 hours.
2. Preheat oven to 325°. Shape dough into 1-in. balls; place 2 in. apart on ungreased baking sheets. Bake until bottoms are brown, 13-16 minutes. Remove to wire racks to cool completely.
3. In a large bowl, beat the first 5 frosting ingredients until blended; beat in enough eggnog to reach desired consistency. Spread over cookies; sprinkle with additional nutmeg. Let stand until set. Store in airtight containers.
1 COOKIE: *167 cal., 9g fat (5g sat. fat), 37mg chol., 66mg sod., 22g carb. (16g sugars, 0 fiber), 1g pro.*

EGGNOG CANDIED ALMONDS

I have come up with so many yummy ideas for different flavored snack nuts. After testing them out, my sister-in-law seemed especially partial to these.
—*Julie Puderbaugh, Berwick, PA*

PREP: 15 min. + cooling • **MAKES:** 10 servings

- 3 Tbsp. eggnog
- 1 Tbsp. rum
- ½ cup sugar
- 2½ cups whole almonds
- 1 tsp. rum extract
- ¼ tsp. salt

Line a baking sheet with foil. Spray lightly with cooking spray; set aside. In a large nonstick skillet, heat eggnog and rum over medium-low heat until hot, 1-2 minutes. Stir in sugar; bring to a simmer, stirring frequently until sugar has dissolved, 2-3 minutes. Add almonds; stir to coat. Increase heat to medium; continue cooking, stirring frequently, until liquid has evaporated and nuts are lightly toasted, 3-5 minutes. Add extract and salt; stir. Spread onto prepared baking sheet. Cool 1 hour. Store in an airtight container.
¼ CUP: *260 cal., 19g fat (2g sat. fat), 3mg chol., 69mg sod., 17g carb. (12g sugars, 4g fiber), 8g pro.*

LOAVES FOR GIVING & SHARING

Sweet or savory, quick or slow-rise, homemade bread is a perfect gift. And these recipes are just right for sharing, because each one makes at least two loaves— one to give away and one to keep for your family!

YUMMY APRICOT PECAN BREAD

Every time I prepare this yummy bread, I receive raves. It's perfect with coffee or as a gift, plus it's really quick and easy to prepare.
—Joan Hallford, North Richland Hills, TX

PREP: 20 min. • **BAKE:** 40 min. + cooling
MAKES: 2 loaves (12 pieces each)

2½ cups all-purpose flour
¾ cup sugar
2 tsp. baking soda
1 tsp. ground cinnamon
¼ tsp. salt
¼ tsp. ground nutmeg
1 cup 2% milk
2 large eggs, room temperature
⅓ cup butter, melted
2 cups shredded cheddar cheese
1 cup finely chopped dried apricots
¾ cup finely chopped pecans
TOPPING
3 Tbsp. packed brown sugar
1 Tbsp. butter
½ tsp. ground cinnamon

1. Preheat oven to 350°. In a large bowl, combine the first 6 ingredients. Beat the milk, eggs and butter; stir into dry ingredients just until moistened. Fold in cheese, apricots and pecans. Spoon into 2 greased 8x4-in. loaf pans. Combine the topping ingredients; sprinkle over batter.
2. Bake 40-45 minutes or until a toothpick inserted in center comes out clean. Cool for 10 minutes before removing from pans to wire racks.
1 PIECE: *189 cal., 9g fat (4g sat. fat), 36mg chol., 223mg sod., 23g carb. (11g sugars, 1g fiber), 5g pro.*

ALMOND & CRANBERRY COCONUT BREAD

Here's an all-around great bread for any season. The red bursts of cranberry lend every slice extra appeal for Christmastime.
—Rosemary Johnson, Irondale, AL

PREP: 20 min. • **BAKE:** 1 hour + cooling
MAKES: 2 loaves (16 pieces each)

2 cups sweetened shredded coconut
1 cup slivered almonds
1 cup butter, softened
1 cup sugar
4 large eggs, room temperature
1 cup vanilla yogurt
1 tsp. almond extract
4½ cups all-purpose flour
3 tsp. baking powder
½ tsp. salt
½ tsp. baking soda
1 can (15 oz.) cream of coconut
1 cup dried cranberries

1. Preheat oven to 350°. Place coconut and almonds in an ungreased 15x10x1-in. pan. Bake for 10-15 minutes or until lightly toasted, stirring occasionally. Cool.
2. In a large bowl, cream butter and sugar until light and fluffy, 5-7 minutes. Add eggs, 1 at a time, beating well after each addition. Beat in yogurt and extract until blended. Combine flour, baking powder, salt and baking soda; add to the creamed mixture alternately with cream of coconut, beating well after each addition. Fold in the cranberries and the toasted coconut and almonds.
3. Transfer to 2 greased and floured 9x5-in. loaf pans. Bake for 60-70 minutes or until a toothpick inserted in the center comes out clean. Cool for 10 minutes before removing from pans to wire racks to cool completely.
1 PIECE: *273 cal., 13g fat (8g sat. fat), 42mg chol., 176mg sod., 36g carb. (21g sugars, 1g fiber), 4g pro.*

ONION FRENCH BREAD LOAVES

Since I love variety in my cooking, I tried adding dried minced onion to my usual recipe in attempts to copy a bread I had tasted, creating these two tasty loaves. Using the bread machine on the dough setting is an easy timesaver.
—Ruth Fueller, Barmstedt, Germany

- -

PREP: 25 min. + rising • **BAKE:** 20 min.
MAKES: 2 loaves (16 pieces each)

- 1 cup water (70° to 80°)
- ½ cup dried minced onion
- 1 Tbsp. sugar
- 2 tsp. salt
- 3 cups bread flour
- 2¼ tsp. active dry yeast
- 1 Tbsp. cornmeal
- 1 large egg yolk, lightly beaten

1. In bread machine pan, place the first 6 ingredients in order suggested by manufacturer. Select dough setting (check after 5 minutes of mixing; add 1-2 Tbsp. water or flour if needed).
2. When cycle is completed, turn dough onto a lightly floured surface. Cover and let rest for 15 minutes. Divide dough in half. Roll each portion into a 15x10-in. rectangle. Roll up jelly-roll style, starting with a long side; pinch seams to seal. Pinch ends to seal and tuck under.
3. Sprinkle cornmeal onto a greased baking sheet. Place loaves on pan. Cover and let rise in a warm place until doubled, about 30 minutes. Brush with egg yolk. Make ¼-in.-deep cuts 2 in. apart in the top of each loaf.
4. Bake at 375° for 20-25 minutes or until crusts are golden brown. Remove from pan to a wire rack.
1 PIECE: *46 cal., 0 fat (0 sat. fat), 7mg chol., 148mg sod., 10g carb. (1g sugars, 0 fiber), 2g pro.*

Holiday Helper

Bread rises quickly when it first goes into the oven (called "oven spring"); scoring the top of the loaf prevents it from cracking. Use a sharp paring knife, a razor blade or a bread lame.

CINNAMON SWIRL BREAKFAST BREAD

My aunt gave me the recipe for these pretty, rich-tasting loaves many years ago. I use my bread machine for the first step in the recipe.
—Peggy Burdick, Burlington, MI

- -

PREP: 20 min. + rising • **BAKE:** 30 min.
MAKES: 2 loaves (16 pieces each)

- 1 cup warm 2% milk (70° to 80°)
- ¼ cup water (70° to 80°)
- 2 large eggs, room temperature
- ¼ cup butter, softened
- 1 tsp. salt
- ¼ cup sugar
- 5 cups bread flour
- 2¼ tsp. active dry yeast
- **FILLING**
- 2 Tbsp. butter, melted
- ⅓ cup sugar
- 1 Tbsp. ground cinnamon
- **GLAZE**
- 1 cup confectioners' sugar
- ½ tsp. vanilla extract
- 4 to 5 tsp. milk

1. In bread machine pan, place the first 8 ingredients in the order suggested by manufacturer. Select dough setting (check dough after 5 minutes of mixing; add 1 to 2 Tbsp. water or flour if needed).
2. When cycle is completed, turn dough onto a lightly floured surface; divide in half. Roll each portion into a 10x8-in. rectangle. Brush with butter. Combine sugar and cinnamon; sprinkle over dough.
3. Roll up tightly jelly-roll style, starting with a short side. Pinch seams and ends to seal. Place seam side down in 2 greased 9x5-in. loaf pans. Cover and let rise in a warm place until doubled, about 1 hour.
4. Bake at 350° for 25 minutes. Cover with foil; bake until golden brown, 5-10 minutes longer. Remove from pans to wire racks to cool completely.
5. Combine confectioners' sugar, vanilla and enough milk to achieve desired consistency; drizzle over warm loaves.
1 PIECE: *121 cal., 3g fat (2g sat. fat), 20mg chol., 104mg sod., 22g carb. (7g sugars, 1g fiber), 3g pro.*

1

2

3a

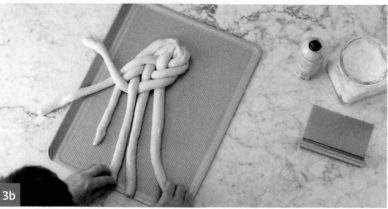

3b

HOW TO BRAID BREAD

A braided loaf looks impressive but it's easy to shape. Keep the braid close set, but not tight—the dough needs space to expand. Too tight a braid will create a distorted shape when the loaf has finished its second rise.

1. On a lightly floured surface, divide dough into desired number of pieces. Roll each into a rope. Add just enough flour so the dough doesn't stick. (If too much flour is added, the dough will just slide back and forth on the counter.)

2. Arrange ropes on a greased baking sheet. Pinch the ropes together at 1 end and tuck the end under.

BRAIDING 3 ROPES

3a. Cross the right rope over the center rope, then the left rope over the center rope. Continue alternating left and right over center until the braid is done. Pinch the ends together and tuck end under for a clean look.

BRAIDING 6 ROPES

3b. Start with the far right rope. Weave to the left—over 2 strands, under 1 strand, over 2 strands. Start again at the (new) far right rope and weave to the left in the same pattern (over 2 strands, under 1 strand, over 2 strands). Repeat until the whole loaf is braided. Pinch the ends together and tuck end under. If you find it more comfortable to weave from the left side toward the right, that's fine—just be sure to always start again from the same side.

CARDAMOM BRAID BREAD

I came across this recipe in 1983 and have been making it for holidays ever since.
—*Rita Bergman, Olympia, WA*

- -

PREP: 30 min. + rising • **BAKE:** 20 min.
MAKES: 2 loaves (20 pieces each)

6   cups all-purpose flour
2   pkg. (¼ oz. each) active dry yeast
1½ tsp. ground cardamom
1   tsp. salt
1½ cups plus 2 Tbsp. 2% milk, divided
½   cup butter, cubed
½   cup honey
2   large eggs, room temperature
2   Tbsp. sugar

1. In a large bowl, combine 2 cups flour, yeast, cardamom and salt. In a small saucepan, heat 1½ cups milk, butter and honey to 120°-130°. Add to the dry ingredients; beat just until moistened. Add eggs; beat until smooth. Stir in enough of the remaining flour to form a firm dough (dough will be sticky).
2. Turn onto a floured surface; knead until smooth and elastic, 6-8 minutes. Place in a greased bowl, turning once to grease top. Cover and let rise in a warm place until doubled, about 45 minutes.
3. Punch dough down. Turn onto a lightly floured surface; divide in half. Divide each portion into thirds. Shape each into a 14-in. rope. Place 3 ropes on a greased

baking sheet and braid (see opposite page); pinch ends to seal and tuck under. Repeat with remaining dough. Cover and let rise until doubled, about 30 minutes.
4. Preheat oven to 375°. Brush loaf with the remaining 2 Tbsp. milk and sprinkle with sugar. Bake until golden brown, 20-25 minutes. Remove from pans to wire racks to cool.

1 PIECE: *114 cal., 3g fat (2g sat. fat), 18mg chol., 91mg sod., 19g carb. (5g sugars, 1g fiber), 3g pro.*

WILD RICE & CRANBERRY LOAVES

This is an incredibly fragrant bread with lots of texture from the wild rice and dried cranberries. It's hearty enough for sandwiches, but with a touch of honey, I could even eat this for dessert!
—Barbara Miller, Oakdale, MN

PREP: 40 min. + rising
BAKE: 40 min. + cooling
MAKES: 2 loaves (16 pieces each)

- 2 cups whole wheat flour
- 2 pkg. (¼ oz. each) quick-rise yeast
- 1 Tbsp. sugar
- 1 Tbsp. grated orange zest
- 2 tsp. aniseed
- 1 tsp. salt
- 1 tsp. caraway seeds
- 4 to 4½ cups bread flour
- 2 cups 2% milk
- ½ cup water
- ¼ cup molasses
- 2 Tbsp. butter
- 1 cup dried cranberries
- 1 cup cooked wild rice, cooled

1. In a large bowl, mix first 7 ingredients and 1½ cups bread flour. In a small saucepan, heat the milk, water, molasses and butter to 120°-130°. Add to the dry ingredients; beat on medium speed for 2 minutes. Stir in cranberries, rice and enough of the remaining bread flour to form a stiff dough (dough will be sticky).
2. Turn the dough onto a floured surface; knead until smooth and elastic, 6-8 minutes. Place in a greased bowl, turning once to grease the top. Cover and let rest 10 minutes.
3. Punch down dough. Turn onto a lightly floured surface; divide in half. Shape into loaves. Place in 2 greased 9x5-in. loaf pans, seam side down. Cover with kitchen towels; let rise in a warm place until almost doubled, about 20 minutes.
4. Bake at 350° until golden brown, 40-45 minutes. Cool in pans 10 minutes; remove to wire racks to cool completely.
1 PIECE: *133 cal., 2g fat (1g sat. fat), 3mg chol., 89mg sod., 26g carb. (7g sugars, 2g fiber), 4g pro.*

BASIL PARMESAN BREAD

The combination of basil, Parmesan cheese and sun-dried tomatoes gives this hearty bread a flavor that will take you right to Tuscany!
—Sherry Hulsman, Louisville, KY

PREP: 25 min. + rising
BAKE: 25 min. + cooling
MAKES: 2 loaves (16 pieces each)

- 1 pkg. (¼ oz.) active dry yeast
- 1½ cups warm water (110° to 115°)
- ½ cup warm 2% milk (110° to 115°)
- 3 Tbsp. sugar
- 3 Tbsp. olive oil
- 2 tsp. salt
- 5 to 6 cups bread flour
- 1 cup shredded Parmesan cheese
- ¼ cup chopped oil-packed sun-dried tomatoes
- 3 tsp. dried basil
- 1 tsp. hot pepper sauce

1. In a large bowl, dissolve yeast in warm water. Add milk, sugar, oil, salt and 4 cups flour. Beat on medium speed until smooth. Stir in cheese, tomatoes, basil, pepper sauce and enough remaining flour to form a soft dough (dough will be sticky).
2. Turn the dough onto a floured surface; knead until smooth and elastic, 6-8 minutes. Place in a greased bowl, turning once to grease top. Cover and let rise in a warm place until doubled, about 1½ hours.
3. Punch down dough. Divide in half and shape into loaves. Place in 2 greased 9x5-in. loaf pans. Cover with kitchen towels; let rise in a warm place until doubled, about 1 hour.
4. Bake at 375° until golden brown, 25-30 minutes. Remove from pans to wire racks to cool.
1 PIECE: *94 cal., 2g fat (1g sat. fat), 2mg chol., 195mg sod., 16g carb. (1g sugars, 1g fiber), 4g pro.*

> ### Holiday Helper
> When using oil-packed sun-dried tomatoes, drain them first, but don't rinse them. If there are tomatoes left in the jar, make sure they're covered with oil, and store in the fridge.

APPLE RAISIN BREAD

I've been making this bread for many years. It smells so good in the oven and tastes even better. I make bread almost every Saturday, and it doesn't stay around long when our sons are home!
—Perlene Hoekema, Lynden, WA

PREP: 25 min. + rising • **BAKE:** 30 min.
MAKES: 3 loaves (16 pieces each)

- 2 pkg. (¼ oz. each) active dry yeast
- 1½ cups warm water (110° to 115°), divided
- 1 tsp. sugar
- 3 large eggs, room temperature, beaten
- 1 cup applesauce
- ½ cup honey
- ½ cup canola oil
- 2 tsp. salt
- 8 to 9 cups all-purpose flour
- 1½ cups diced peeled apples
- 1½ cups raisins
- 2 Tbsp. lemon juice
- 2 Tbsp. cornmeal
- GLAZE
- 1 large egg, beaten
  Sugar

1. In a small bowl, combine yeast, ½ cup water and the sugar; set aside. In a large bowl, combine eggs, applesauce, honey, oil, salt and remaining 1 cup water; mix well. Stir in yeast mixture. Gradually add enough flour to form a soft dough.
2. Turn dough onto a floured surface; knead until smooth and elastic, about 10 minutes. Place dough in a greased bowl, turning once to grease top. Cover and let rise in a warm place until doubled, about 1 hour.
3. Punch down dough and turn over in bowl. Cover and let rise 30 minutes.
4. In a small bowl, combine the apples, raisins and lemon juice. Divide dough into 3 parts; knead a third of the apple mixture into each part. Shape each into a round flat ball. Place each in a greased 8-in. round baking pan that has been sprinkled with cornmeal. Cover and let rise until doubled, about 1 hour.
5. Brush the top of each loaf with egg and sprinkle with sugar. Bake at 350° for 30-35 minutes or until bread sounds hollow when tapped.
1 PIECE: *135 cal., 3g fat (0 sat. fat), 18mg chol., 105mg sod., 25g carb. (8g sugars, 1g fiber), 3g pro.*

WALNUT DATE BREAD

Many years ago when I was sick, a dear friend stopped in with a pot of soup and this beautiful bread. Every cook should have a copy of this traditional quick bread recipe in his or her files.
—Janet Backie, Rogers, AR

PREP: 15 min. • **BAKE:** 45 min. + cooling
MAKES: 2 loaves (12 pieces each)

- 1½ cups chopped dates
- 1½ cups hot water
- 2 Tbsp. butter, softened
- 2¼ cups all-purpose flour
- 1½ cups sugar
- ¾ cup coarsely chopped walnuts
- 1½ tsp. baking soda
- 1½ tsp. salt
- 2 large eggs, room temperature, lightly beaten
- 1½ tsp. vanilla extract

1. Preheat oven to 375°. In a large bowl, combine the dates, water and butter; let stand for 5 minutes. In a large bowl, combine the flour, sugar, walnuts, baking soda and salt. In a small bowl, combine eggs, vanilla and the date mixture. Stir into the dry ingredients just until moistened.
2. Pour batter into 2 greased 8x4-in. loaf pans. Bake until a toothpick comes out clean, 45-50 minutes. Cover loosely with foil if top browns too quickly. Cool for 10 minutes before removing from pans to wire racks.
1 PIECE: *120 cal., 3g fat (1g sat. fat), 15mg chol., 181mg sod., 23g carb. (15g sugars, 1g fiber), 2g pro.*

SWEET POTATO SPICE BREAD

It's a good thing this recipe makes two mini loaves, because they'll go fast. For a small household, eat one loaf now and freeze the other for later—or give it to a friend!
—Ronnie Littles, Virginia Beach, VA

PREP: 15 min. • **BAKE:** 25 min. + cooling
MAKES: 2 mini loaves (6 pieces each)

- 1 cup all-purpose flour
- 1½ tsp. baking powder
- ¼ tsp. each ground cinnamon, nutmeg and allspice
- ⅛ tsp. salt
- 1 large egg, room temperature
- ⅓ cup mashed sweet potato
- ⅓ cup honey
- 3 Tbsp. canola oil
- 2 Tbsp. molasses
- ⅓ cup chopped walnuts

1. Preheat oven to 325°. In a small bowl, combine the flour, baking powder, spices and salt. In another small bowl, whisk the egg, sweet potato, honey, oil and molasses. Stir into dry ingredients just until moistened. Fold in walnuts.
2. Transfer batter to 2 greased 5¾x3x2-in. loaf pans. Bake for 25-30 minutes or until a toothpick inserted in the center comes out clean. Cool for 10 minutes before removing from pans to wire racks.
1 PIECE: *142 cal., 6g fat (1g sat. fat), 18mg chol., 85mg sod., 20g carb. (10g sugars, 1g fiber), 3g pro.*

HONEY CHALLAH

I use these shiny beautiful loaves as the centerpiece of my spread. I love the taste of honey, but you can also add chocolate chips, cinnamon, orange zest or almonds. Leftover slices work well in bread pudding or for French toast.
—*Jennifer Newfield, Los Angeles, CA*

PREP: 45 min. + rising
BAKE: 30 min. + cooling
MAKES: 2 loaves (24 pieces each)

- 2 pkg. (¼ oz. each) active dry yeast
- ½ tsp. sugar
- 1½ cups warm water (110° to 115°), divided
- 5 large eggs, room temperature
- ⅔ cup plus 1 tsp. honey, divided
- ½ cup canola oil
- 2 tsp. salt
- 6 to 7 cups bread flour
- 1 cup boiling water
- 2 cups golden raisins
- 1 Tbsp. water
- 1 Tbsp. sesame seeds

1. In a small bowl, dissolve yeast and sugar in 1 cup warm water. Separate 2 eggs; refrigerate the whites. Place egg yolks and remaining 3 whole eggs in a large bowl. Add ⅔ cup honey, oil, salt, yeast mixture, 3 cups flour and the remaining ½ cup warm water; beat on medium speed 3 minutes. Stir in enough of the remaining flour to form a soft dough (dough will be sticky).
2. Pour boiling water over raisins in a small bowl; let stand 5 minutes. Drain and pat dry. Turn the dough onto a floured surface; knead until smooth and elastic, 6-8 minutes. Knead in raisins. Place in a greased bowl, turning once to grease the top. Cover and let rise in a warm place until almost doubled, about 1½ hours.
3. Punch down dough. Turn onto a lightly floured surface. Divide dough in half. Divide 1 portion into 6 pieces. Roll each into a 16-in. rope. Place ropes parallel on a greased baking sheet; pinch ropes together at the top.
4. To braid, take the rope on the left and carry it over the 2 ropes beside it, then slip it under the middle rope and carry it over the last 2 ropes. Lay the rope down parallel to the other ropes; it is now on

the far right side. Repeat these steps until you reach the end. As the braid moves to the right, you can pick up the loaf and recenter it on the work surface if needed. Pinch ends to seal and tuck under. For a fuller loaf, using your hands, push the ends of the loaf closer together. Repeat process with remaining dough. Cover with kitchen towels; let rise in a warm place until almost doubled, about 30 minutes.
5. Preheat oven to 350°. In a small bowl, whisk the 2 chilled egg whites and honey with water; brush over loaves. Sprinkle with sesame seeds. Bake 30-35 minutes or until bread is golden brown and sounds hollow when tapped. Remove from pans to a wire rack to cool.

1 PIECE: *125 cal., 3g fat (0 sat. fat), 19mg chol., 107mg sod., 21g carb. (8g sugars, 1g fiber), 3g pro.*

Holiday Helper

- You can leave challah dough in the refrigerator overnight during the first rise for a slower process that will help the bread develop a great flavor. Be careful with the second rise, though—leaving it for too long can cause the loaf to collapse and give it a dense texture.
- If the challah is dry, it could be because you added a little too much flour. Next time, let the dough stay sticky! It may be a little harder to work with, but sticky dough means you've used just the right ratio of water, oil and flour.

LEMON-TWIST LOAVES

Christmas at our house just wouldn't be the same without this mouthwateringly tangy twist and its pretty glaze.
—Audrey Thibodeau, Gilbert, AZ

PREP: 30 min. + rising • **BAKE:** 25 min.
MAKES: 3 loaves (12 pieces each)

- 2 pkg. (¼ oz. each) active dry yeast
- 2 cups warm water (110° to 115°), divided
- 3 cups sugar, divided
- 1 cup butter, melted and cooled, divided
- ¾ tsp. salt
- 1 large egg, room temperature
- 1 large egg yolk, room temperature
- 7 cups all-purpose flour
- 1 cup sliced almonds, chopped
- 3 Tbsp. grated lemon zest

GLAZE
- 3 cups confectioners' sugar
- 3 Tbsp. grated lemon zest
- 1 tsp. lemon extract
- 3 to 4 Tbsp. milk
- 1 cup sliced almonds, toasted

1. In a large bowl, dissolve yeast in ½ cup warm water. Add 1 cup sugar, ½ cup butter, salt, egg, egg yolk and remaining 1½ cups water. Beat until blended. Add 4 cups flour. Beat until smooth. Stir in enough of the remaining flour to form a soft dough.
2. Turn onto a floured surface; knead until smooth and elastic, 6-8 minutes. Place in a greased bowl, turning over once to grease top. Cover and refrigerate 8 hours.
3. Punch dough down. Turn onto a lightly floured surface; divide into thirds. Roll each piece into a 16x10-in. rectangle. Spread remaining ½ cup melted butter over dough. Combine the chopped almonds, lemon zest and remaining 2 cups sugar; sprinkle over butter. Roll up each rectangle jelly-roll style, starting with a long side; pinch seams and ends to seal. Place rolls seam side down on greased baking sheets. With a knife, cut loaves in half lengthwise to within 1 in. of one end. Holding the uncut end, loosely twist strips together. Cover and let rise until doubled, about 1½ hours. Preheat oven to 350°.
4. Bake until bread sounds hollow when tapped, 25-30 minutes. Remove from pans to wire racks.
5. For glaze, combine the confectioners' sugar, lemon zest, extract and enough milk to achieve spreading consistency; spread over warm bread. Sprinkle with toasted almonds.
1 PIECE: *274 cal., 8g fat (4g sat. fat), 26mg chol., 104mg sod., 47g carb. (26g sugars, 1g fiber), 4g pro.*

POLISH POPPY SEED LOAVES

Traditionally, these loaves were eaten after sundown on Christmas Eve as part of a 12-course meal. At our home, we never can wait that long to bite into this tender treat that's similar to coffee cake.
—Linda Gronewaller, Hutchinson, KS

PREP: 50 min. + rising • **BAKE:** 35 min. + cooling
MAKES: 2 loaves (12 pieces each)

- 2 pkg. (¼ oz. each) active dry yeast
- ½ cup warm water (110° to 115°)
- 4½ cups all-purpose flour
- ¾ cup sugar
- ½ tsp. salt
- ½ cup cold butter
- 2 large eggs, room temperature
- 2 large egg yolks, room temperature
- ½ cup sour cream
- 1 tsp. vanilla extract

FILLING
- 3 Tbsp. poppy seeds
- 2 Tbsp. butter
- ¼ cup raisins
- 2 Tbsp. honey
- 2 tsp. lemon juice
- ¼ cup finely chopped candied orange peel
- 2 tsp. grated lemon zest
- 2 large egg whites, room temperature
- ½ cup sugar

ICING
- 1 cup confectioners' sugar
- 2 Tbsp. lemon juice

1. Dissolve yeast in warm water. In a large bowl, combine the flour, sugar and salt; cut in butter until mixture resembles fine crumbs. Combine eggs, yolks and yeast mixture; add to crumb mixture and mix well. Beat in sour cream and vanilla until smooth.
2. Turn dough onto a floured surface; knead until smooth and elastic, 6-8 minutes. Do not let rise. Divide in half. Roll out into two 12-in. squares; cover.
3. In a small skillet, cook and stir poppy seeds and butter over medium heat for 3 minutes. Stir in the raisins, honey and lemon juice. Transfer to a bowl; cool for 10 minutes. Stir in candied orange peel and lemon zest.
4. In a small bowl, beat egg whites until foamy. On high speed, gradually beat in sugar, 1 Tbsp. at a time, just until stiff peaks form and sugar is dissolved. Fold into poppy seed mixture. Spread over squares to within ½ in. of edges. Roll up each square jelly-roll style; pinch seams to seal. Place on a greased baking sheet. Cover and let rise until nearly doubled, about 45 minutes.
5. Bake at 350° for 35-40 minutes or until golden brown. Remove from pan to a wire rack to cool completely. Combine icing ingredients; drizzle over cooled loaves.
1 PIECE: *234 cal., 7g fat (4g sat. fat), 52mg chol., 118mg sod., 39g carb. (20g sugars, 1g fiber), 4g pro.*

A BIT NUTTY BOSTON BROWN BREAD

Hearty and dense, my homemade Boston brown bread features hazelnuts for a delightfully nutty taste. Thick slices pair well with just about anything, including soups, stews, roasts and casseroles.
—Lorraine Caland, Shuniah, ON

- -

PREP: 30 min. • **BAKE:** 45 min. + cooling
MAKES: 2 loaves (12 pieces each)

3	cups whole wheat flour
1	cup all-purpose flour
2½	tsp. baking soda
1	tsp. salt
2½	cups buttermilk
1	cup molasses
1	cup golden raisins
¾	cup chopped hazelnuts

1. Preheat oven to 350°. In a large bowl, combine the flours, baking soda and salt. In a small bowl, whisk buttermilk and molasses. Stir into dry ingredients just until moistened. Fold in raisins and nuts. Transfer to 2 greased 8x4-in. loaf pans.
2. Bake for 45-50 minutes or until a toothpick inserted in the center comes out clean. Cool for 10 minutes before removing from pans to wire racks.
NOTE: *To toast nuts, bake in a shallow pan in a 350° oven for 5-10 minutes or cook in a skillet over low heat until lightly browned, stirring occasionally.*
1 PIECE: *159 cal., 3g fat (0 sat. fat), 1mg chol., 263mg sod., 31g carb. (13g sugars, 3g fiber), 4g pro.*

PUMPKIN PECAN LOAVES

Among all my pumpkin bread recipes, this caramel-glazed creation is the pick of the crop. Often, I'll wrap up a lovely loaf as a homemade gift for teachers and Sunday school leaders.
—Brenda Jackson, Garden City, KS

- -

PREP: 15 min. • **BAKE:** 1 hour + cooling
MAKES: 2 loaves (16 pieces each)

3⅓	cups all-purpose flour
3	cups sugar
2	tsp. baking soda
1½	tsp. salt
1	tsp. ground cinnamon
1	tsp. ground nutmeg
1	can (15 oz.) pumpkin
1	cup vegetable oil
4	large eggs, room temperature, lightly beaten
⅔	cup water
½	cup chopped pecans

CARAMEL GLAZE

¼	cup butter
¼	cup sugar
¼	cup packed brown sugar
¼	cup heavy whipping cream
⅔	cup confectioners' sugar
1	tsp. vanilla extract

1. Preheat oven to 350°. Combine the first 6 ingredients. In a separate bowl, combine pumpkin, oil, eggs and water; mix well. Stir into dry ingredients just until combined; fold in the pecans.
2. Spoon into 2 greased 9x5-in. loaf pans. Bake for 60-65 minutes or until a toothpick inserted in the center comes out clean. Cool for 10 minutes before removing from pans to wire racks.
3. For glaze, combine the butter, sugar, brown sugar and cream in a saucepan. Cook until sugar is dissolved. Cool for 20 minutes. Stir in the confectioners' sugar and vanilla until smooth. Drizzle over cooled loaves.
1 PIECE: *249 cal., 11g fat (3g sat. fat), 29mg chol., 212mg sod., 36g carb. (25g sugars, 1g fiber), 3g pro.*

CHOCOLATE BABKA

I love this chocolate babka. It's a rewarding recipe for taking the next step in your bread baking. Even if it's slightly imperfect going into the oven, it turns out gorgeous. Look at those swirls!
—Lisa Kaminski, Wauwatosa, WI

PREP: 20 min. + chilling • **BAKE:** 35 min. + cooling
MAKES: 2 loaves (16 pieces each)

- 4¼ to 4¾ cups all-purpose flour
- ½ cup sugar
- 2½ tsp. quick-rise yeast
- ¾ tsp. salt
- ⅔ cup butter
- ½ cup water
- 3 large eggs plus 1 large egg yolk, room temperature, beaten
- 2 Tbsp. grated orange zest

FILLING
- ½ cup butter, cubed
- 5 oz. dark chocolate chips
- ½ cup confectioners' sugar
- ⅓ cup baking cocoa
- ¼ tsp. salt

GLAZE
- ¼ cup sugar
- ¼ cup water

1. In a large bowl, mix 2 cups flour, sugar, yeast and salt. Cut in butter until crumbly. In a small saucepan, heat water to 120°-130°; stir into dry ingredients. Stir in eggs and yolk, orange zest and enough remaining flour to form a soft dough (dough will be sticky).

2. Turn dough onto a floured surface; knead until smooth and elastic, 6-8 minutes. Place in a greased bowl, turning once to grease the top. Cover and refrigerate 8 hours or overnight.

3. Turn out dough onto a lightly floured surface; divide in half. Roll each half into a 12x10-in. rectangle. For filling, in a microwave, melt butter and chocolate chips; stir until smooth. Stir in confectioners' sugar, cocoa and salt. Spread filling to within ½ in. of edges. Roll up jelly-roll style, starting with a long side; pinch seam and ends to seal.

4. Using a sharp knife, cut each roll lengthwise in half; carefully turn each half cut side up. Loosely twist strips around each other, keeping the cut surfaces facing up; pinch ends together to seal. Place in 2 greased 9x5-in. loaf pans, cut side up. Cover with kitchen towels; let rise in a warm place until almost doubled, about 1 hour.

5. Bake at 375° until golden brown, 35-45 minutes, tenting with foil halfway through baking. Meanwhile, in a saucepan, combine sugar and water; bring to a boil. Reduce heat; simmer, uncovered, 10 minutes. Brush over warm babka. Cool 10 minutes before removing from pans to wire racks.

1 PIECE: *181 cal., 9g fat (5g sat. fat), 41mg chol., 136mg sod., 23g carb. (10g sugars, 1g fiber), 3g pro.*

BACON & CHEESE FILLED LOAVES

When I entered this bread for a Los Angeles County Fair contest, I won third place! The soft braided bread is wonderful served with a hot bowl of soup.
—Marina Castle-Kelley, Canyon Country, CA

PREP: 30 min. + rising • **BAKE:** 25 min.
MAKES: 2 loaves (8 pieces each)

- 10 bacon strips, chopped
- ¼ cup finely chopped onion
- ⅔ cup sour cream
- ⅔ cup shredded cheddar cheese
- 2 loaves (1 lb. each) frozen bread dough, thawed
- 1 large egg, room temperature, lightly beaten
- ½ tsp. dried parsley flakes
- ⅛ tsp. poppy seeds

1. In a large skillet, cook bacon and onion over medium heat until bacon is crisp. Remove with a slotted spoon; drain on paper towels. Cool slightly.
2. In a small bowl, mix sour cream, cheese and bacon mixture. On 2 greased baking sheets, roll each loaf of dough into a 16x10-in. rectangle. Spoon half of the filling lengthwise down the center third of each rectangle.
3. On each long side, beginning at the edge, cut ¾-in.-wide strips about 2½ in. into the center. Starting at 1 end, fold alternating strips at an angle across filling. Pinch both ends to seal.
4. Cover with kitchen towels; let rise in a warm place until doubled, about 1 hour. Preheat oven to 350°.
5. Brush loaves with egg; sprinkle with parsley and poppy seeds. Bake until golden brown, 25-30 minutes. Remove from pans to wire racks to cool.
1 PIECE: 222 cal., 7g fat (3g sat. fat), 29mg chol., 445mg sod., 28g carb. (3g sugars, 2g fiber), 9g pro.

FRESH PEAR BREAD

When our trees are loaded with ripe juicy pears, I treat my family and friends to loaves of this cinnamony bread that's richly studded with walnuts and pears. I always receive raves and requests for the recipe.
—Linda Patrick, Houston, TX

PREP: 15 min. • **BAKE:** 55 min. + cooling
MAKES: 2 loaves (16 pieces each)

- 3 large eggs, room temperature
- 1½ cups sugar
- ¾ cup vegetable oil
- 1 tsp. vanilla extract
- 3 cups all-purpose flour
- 2 tsp. baking powder
- 2 tsp. ground cinnamon
- 1 tsp. baking soda
- 1 tsp. salt
- 4 cups finely chopped peeled ripe pears (about 4 medium)
- 1 tsp. lemon juice
- 1 cup chopped walnuts

1. Preheat oven to 350°. Combine the eggs, sugar, oil and vanilla; mix well. Combine flour, baking powder, cinnamon, baking soda and salt; stir into the egg mixture just until moistened. Toss pears with lemon juice. Stir pears and walnuts into batter (the batter will be thick).
2. Spoon into 2 greased 9x5-in. loaf pans. Bake for 55-60 minutes or until a toothpick inserted in the center comes out clean. Cool for 10 minutes before removing from pans to wire racks.
1 PIECE: 168 cal., 8g fat (1g sat. fat), 20mg chol., 144mg sod., 22g carb. (12g sugars, 1g fiber), 3g pro.

CHOCOLATE CHAI MINI LOAVES

This bread is irresistible! A friend gets mad when I make it because I give her a loaf and she can't help but eat the whole thing!
—Lisa Christensen, Poplar Grove, IL

- -

PREP: 25 min. • **BAKE:** 35 min. + cooling
MAKES: 3 mini loaves (6 pieces each)

- 2 oz. semisweet chocolate, chopped
- ½ cup water
- ½ cup butter, softened
- 1 cup packed brown sugar
- 2 large eggs, room temperature
- 1 tsp. vanilla extract
- 1½ cups all-purpose flour
- 3 Tbsp. chai tea latte mix
- 1 tsp. baking soda
- ½ tsp. salt
- ½ cup sour cream

FROSTING

- 1 cup confectioners' sugar
- 1 Tbsp. butter, softened
- 1 Tbsp. chai tea latte mix
- ½ tsp. vanilla extract
- 4 to 5 tsp. 2% milk

1. Preheat oven to 350°. In a microwave, melt chocolate with the water; stir until smooth. Cool slightly. In a large bowl, cream butter and brown sugar until light and fluffy, 5-7 minutes. Add eggs, 1 at a time, beating well after each addition. Beat in vanilla, then the chocolate mixture.
2. Combine the flour, latte mix, baking soda and salt; add to creamed mixture alternately with sour cream.
3. Transfer to 3 greased 5¾x3x2-in. loaf pans. Bake for 35-40 minutes or until a toothpick inserted in the center comes out clean. Cool for 10 minutes before removing from pans to a wire rack to cool completely.
4. For frosting, combine confectioners' sugar, butter, latte mix, vanilla and enough milk to achieve desired consistency. Frost tops of loaves.
NOTE: *Skip the frosting and dust the top of these loaves with confectioners' sugar to cut calories by almost 20%.*
1 PIECE: *208 cal., 9g fat (5g sat. fat), 43mg chol., 206mg sod., 30g carb. (21g sugars, 1g fiber), 3g pro.*

CRANBERRY ZUCCHINI BREAD

Nutmeg and cinnamon add spice to these flavorful loaves. The flecks of green zucchini and red cranberries give each slice a look that's just right for the holidays.
—Alice Manzo, South Easton, MA

- -

PREP: 15 min. • **BAKE:** 1 hour + cooling
MAKES: 2 loaves (12 pieces each)

- 3 cups all-purpose flour
- 2 cups sugar
- 2½ tsp. ground cinnamon
- 1¼ tsp. salt
- 1 tsp. baking soda
- ½ tsp. baking powder
- ¼ tsp. ground nutmeg
- 3 large eggs
- 1½ cups shredded zucchini
- 1 cup vegetable oil
- 1 Tbsp. vanilla extract
- 1 cup chopped fresh or frozen cranberries
- ½ cup chopped walnuts

1. Preheat oven to 350°. Combine the first 7 ingredients. In another bowl, beat eggs; add zucchini, oil and vanilla. Stir into the dry ingredients just until blended. Fold in cranberries and walnuts. Pour into 2 greased and floured 8x4-in. loaf pans.
2. Bake 60-65 minutes or until a toothpick inserted in center comes out clean. Cool 10 minutes before removing from pans to wire racks.
1 PIECE: *234 cal., 11g fat (2g sat. fat), 23mg chol., 196mg sod., 30g carb. (17g sugars, 1g fiber), 3g pro.*

HALLMARK MOVIE MARATHON

Sentimental movies are a seasonal tradition—where everyone finds romance just in time for the holidays! Invite friends over to watch the show, with a spread to suit the occasion...oh, so sweet with just the right amount of spice!

NANA'S CHOCOLATE CUPCAKES WITH MINT FROSTING

My Nana used to make these cupcakes at Christmas every year, and it brings me joy to bake them now. For a more indulgent version, double the frosting and pile it high on top of each cupcake.
—Chekota Hunter, Cassville, MO

PREP: 25 min. • **BAKE:** 15 min. + cooling
MAKES: 1 dozen

- ½ cup baking cocoa
- 1 cup boiling water
- ¼ cup butter, softened
- 1 cup sugar
- 2 large eggs, room temperature
- 1⅓ cups all-purpose flour
- 2 tsp. baking powder
- ¼ tsp. salt
- ¼ cup unsweetened applesauce

FROSTING
- 1 cup confectioners' sugar
- 3 Tbsp. butter, softened
- 4 tsp. heavy whipping cream
  Dash peppermint extract
- 1 drop green food coloring, optional
- 2 Tbsp. miniature semisweet chocolate chips
  Mint Andes candies, optional

1. Preheat oven to 375°. Line 12 muffin cups with paper or foil liners. Mix cocoa and boiling water until smooth; cool completely.

2. Beat butter and sugar until blended. Beat in eggs, 1 at a time. In another bowl, whisk together flour, baking powder and salt; add to the butter mixture alternately with applesauce, beating well after each addition. Beat in the cocoa mixture.

3. Fill prepared muffin cups three-fourths full. Bake until a toothpick inserted in center comes out clean, 15-18 minutes. Cool 10 minutes before removing to a wire rack to cool completely.

4. For frosting, beat confectioners' sugar, butter, cream and extract until smooth. If desired, tint frosting with food coloring. Stir in the chocolate chips. Spread over cupcakes. If desired, top with candies.

1 CUPCAKE: *253 cal., 9g fat (5g sat. fat), 51mg chol., 196mg sod., 41g carb. (28g sugars, 1g fiber), 3g pro.*

SEAFOOD CHEESE DIP

This cheesy recipe has a nice combination of seafood flavors and clings beautifully to slices of bread.
—Michelle Domm, Atlanta, NY

PREP: 15 min. • **COOK:** 1½ hours
MAKES: 5 cups

- 1 pkg. (32 oz.) Velveeta, cubed
- 2 cans (6 oz. each) lump crabmeat, drained
- 1 can (10 oz.) diced tomatoes and green chiles, undrained
- 1 cup frozen cooked salad shrimp, thawed
  French bread baguette, sliced and toasted, and assorted fresh vegetables

In a greased 3-qt. slow cooker, combine the cheese, crab, tomatoes and shrimp. Cover and cook on low for 1½-2 hours or until the cheese is melted, stirring occasionally. Serve with baguette slices and vegetables.

¼ CUP: *172 cal., 12g fat (7g sat. fat), 77mg chol., 791mg sod., 4g carb. (3g sugars, 0 fiber), 12g pro.*

GARBANZO-STUFFED MINI PEPPERS

Mini peppers are so colorful and are the perfect size for a two-bite appetizer. They have all the crunch of a pita chip, without the extra calories.
—Christine Hanover, Lewiston, CA

TAKES: 20 min. • **MAKES:** 32 appetizers

- 1 tsp. cumin seeds
- 1 can (15 oz.) garbanzo beans or chickpeas, rinsed and drained
- ¼ cup fresh cilantro leaves
- 3 Tbsp. water
- 3 Tbsp. cider vinegar
- ¼ tsp. salt
- 16 miniature sweet peppers, halved lengthwise
  Additional fresh cilantro leaves

1. In a small dry skillet over medium heat, toast cumin seeds until aromatic, 1-2 minutes, stirring frequently. Transfer to a food processor. Add garbanzo beans, cilantro, water, vinegar and salt; pulse until blended.

2. Spoon garbanzo bean mixture into pepper halves. Top with additional cilantro. Refrigerate until serving.

1 APPETIZER: *15 cal., 0 fat (0 sat. fat), 0 chol., 36mg sod., 3g carb. (1g sugars, 1g fiber), 1g pro.*

SPICY BUTTERSCOTCH WINGS

*We love big-time spicy chicken wings!
I make a caramel sauce to balance the heat,
but you could also glaze the wings with
melted brown sugar.*
—Aaron Salazar, Westminster, CO

PREP: 25 min. • **BAKE:** 25 min.
MAKES: 20 servings

- 2 lbs. chicken wings
- 2 Tbsp. soy sauce
- 2 Tbsp. ketchup
- 2 Tbsp. Sriracha chili sauce
- 1 tsp. pepper
- 1 tsp. crushed red pepper flakes
- 1 tsp. onion powder
- ½ tsp. salt

BUTTERSCOTCH SAUCE
- ½ cup sugar
- ½ cup 2% milk, warmed
- 2 Tbsp. butter

CRUMB TOPPING
- 1 Tbsp. butter
- ½ cup panko bread crumbs

- 2 green onions, sliced diagonally, divided
- 1 garlic clove, minced
- ½ tsp. salt
- ½ tsp. pepper
- 2 red bird's eye chili peppers, sliced, optional

1. Preheat oven to 400°. Using a sharp knife, cut through the 2 wing joints; discard wing tips. Combine the next 7 ingredients; add wings and toss to coat.
2. Line a 15x10x1-in. pan with foil; grease with cooking spray. Bake the wings in prepared pan 10 minutes; reduce heat to 350° and bake until juices run clear, 12-15 minutes longer. Remove from oven; keep warm.
3. In a small skillet, spread sugar; cook, without stirring, over medium heat until it begins to melt. Gently drag melted sugar to center of pan so it melts evenly. Cook, without stirring, until melted sugar turns amber. Carefully stir in warm milk and butter. Simmer, stirring frequently, until thickened, 5-7 minutes. Keep warm.

4. For the topping, in a large skillet over medium heat, melt butter; add bread crumbs, 1 green onion, garlic, salt and pepper. Cook and stir until crumbs are golden brown, about 2 minutes. Set aside.
5. To serve, toss wings in butterscotch sauce. Sprinkle with crumb topping, remaining green onion and, if desired, sliced peppers. Serve hot.

1 PIECE: 100 cal., 5g fat (2g sat. fat), 20mg chol., 312mg sod., 8g carb. (6g sugars, 0 fiber), 5g pro.

Holiday Helper

Bird's eye chili peppers are small, round peppers that originated in Cambodia, Vietnam, Thailand, the Philippines and surrounding countries. At 50,000–100,000 on the Scoville scale, these little peppers are 10 to 20 times hotter than the average jalapeno! If you can't find bird's eye chilis and are looking for something with comparable heat, try a habanero.

HONEY-KISSED SAVORY SHORTBREAD CRACKERS

It may seem like a lot of work to make homemade crackers. However, after you've tasted these sweet and savory shortbread crackers, I think you'll admit that they're worth every minute you spent making them. They're crispy, cheesy, salty, and have a lovely sweet honey finish. They are basically cracker perfection.
—Colleen Delawder, Herndon, VA

- -

PREP: 45 min. • **BAKE:** 15 min./batch + cooling • **MAKES:** 7 dozen

- 1 cup unsalted butter, softened
- ⅓ cup minced fresh parsley
- 2 cups all-purpose flour
- 1 Tbsp. sugar
- 1 tsp. paprika
- ½ tsp. kosher salt
- ½ tsp. garlic powder
- ½ tsp. pepper
- 1 cup grated shredded cheddar cheese
- ¼ cup heavy whipping cream

HONEY-KISSED TOPPING
- 1 Tbsp. unsalted butter
- 1 Tbsp. honey
- ⅔ cup confectioners' sugar
- ⅓ cup minced fresh parsley
  Flaky sea salt, such as Maldon, optional

1. Preheat oven to 350°. In a large bowl, beat the butter for 2 minutes. Mix in parsley. In another bowl, whisk flour, sugar, paprika, kosher salt, garlic powder and pepper. Add cheese; toss to coat. Add to butter mixture alternately with cream, beating until mixture comes together. Divide dough into 3 portions.
2. On a lightly floured surface, roll each portion of dough to ¼-in. thickness. Cut with a floured 1½-in. round cookie cutter. Place 1 in. apart on parchment-lined baking sheets. Reroll and chill scraps as needed. Bake until crisp, 15-20 minutes. Cool completely on wire racks.
3. For topping, in a microwave, melt butter and honey; stir until smooth. Stir in confectioners' sugar until smooth; fold in parsley. Top crackers with honey mixture; if desired, sprinkle with flaky sea salt. Let stand until set. Store between layers of waxed paper in an airtight container at room temperature.
1 CRACKER: *45 cal., 3g fat (2g sat. fat), 8mg chol., 21mg sod., 4g carb. (1g sugars, 0 fiber), 1g pro.*

Holiday Helper
Flaky sea salts are coarse-grained salts that are used as finishing salts—sprinkled on a dish before serving for a pop of flavor and texture. The shape of the grains is often unique to the site it's harvested from—Maldon salt from England has a distinctive pyramid shape. You can also find good flake salt from Wales, France, Cyprus, Australia and New Zealand.

BRIE CHERRY PASTRY CUPS

Golden brown and flaky, these bite-sized puff pastries with creamy Brie and sweet cherry preserves could easily double as a scrumptious dessert.
—Marilyn McSween, Mentor, OH

- -

TAKES: 30 min. • **MAKES:** 3 dozen

- 1 sheet frozen puff pastry, thawed
- ½ cup cherry preserves
- 4 oz. Brie cheese, cut into ½-in. cubes
- ¼ cup chopped pecans or walnuts
- 2 Tbsp. minced chives

1. Preheat oven to 375°. Unfold puff pastry; cut into 36 squares. Gently press squares onto the bottoms of 36 greased miniature muffin cups.
2. Bake for 10 minutes. Using the end of a wooden spoon handle, make a ½-in.-deep indentation in the center of each. Bake until golden brown, 6-8 minutes longer. With spoon handle, press squares down again.
3. Spoon ½ rounded tsp. preserves into each cup. Top with cheese; sprinkle with nuts and chives. Bake until cheese is melted, 3-5 minutes.
1 APPETIZER: *61 cal., 3g fat (1g sat. fat), 3mg chol., 42mg sod., 7g carb. (3g sugars, 1g fiber), 1g pro.*

HOLIDAY HOT CHOCOLATE MIX

This is the recipe I make for holiday gifts. I put it in decorative jars and tie pretty ribbons around the jars for a festive-looking gift.
—Debbie Klejeski, Sturgeon Lake, MN

TAKES: 10 min. • **MAKES:** 3 qt. mix

- 1 pkg. (25.6 oz.) nonfat dry milk powder, about 10 cups
- 1 jar (6 oz.) nondairy coffee creamer, about 1¾ cups
- 3¾ cups instant chocolate drink mix
- ½ cup confectioners' sugar

Place all the ingredients in a very large bowl. Stir until well blended. Store in an airtight container or pack into small gift containers. To serve, add ¼ cup chocolate mix to ⅔ cup hot water.

¼ CUP MIX: 316 cal., 2g fat (1g sat. fat), 8mg chol., 305mg sod., 57g carb. (53g sugars, 2g fiber), 17g pro.

CRAFTY CUPS

As a special festive party favor, serve your guests hot chocolate in their own personalized mug! In addition to a drawn or stenciled pattern, you can inscribe each cup with a guest's name.

WHAT YOU'LL NEED
- White mugs
- Oil-based paint markers

INSTRUCTIONS
1. With oil-based paint markers, doodle to your heart's desire on white mugs. Let dry for a few hours or overnight.
2. Bake at 350° for 30 minutes, leaving mugs in the oven as it heats and cools to prevent cracking. (Bake twice if desired.)
3. Wash in the sink, rather than the dishwasher, to preserve the pattern.

HOMEMADE MARSHMALLOW POPS

Homemade marshmallows are fun to eat on a stick or to stir into your favorite hot chocolate. Their melt-in-your-mouth texture appeals to the young and the young at heart.
—*Jennifer Andrzejewski, Carmel Valley, CA*

- -

PREP: 55 min. + standing
MAKES: 15 marshmallows

- ½ **cup cold water**
- 3 **envelopes unflavored gelatin**
- 2 **cups sugar**
- 1 **cup light corn syrup**
- ½ **cup water**
- ¼ **tsp. salt**
- 1 **tsp. almond extract**
- ½ **cup confectioners' sugar, divided**
   Lollipop sticks

1. In a large bowl, combine cold water and gelatin; set aside.

2. In a large heavy saucepan over medium heat, combine the sugar, corn syrup, water and salt. Bring to a boil, stirring occasionally. Cook, covered, for 2 minutes to dissolve sugar crystals; uncover and cook on medium-high heat, without stirring, until a candy thermometer reads 240° (soft-ball stage).

3. Remove from heat and gradually add to the gelatin. Beat on medium speed for 14 minutes. Add almond extract; beat 1 minute longer.

4. Sprinkle 2 Tbsp. confectioners' sugar into a greased 13x9-in. pan. With greased hands, spread the marshmallow mixture into the prepared pan. Top with 2 Tbsp. confectioners' sugar. Cover and cool at room temperature for 6 hours or overnight.

5. Cut 15 snowflakes with a greased 2½-in. snowflake-shaped cookie cutter; toss marshmallows in remaining confectioners' sugar. If desired, gently press lollipop stick into each snowflake. Store in an airtight container in a cool, dry place.

1 MARSHMALLOW: *82 cal., 0 fat (0 sat. fat), 0 chol., 24mg sod., 21g carb. (16g sugars, 0 fiber), 1g pro.*

HOT CHOCOLATE BOMBS

These hot chocolate-filled spheres are all the rage! Make them ahead of time as a holiday gift or to have on hand when you have a hot chocolate craving.
—Rashanda Cobbins, Milwaukee, WI

PREP: 45 min. + chilling + decorating
MAKES: 6 chocolate bombs

- 22 oz. semisweet chocolate, such as Baker's Chocolate, finely chopped
- ½ cup baking cocoa
- ½ cup nonfat dry milk powder
- ¼ cup confectioners' sugar
- 6 Tbsp. vanilla marshmallow bits (not miniature marshmallows)
  Optional: Sprinkles, colored sanding sugar and melted candy melts

1. In a microwave-safe bowl, microwave the chocolate, uncovered, on high for 1 minute; stir. Microwave, stirring every 30 seconds, until chocolate is melted and smooth, 1-2 minutes longer. Chocolate should not exceed 90°.

2. Add 1 Tbsp. melted chocolate to each depression in a silicone sphere-shaped mold (2½-in. diameter). Brush chocolate evenly inside molds, all the way to the edges, rewarming chocolate as needed. Refrigerate molds until chocolate is set, 3-5 minutes. Brush a thin second layer of chocolate in molds. Refrigerate until set, 8-10 minutes. Place the remaining melted chocolate into a piping bag fitted with a small round decorating tip; set aside.

3. Remove chocolate hemispheres from molds. In a medium bowl, whisk together baking cocoa, milk powder and confectioners' sugar. Place 3 Tbsp. cocoa mixture into each of 6 chocolate hemispheres. Top each with 1 Tbsp. marshmallow bits.

4. Pipe a small amount of the melted chocolate on edges of the remaining 6 hemispheres; carefully adhere to filled halves, pressing lightly to seal, using additional melted chocolate if necessary. If desired, decorate with the optional ingredients. Refrigerate until set. Store in a tightly sealed container.

5. To prepare hot chocolate: Place hot chocolate bomb in a mug; add 1 cup hot milk and stir to dissolve.

1 CHOCOLATE BOMB: *619 cal., 34g fat (20g sat. fat), 1mg chol., 31mg sod., 36g carb. (29g sugars, 4g fiber), 10g pro.*

SALTED CARAMEL HOT CHOCOLATE BOMBS: *Fill spheres with hot cocoa mix, 1 Tbsp. caramel chips and a pinch of flake sea salt. Drizzle outside with melted dark chocolate and melted caramel chips; sprinkle with flake sea salt.*

PEPPERMINT HOT CHOCOLATE BOMBS: *Fill spheres with hot cocoa mix, 1 Tbsp. white baking chips and 1 Tbsp. finely crushed peppermint candies. Drizzle outside with melted white chocolate tinted pink and red; top with additional crushed peppermint candies.*

Holiday Helper
Use 1¼ cups of prepared hot cocoa mix from the grocery store instead of making your own.

CHOCOLATE-DIPPED BEVERAGE SPOONS

These spoons make cute gifts during the holidays. To set the chocolate quickly, simply pop the dipped spoons in the freezer.
—Marcy Boswell, Menifee, CA

PREP: 45 min. + chilling • **MAKES:** 2 dozen

1 cup milk chocolate chips
3½ tsp. shortening, divided
1 cup white baking chips
24 metal, wooden or plastic spoons
   Optional: Coarse sugar or chocolate sprinkles

1. In a microwave-safe bowl, melt milk chocolate chips with 2 tsp. shortening; stir until smooth. Repeat with white baking chips and remaining shortening.
2. Dip spoons into either mixture, tapping handles on bowl edges to remove excess. Place on a waxed paper-lined baking sheet. Pipe or drizzle milk chocolate over white-dipped spoons and white mixture over milk chocolate-dipped spoons. Use a toothpick or skewer to swirl chocolate. If desired, decorate with coarse sugar or sprinkles.
3. Chill for 5 minutes or until set. Use as stirring spoons for coffee or cocoa.
1 SPOON: *81 cal., 5g fat (3g sat. fat), 3mg chol., 12mg sod., 8g carb. (8g sugars, 0 fiber), 1g pro.*

HOT COCOA BOARD FILLERS

Once you've arranged your homemade goodies on your sweet board, fill in the spaces with store-bought items. Here are some ideas:

WHAT DO I ADD?

- Buttermints
- Candy-coated pretzels
- Caramel candies & caramel bits
- Chocolate & white baking chips
- Chocolate Kisses
- Liqueurs: Bailey's Irish Cream or Kahlua
- Peppermint sticks
- Biscotti & Pirouette cookies
- Whipped cream
- Chocolate-covered Oreos
- Peppermint bark

CRANBERRY-JALAPENO MARTINI

I describe this cocktail as slightly tart, a little sassy and completely delicious. I make a big batch when I'm hosting a party because it tends to disappear quickly. Garnish with fresh mint and cranberries for an extra-special touch.
—Kelli Haetinger, Virginia Beach, VA

PREP: 30 min. + chilling • **MAKES:** 16 servings

- 1 cup turbinado (washed raw) sugar
- 1½ cups cranberry juice, divided
- ½ cup fresh or frozen cranberries
- ½ tsp. chopped seeded jalapeno pepper
  Ice cubes
- 6 cups vodka
  Optional: Fresh mint leaves and additional cranberries

1. In a large saucepan, combine the sugar, ½ cup cranberry juice, cranberries and jalapeno. Bring to a boil. Reduce heat; simmer, uncovered, for 3 minutes or until sugar is dissolved. Remove from the heat. Cover and let stand for 20 minutes.

2. Strain, discarding cranberries and jalapeno. Cover and refrigerate syrup for at least 2 hours or until chilled.

3. For each serving, fill a mixing glass or tumbler three-fourths full with ice. Add 3 oz. vodka, 1 Tbsp. cranberry juice and 1 Tbsp. cranberry-jalapeno syrup; stir until condensation forms on outside of glass. Strain into a chilled cocktail glass. Garnish with mint and cranberries if desired.

NOTE: *Wear disposable gloves when cutting hot peppers; the oils can burn skin. Avoid touching your face.*

1 MARTINI: *252 cal., 0 fat (0 sat. fat), 0 chol., 1mg sod., 15g carb. (15g sugars, 0 fiber), 0 pro.*

FLANK STEAK CROSTINI

This recipe is perfect for gatherings, holidays, or as a special Sunday football snack. My kids love it and so do my friends and family. You can substitute butter for the olive oil, or any kind of steak for the flank steak.
—Donna Evaro, Casper, WY

PREP: 20 min. • **GRILL:** 10 min. • **MAKES:** 2 dozen

- ¾ lb. beef flank steak
- ¼ tsp. salt
- ¼ tsp. pepper
- 3 Tbsp. olive oil
- 3 garlic cloves, minced
- 1 tsp. dried basil
- 24 slices French bread baguette (¼ in. thick)
- ½ cup finely chopped fresh portobello mushrooms
- ¼ cup shredded part-skim mozzarella cheese
- 2 Tbsp. grated Parmesan cheese
- 1 Tbsp. minced chives

1. Sprinkle beef with salt and pepper. Grill beef, covered, over medium heat or broil 4 in. from the heat for 4-6 minutes on each side or until meat reaches desired doneness (for medium-rare, a thermometer should read 135°; medium, 140°; medium-well, 145°). Let stand for 5 minutes. Thinly slice across the grain.

2. Meanwhile, in a small bowl, combine the oil, garlic and basil; brush lightly over baguette slices. Place on baking sheets. Bake at 400° for 5 minutes. Top with mushrooms and mozzarella cheese. Bake 2-3 minutes longer or until cheese is melted.

3. Top with sliced steak, Parmesan cheese and chives. Serve immediately.

1 APPETIZER: *63 cal., 3g fat (1g sat. fat), 8mg chol., 101mg sod., 5g carb. (0 sugars, 0 fiber), 4g pro.*

ROSEMARY WALNUTS

My Aunt Mary started making this recipe years ago, and she would have a batch ready for us each time we visited her. The cayenne adds an unexpected zing to the savory combo of rosemary and walnuts.
—Renee D. Ciancio, New Bern, NC

- -

TAKES: 20 min. • **MAKES:** 2 cups

- 2 **cups walnut halves**
  Cooking spray
- 2 **tsp. dried rosemary, crushed**
- ½ **tsp. kosher salt**
- ¼ **to ½ tsp. cayenne pepper**

1. Place walnuts in a small bowl. Spritz with cooking spray. Add the seasonings; toss to coat. Place in a single layer on a baking sheet.
2. Bake at 350° for 10 minutes. Serve warm, or cool completely and store in an airtight container.

¼ **CUP:** *166 cal., 17g fat (2g sat. fat), 0 chol., 118mg sod., 4g carb. (1g sugars, 2g fiber), 4g pro.* **DIABETIC EXCHANGES:** 3 fat.

JALAPENO-PECAN CHEESE SPREAD

I like to shape this cheesy spread like a Christmas tree around the holidays, but it's a recipe I make year-round.
—Charolette Westfall, Houston, TX

- -

PREP: 15 min. + chilling • **COOK:** 5 min.
MAKES: 2 cups

- 1 **pkg. (8 oz.) cream cheese, softened**
- 1 **cup shredded sharp white cheddar cheese**
- 1 **cup finely chopped pecans**
- 4 **green onions, finely chopped**
- ¼ **cup jalapeno pepper jelly**
  Assorted crackers

1. In a bowl, beat cream cheese, cheddar cheese, pecans and green onions until blended. On a serving plate, form mixture into desired shape. Refrigerate, covered, at least 2 hours.
2. In a microwave, warm jelly until melted; spread over cheese spread. Serve with crackers.

2 **TBSP.:** *139 cal., 12g fat (5g sat. fat), 23mg chol., 99mg sod., 6g carb. (1g sugars, 1g fiber), 3g pro.*

LEMON-ROSEMARY CUTOUT TREES

I love snuggling up on the sofa with tea, cookies and a holiday movie, and these are the cookies for the occasion. They're not too sweet and you can eat a lot of them!
—Sarah Reynolds, Victoria, BC

- -

PREP: 40 min.
BAKE: 20 min./batch + cooling
MAKES: 2½ dozen

- ½ **cup butter, softened**
- ½ **cup sugar**
- 1 **large egg, room temperature**
- 1 **tsp. vanilla extract**
- 1¾ **cups all-purpose flour**
- 2 **Tbsp. minced fresh rosemary**
- 1 **Tbsp. grated lemon zest**
- ½ **tsp. salt**
  Coarse sugar, optional
- 1 **to 2 Tbsp. vanilla frosting**

1. Preheat oven to 350°. In a large bowl, cream butter and sugar until light and fluffy, 5-7 minutes. Beat in egg and vanilla. In another bowl, whisk flour, rosemary, lemon zest and salt; gradually beat into the creamed mixture.

2. On a lightly floured surface, roll dough to ⅛-in. thickness. Cut out 30 trees, using a floured 3-in. tree-shaped cookie cutter; cut out 30 stars, using a floured ½-in. star-shaped cookie cutter.
3. Place trees 1 in. apart on ungreased baking sheets. If desired, sprinkle with coarse sugar. Bake 10-12 minutes or until golden brown. Remove from pans to wire racks to cool completely.
4. Place stars 1 in. apart on an ungreased baking sheet. If desired, sprinkle with coarse sugar. Bake 6-8 minutes or until golden brown. Cool completely on pan. Attach stars to trees with frosting.

1 **COOKIE:** *72 cal., 3g fat (2g sat. fat), 14mg chol., 67mg sod., 9g carb. (4g sugars, 0 fiber), 1g pro.*

Holiday Helper

Chilling your dough will make it easier to roll out and less likely to stick. Then, before you bake your cookies, chill them for about 30 minutes; cold dough won't spread as quickly in the oven and the finished cookie will have a cleaner edge.

REGIONAL CHRISTMAS COOKIES

Christmas cookies are far from "cookie cutter," with different regions of the country embracing distinct ingredients, traditions and flavors. Do a little exploring with some of these surprising holiday gems!

COOKIE JAR GINGERSNAPS

A classic New England cookie, gingersnaps are now universal. My grandma kept two cookie jars in her pantry. One always had these crisp and chewy gingersnaps in it. They're still my favorite cookie. My daughter, Becky, won a blue ribbon for this recipe at a 4-H fair.
—Deb Handy, Pomona, KS

PREP: 20 min. • **BAKE:** 15 min./batch • **MAKES:** 3 dozen

- ¾ cup shortening
- 1 cup plus 2 Tbsp. sugar, divided
- 1 large egg, room temperature
- ¼ cup molasses
- 2 cups all-purpose flour
- 2 tsp. baking soda
- 1½ tsp. ground ginger
- 1 tsp. ground cinnamon
- ½ tsp. salt

1. Preheat oven to 350°. Cream shortening and 1 cup sugar until light and fluffy, 5-7 minutes. Beat in egg and molasses. In another bowl, combine next 5 ingredients; gradually add to the creamed mixture and mix well.

2. Shape level tablespoons of dough into balls. Dip 1 side of each ball into remaining 2 Tbsp. sugar; place 2 in. apart, sugary side up, on greased baking sheets. Bake until lightly browned and crinkly, 12-15 minutes. Remove cookies to wire racks to cool.

1 COOKIE: *92 cal., 4g fat (1g sat. fat), 5mg chol., 106mg sod., 13g carb. (7g sugars, 0 fiber), 1g pro.*

BUTTERY POTATO CHIP COOKIES

Potato chip cookies got their start in the spud-proud region of Idaho and the western U.S. This recipe makes plenty of crisp cookies and will keep people guessing about the secret ingredient.
—Rachel Roberts, Lemoore, CA

PREP: 15 min. • **BAKE:** 10 min./batch • **MAKES:** 4½ dozen

- 2 cups butter, softened
- 1 cup sugar
- 1 tsp. vanilla extract
- 3½ cups all-purpose flour
- 2 cups crushed potato chips
- ¾ cup chopped walnuts

1. Preheat oven to 350°. Cream butter and sugar until light and fluffy, 5-7 minutes. Beat in vanilla. Gradually add flour to creamed mixture and mix well. Stir in potato chips and walnuts.

2. Drop by rounded tablespoonfuls 2 in. apart onto ungreased baking sheets. Bake 10-12 minutes or until lightly browned. Cool 2 minutes before removing from pans to wire racks.

1 COOKIE: *126 cal., 9g fat (5g sat. fat), 18mg chol., 67mg sod., 11g carb. (4g sugars, 0 fiber), 1g pro.*

Holiday Helper

There is a huge variety of potato chips in the snack aisle—pick one you'd actually want to eat. Avoid thin chips with a high grease factor and go for a sturdier ridged chip for a better texture. You can substitute the nuts for a flavored candy chip—cinnamon or butterscotch would do nicely!

KEY LIME BUTTER COOKIES

I love limes so much that if a recipe calls for lemons, I almost always use limes instead. With their hints of delicate green color, these cookies are perfect for Christmas—you can also make them as sandwich cookies and use lime curd for the filling.
—*Deirdre Cox, Kansas City, MO*

PREP: 25 min. • **BAKE:** 10 min./batch + cooling • **MAKES:** 3 dozen

- 1 cup butter, softened
- ½ cup confectioners' sugar
- 1 Tbsp. grated lime zest
- ½ tsp. vanilla extract
- 1¾ cups all-purpose flour
- ¼ cup cornstarch
  Sugar

GLAZE
- ½ cup confectioners' sugar
- 4 tsp. Key lime or regular lime juice
- 1 tsp. grated lime zest

1. Preheat oven to 350°. In a large bowl, cream the butter and confectioners' sugar until light and fluffy. Beat in lime zest and vanilla. In another bowl, whisk flour and cornstarch; gradually beat into creamed mixture.
2. Shape dough into 1-in. balls; place 1 in. apart on ungreased baking sheets. Flatten to ¼-in. thickness with the bottom of a glass dipped in sugar.
3. Bake 8-10 minutes or until bottoms are light brown. Remove the cookies from the pans to wire racks to cool completely.
4. For glaze, mix confectioners' sugar, lime juice and zest. Brush over cookies. Let stand until set.
1 COOKIE: *84 cal., 5g fat (3g sat. fat), 14mg chol., 41mg sod., 9g carb. (3g sugars, 0 fiber), 1g pro.*

RAISIN SWEET POTATO COOKIES

Cozy up to the fire with a plate of satisfyingly sweet cookies that taste like home. Serve them with a mug of hot chai tea or ice-cold milk, and no one will be able to resist them.
—*Jacque Sue Meyer, Lohman, MO*

PREP: 25 min. • **BAKE:** 10 min./batch + cooling • **MAKES:** 5 dozen

- 1 cup butter, softened
- 1 cup sugar
- 1 large egg, room temperature
- 1 cup mashed sweet potato
- 1 tsp. vanilla extract
- 2 cups all-purpose flour
- 1 tsp. baking powder
- 1 tsp. ground cinnamon
- ½ tsp. baking soda
- ½ tsp. salt
- ½ tsp. ground allspice
- 1 cup chopped pecans
- 1 cup raisins

1. Preheat oven to 375°. In a large bowl, cream butter and sugar until light and fluffy, 5-7 minutes. Beat in the egg, sweet potato and vanilla. Combine the flour, baking powder, cinnamon, baking soda, salt and allspice; gradually add to the creamed mixture and mix well. Fold in pecans and raisins.
2. Drop by tablespoonfuls 1 in. apart onto ungreased baking sheets. Bake until edges begin to brown, 10-12 minutes. Cool on pans for 1 minute before removing to wire racks to cool completely. Store in an airtight container.
1 COOKIE: *81 cal., 5g fat (2g sat. fat), 12mg chol., 61mg sod., 10g carb. (5g sugars, 1g fiber), 1g pro.*

BISCOCHITOS

This recipe has been handed down to family members since the early 1880s by Hispanic settlers in our area. In our heritage, biscochitos are for young and old.
—Martha Abeyta, Antonito, CO

PREP: 30 min. + standing
BAKE: 10 min./batch + cooling
MAKES: about 8 dozen

- 1 large egg
- 1 large egg yolk
- 6 cups all-purpose flour, sifted
- 2 tsp. baking powder
- 1 tsp. salt
- ¼ tsp. baking soda
- 2 cups lard
- 1 cup sugar
- 2 tsp. aniseed
- ½ cup orange juice

COATING
- 1 cup sugar
- 1½ Tbsp. ground cinnamon

1. In a small bowl, stir together the whole egg and the egg yolk; let stand at room temperature for 30 minutes. In another bowl, whisk the flour, baking powder, salt and baking soda; set aside.
2. Preheat oven to 375°. In a large bowl, beat the lard and sugar until creamy, 5-7 minutes. Add eggs and aniseed.
3. Add flour mixture, alternately with orange juice, beginning and ending with flour; do not overmix. Turn onto a lightly floured surface; knead gently 8-10 times.
4. On a lightly floured surface, roll out dough to ¼-in. thickness. Cut with 2-in. fluted round cookie cutter. Place 1 in. apart on parchment lined baking sheets. Bake until golden brown, 8-10 minutes. Cool on pans 5 minutes.
5. In a small bowl, mix sugar and cinnamon. Press warm cookies in the cinnamon sugar. Cool completely on wire racks.
1 COOKIE: *80 cal., 5g fat (2g sat. fat), 8mg chol., 39mg sod., 9g carb. (3g sugars, 0 fiber), 1g pro.*

PECAN PIE COOKIES

Like many people in the South, my family loves pecans. In fact, having pecan pie at Thanksgiving isn't enough—we'll follow it with these pecan cookies at Christmas.
—Julie McQuiston, Bradenton, FL

PREP: 45 min. • **BAKE:** 10 min./batch
MAKES: 3 dozen

- ¾ cup shortening
- 1½ cups packed brown sugar, divided
- 1 large egg, room temperature
- 2 tsp. vanilla extract, divided
- 2 cups all-purpose flour
- 1 tsp. baking powder
- ½ tsp. salt
- 1 cup finely chopped pecans
- ¼ cup heavy whipping cream
  Frosting of choice, optional

1. Preheat oven to 350°. In a large bowl, cream shortening and 1 cup brown sugar until light and fluffy, 5-7 minutes. Beat in egg and 1 tsp. vanilla. In a second bowl, combine the flour, baking powder and salt; gradually add to the creamed mixture and mix well.
2. Shape dough into 1-in. balls. Place 2 in. apart on ungreased baking sheets. Using the end of a wooden spoon handle, make a ½-in.-deep indentation in the center of each ball.
3. Combine pecans, remaining ½ cup brown sugar, cream and remaining 1 tsp. vanilla; spoon into indentations.
4. Bake for 9-11 minutes or until lightly browned. Cool for 1 minute before removing from pans to wire racks. If desired, top with frosting.
1 COOKIE: *128 cal., 7g fat (2g sat. fat), 8mg chol., 50mg sod., 15g carb. (9g sugars, 1g fiber), 1g pro.*

OATMEAL MOLASSES CRISPS

When I found this recipe in an Amish cookbook, I had to try it. It's traditional in regions with Amish populations—Pennsylvania, Ohio and the Upper Midwest. Now it's a staple for our family and the folks at our church fellowship, too.
—Jori Schellenberger, Everett, WA

PREP: 45 min. • **BAKE:** 10 min./batch • **MAKES:** about 15 dozen

2½ cups butter, softened
5 cups sugar
4 large eggs, room temperature
⅓ cup dark molasses
3 tsp. vanilla extract
4⅓ cups all-purpose flour
4 tsp. baking powder
3 tsp. ground cinnamon
2 tsp. salt
1 tsp. baking soda
4¾ cups old-fashioned oats
2 cups finely chopped pecans

1. Preheat oven to 375°. In a large bowl, cream butter and sugar until light and fluffy, 5-7 minutes. Beat in eggs, 1 at a time. Beat in molasses and vanilla. In another bowl, whisk together flour, baking powder, cinnamon, salt and baking soda; gradually add to the creamed mixture. Stir in oats and pecans.
2. Drop dough by tablespoonfuls 2 in. apart onto greased baking sheets. Bake until edges are firm, 10-12 minutes. Cool on pans for 3 minutes. Remove to wire racks to cool.
1 COOKIE: *75 cal., 4g fat (2g sat. fat), 11mg chol., 66mg sod., 10g carb. (6g sugars, 0 fiber), 1g pro.*

MAPLE-WALNUT SPRITZ COOKIES

After taking a trip to Vermont during maple harvest season and tasting delicious maple goodies, I just had to make something using maple syrup. I love the combination of maple syrup, walnuts and spritz cookies, so I used all three of those elements to create these perfectly delicious bites. I just love the aroma when these are baking — it takes me back to Vermont and the good times I had there.
—Paula Marchesi, Lenhartsville, PA

PREP: 30 min. • **BAKE:** 10 min./batch + cooling • **MAKES:** 6½ dozen

½ cup butter, softened
⅓ cup packed brown sugar
1 large egg, room temperature
¼ cup maple syrup
1 tsp. vanilla extract
1½ cups all-purpose flour
⅔ cup ground walnuts
½ tsp. baking powder
¼ tsp. salt
  Coarse sugar
⅔ cup walnut pieces

1. Preheat oven to 350°. In a bowl, cream butter and brown sugar until light and fluffy, 5-7 minutes. Beat in egg, maple syrup and vanilla. In another bowl, whisk the flour, ground walnuts, baking powder and salt; gradually beat into the creamed mixture (dough will be soft).
2. Using a cookie press fitted with a flower or star disk, press dough 1 in. apart onto ungreased baking sheets. Sprinkle with coarse sugar. Top with walnuts.
3. Bake for 10-12 minutes or until bottoms are light brown. Cool on pans 2 minutes. Remove to wire racks to cool completely.
1 COOKIE: *38 cal., 2g fat (1g sat. fat), 6mg chol., 21mg sod., 4g carb. (2g sugars, 0 fiber), 1g pro.*

WYOMING COWBOY COOKIES

These cookies are very popular here in Wyoming. Mix up a batch for your crew and see why!
—Patsy Steenbock, Shoshoni, WY

PREP: 25 min. • **BAKE:** 15 min.
MAKES: 6 dozen

- 1   cup sweetened shredded coconut
- ¾   cup chopped pecans
- 1   cup butter, softened
- 1½   cups packed brown sugar
- ½   cup sugar
- 2   large eggs, room temperature
- 1½   tsp. vanilla extract
- 2   cups all-purpose flour
- 1   tsp. baking soda
- ½   tsp. salt
- 2   cups old-fashioned oats
- 2   cups (12 oz.) chocolate chips

1. Preheat oven to 350°. Place coconut and pecans on a 15x10x1-in. baking pan. Bake for 6-8 minutes or until toasted, stirring every 2 minutes. Set aside to cool.
2. In a large bowl, cream the butter and sugars until light and fluffy, 5-7 minutes. Add eggs and vanilla; beat well. In another bowl, combine the flour, baking soda and salt. Add to creamed mixture; beat well. Stir in the oats, chocolate chips and toasted coconut and pecans.
3. Drop dough by rounded teaspoonfuls onto greased baking sheets. Bake for 12 minutes or until browned. Remove to wire racks to cool.

1 COOKIE: *105 cal., 6g fat (3g sat. fat), 12mg chol., 61mg sod., 14g carb. (9g sugars, 1g fiber), 1g pro.*

Holiday Helper

You can double the size of these cookies—just increase the oven time, baking until they're golden brown. Be sure not to overbake, though. They should be crunchy on the outside and chewy on the inside. These cookies are great crumbled over ice cream!

SNICKERDOODLE CRISPS

This classic cookie from New England can be made two ways: soft or crunchy. My happy version with cinnamon, ginger and nutmeg is crispy to perfection.
—Jenni Sharp, Milwaukee, WI

PREP: 20 min. + chilling
BAKE: 10 min./batch + cooling
MAKES: about 5 dozen

- 1   cup butter, softened
- 2   cups sugar
- 2   large eggs, room temperature
- 2   tsp. vanilla extract
- 3   cups all-purpose flour
- 4   tsp. ground cinnamon
- 2   tsp. ground ginger
- ¾   tsp. ground nutmeg
- ½   tsp. ground allspice
- 2   tsp. cream of tartar
- 1   tsp. baking soda
- ½   tsp. salt
- **SPICED SUGAR**
- ⅓   cup sugar
- 1   tsp. ground cinnamon
- ¾   tsp. ground ginger
- ¼   tsp. ground nutmeg
- ¼   tsp. ground allspice

1. In a large bowl, cream butter and sugar until light and fluffy, 5-7 minutes. Beat in eggs and vanilla. In another bowl, whisk the flour, spices, cream of tartar, baking soda and salt; gradually beat into the creamed mixture.
2. Divide dough in half; shape each into an 8-in.-long roll. Wrap and refrigerate for 2 hours or until firm.
3. Preheat oven to 350°. In a small bowl, mix spiced sugar ingredients. Unwrap and cut the dough crosswise into ¼-in. slices; press cookies into spiced sugar mixture to coat both sides or sprinkle sugar mixture over cookies. Place 2 in. apart on greased baking sheets. Bake 7-9 minutes or until edges are light brown. Cool on pans for 2 minutes before removing to wire racks to cool completely.

1 COOKIE: *84 cal., 3g fat (2g sat. fat), 14mg chol., 68mg sod., 13g carb. (8g sugars, 0 fiber), 1g pro.*

PEANUTTY LACE COOKIES

The fluffy filling sandwiched by crunchy, nutty cookies make these different from your typical treat. People always want seconds!
—Scarlett Elrod, Newnan, GA

PREP: 35 min. • **BAKE:** 10 min. + cooling • **MAKES:** about 1½ dozen

- ¾ cup packed brown sugar
- ⅔ cup butter, melted
- 1 large egg, room temperature
- 1 tsp. vanilla extract
- 2 cups quick-cooking oats
- ¼ cup all-purpose flour
- ¼ tsp. salt
- ¼ tsp. baking powder
- ½ cup finely chopped dry roasted peanuts

FILLING
- 2 cups confectioners' sugar
- 1 jar (7 oz.) marshmallow creme
- ½ cup butter, softened
- 1 Tbsp. 2% milk
- 2 tsp. vanilla extract

1. Preheat oven to 350°. In a large bowl, beat brown sugar and melted butter until blended. Beat in egg and vanilla. In another bowl, whisk oats, flour, salt and baking powder; gradually beat into the sugar mixture. Stir in peanuts.
2. Drop by tablespoonfuls 4 in. apart onto parchment paper-lined baking sheets; spread into 3-in. circles. Bake for 8-10 minutes or until edges are golden brown. Remove from pans to wire racks to cool completely.
3. In a large bowl, beat filling ingredients until fluffy. Spread on bottoms of half of the cookies; cover with the remaining cookies.
1 SANDWICH COOKIE: *270 cal., 13g fat (7g sat. fat), 38mg chol., 164mg sod., 34g carb. (26g sugars, 1g fiber), 3g pro.*

SAND DOLLAR COOKIES

Before the military relocated our family, my children had never lived near the ocean. I came up with this special treat with a beach theme—it made our move even more fun!
—Michelle Duncan, Callaway, FL

PREP: 15 min. + chilling • **BAKE:** 15 min./batch
MAKES: about 1½ dozen

- 1½ cups butter, softened
- ⅔ cup confectioners' sugar
- 3 Tbsp. sugar
- 4 tsp. almond extract
- 2⅔ cups all-purpose flour
- ½ tsp. salt
- 2 large eggs, lightly beaten
  Slivered almonds and cinnamon sugar

1. In a large bowl, cream butter and sugars until light and fluffy, 5-7 minutes. Beat in almond extract. In another bowl, combine the flour and salt; gradually add to the creamed mixture and mix well. Divide dough in half. Shape each half into a disk; wrap and refrigerate 1 hour or until firm enough to roll.
2. Preheat oven to 325°. Roll each portion of dough between layers of waxed paper to ⅛-in. thickness. Cut with a 3½-in. round cookie cutter dipped in flour. Using a floured spatula, place 1 in. apart on ungreased baking sheets. Brush with egg. Decorate with almonds to resemble sand dollars; sprinkle with cinnamon sugar.
3. Bake 12-16 minutes or until edges begin to brown. Cool on pans for 2 minutes before removing to wire racks.
1 COOKIE: *240 cal., 16g fat (10g sat. fat), 64mg chol., 227mg sod., 21g carb. (7g sugars, 0 fiber), 3g pro.*

BERGER COOKIES

After a friend who had recently traveled to Baltimore sent me a package of Berger cookies, I was hooked. They disappeared so quickly, I decided to try to re-create them at home. After many tests and tweaks, my husband and I gained 6 pounds between the two of us, but it was worth it—I landed on a reproduction of the famous cookie I'm so proud of.
—Marina Castle-Kelley, Canyon Country, CA

PREP: 15 min. • **BAKE:** 10 min./batch + cooling • **MAKES:** 35 cookies

1 cup unsalted butter, softened
1 Tbsp. baking powder
1½ tsp. salt
2 tsp. vanilla extract
1½ cups sugar
3 large eggs, room temperature
4½ cups all-purpose flour
1 cup sour cream
CHOCOLATE ICING
4 Tbsp. unsalted butter
3½ cups semisweet chocolate chips
4 oz. unsweetened chocolate, chopped
2 Tbsp. light corn syrup
1½ cups sour cream

1. Preheat oven to 400°. Beat butter, baking powder, salt and vanilla until combined. Add sugar; beat until light and fluffy, 5-7 minutes. Add eggs, 1 at a time, beating well after each addition. Add flour alternately with the sour cream, beginning and ending with flour; do not overmix.
2. Drop by 3 tablespoonfuls onto greased baking sheets. With wet fingers, flatten each into a 3-in. circle.
3. Bake 10 minutes or until edges start to brown. Cool on pan 5 minutes; remove to wire racks to cool completely.
4. For icing: In a small saucepan, stir ingredients over low heat just until chocolate melts and mixture is smooth. Remove from heat; cool to room temperature. Using a hand mixer, beat on high until mixture thickens and becomes lighter in color, 6-7 minutes.
5. Spread 2 Tbsp. icing over the flat side of each cookie; let stand until set. Store in an airtight container in the refrigerator.
1 COOKIE: *296 cal., 17g fat (10g sat. fat), 37mg chol., 159mg sod., 34g carb. (19g sugars, 2g fiber), 4g pro.*

Holiday Helper
To test cookie doneness, use a spatula and gently lift the edge of the cookie. While the top may not be brown when they are done, the edges will be slightly brown.

BENNE SEED WAFERS

Crisp, chewy, nutty and caramelized benne cookies, aka sesame cookies or benne wafers, are perfect for Kwanzaa or holiday celebrations. For a traditional cookie, leave them plain; to dress them up, drizzle them with melted chocolate. Both ways are equally delicious!
—April Wright, Elkridge, MD

PREP: 30 min.
BAKE: 20 min./batch + cooling
MAKES: 8 dozen

- 1 cup sesame seeds
- 1¼ cups packed light brown sugar
- ½ cup unsalted butter, softened
- 1 large egg, room temperature
- 1 tsp. vanilla extract
- ¾ cup all-purpose flour
- ¼ tsp. salt
- ⅛ tsp. baking powder

OPTIONAL CHOCOLATE DRIZZLE

- 1¼ to 2½ cups 60% cacao bittersweet chocolate baking chips
- 2 tsp. shortening or coconut oil

1. Preheat oven to 350°. Place sesame seeds on an ungreased baking sheet. Bake until fragrant and lightly browned, 10-15 minutes; cool.

2. Reduce oven temperature to 300°. In a large bowl, beat brown sugar and butter until crumbly. Beat in the egg and vanilla extract. In a small bowl, whisk together flour, salt and baking powder. Gradually beat into the sugar mixture. Add cooled sesame seeds and stir to combine.

3. Roll level teaspoons of dough into balls. Place 2 in. apart onto parchment-lined baking sheets. Reduce the oven temperature to 275°; bake until set but still soft, 18-20 minutes. Cool on pan 5 minutes before removing to a wire rack to cool completely.

4. For chocolate drizzle, in a large microwave-safe bowl, melt chocolate, uncovered, at 50% power until chips are melted, stirring every 30 seconds for 1-1½ minutes. Add the shortening and stir until melted. Drizzle over cookies; let stand until set.

1 WAFER: *32 cal., 2g fat (1g sat. fat), 4mg chol., 9mg sod., 4g carb. (3g sugars, 0 fiber), 0 pro.*

Holiday Helper

A light-colored baking sheet will help keep these cookies from browning too much. If using a dark-colored pan, check cookies a minute earlier. Lining baking sheet with parchment paper helps keep the cookies from spreading too much.

GRANDMA'S SCOTTISH SHORTBREAD

My Scottish grandmother was renowned for her baked goods, and these shortbread bars are an example of why. While widely known and loved, shortbread is particularly deeply rooted in areas where Scottish immigrants settled, such as New England and Appalachia.
—Jane Kelly, Wayland, MA

PREP: 15 min. • **BAKE:** 45 min. + cooling
MAKES: 4 dozen

- 1 **lb. butter, softened**
- 8 **oz. superfine sugar (about 1¼ cups)**
- 1 **lb. all-purpose flour (3⅔ cups)**
- 8 **oz. white rice flour (1⅓ cups)**

1. Preheat oven to 300°. Cream the butter and sugar until light and fluffy, 5-7 minutes. Combine flours; gradually beat into creamed mixture. Press dough into an ungreased 13x9-in. baking pan. Prick with a fork.
2. Bake until light brown, 45-50 minutes. Cut into 48 bars or triangles while still warm. Cool completely on a wire rack.
1 BAR: *139 cal., 8g fat (5g sat. fat), 20mg chol., 61mg sod., 16g carb. (5g sugars, 0 fiber), 1g pro.*

TEA CAKES

I've baked many batches of cookies through the years, but family and friends tell me these southern treats are the best. The simple buttery flavor appeals to all.
—Doris McGough, Dothan, AL

PREP: 10 min. • **BAKE:** 10 min./batch
MAKES: 5 dozen

- 1 **cup butter, softened**
- 1½ **cups sugar**
- 3 **large eggs, room temperature**
- 1 **Tbsp. vanilla extract**
- 3 **cups all-purpose flour**
- 2 **tsp. baking powder**
- ¼ **tsp. salt**

1. Preheat oven to 375°. In a large bowl, cream butter and sugar until light and fluffy, 5-7 minutes. Add eggs, 1 at a time, beating well after each addition. Beat in vanilla. Combine the flour, baking powder and salt; gradually add to the creamed mixture (the dough will be soft).
2. Drop by tablespoonfuls 2 in. apart onto greased baking sheets. Bake until the edges are golden brown, 7-8 minutes. Remove from pans to wire racks to cool.
1 TEA CAKE: *74 cal., 3g fat (2g sat. fat), 17mg chol., 54mg sod., 10g carb. (5g sugars, 0 fiber), 1g pro.*

WHITE CHOCOLATE MACADAMIA COOKIES

Hawaiian macadamia nuts and white baking chips make a fantastic combination in these buttery cookies.
—Cathy Lennon, Newport, TN

PREP: 15 min.
BAKE: 10 min./batch + cooling
MAKES: 4½ dozen

- ½ **cup butter, softened**
- ⅔ **cup sugar**
- 1 **large egg, room temperature**
- 1 **tsp. vanilla extract**
- 1 **cup plus 2 Tbsp. all-purpose flour**
- ½ **tsp. baking soda**
- 1 **cup macadamia nuts, chopped**
- 1 **cup white baking chips**

1. Preheat oven to 350°. In a large bowl, cream butter and sugar until light and fluffy, 5-7 minutes. Beat in egg and vanilla. In another bowl, whisk flour and baking soda; gradually beat into the creamed mixture. Stir in nuts and baking chips.
2. Drop by heaping teaspoonfuls 2 in. apart onto ungreased baking sheets. Bake 10-12 minutes or until golden brown. Cool on pans 1 minute before removing to wire racks to cool completely.
1 COOKIE: *70 cal., 5g fat (2g sat. fat), 9mg chol., 38mg sod., 7g carb. (4g sugars, 0 fiber), 1g pro.*

ORANGE-CHILI CHOCOLATE COOKIES

Whenever I make these cookies I'm always asked for the recipe—we love a bit of spice in our chocolate in the Southwest! Because they start with a packaged sugar cookie mix, these favorites are super easy to make.
—Debbie Blunt, Wickenburg, AZ

PREP: 15 min. • **BAKE:** 10 min./batch
MAKES: 3 dozen

- 1 pkg. (17½ oz.) sugar cookie mix
- ⅓ cup baking cocoa
- 4 tsp. grated orange zest
- ½ tsp. ground cinnamon
- ¼ to ½ tsp. cayenne pepper
- ½ cup butter, softened
- 1 large egg, room temperature
- 1 tsp. vanilla extract
- 1 tsp. Triple Sec, optional

TOPPING
- 2 Tbsp. sugar
- 1 tsp. ground cinnamon

1. Preheat oven to 350°. Combine cookie mix, cocoa, orange zest, cinnamon and cayenne. Beat in butter, egg, vanilla and, if desired, Triple Sec.
2. Mix sugar and cinnamon. Roll dough into 1-in. balls; roll balls in sugar mixture. Place 2 in. apart on ungreased baking sheets. Bake until set, 8-10 minutes. Remove from pans to wire racks to cool.
1 COOKIE: *89 cal., 4g fat (2g sat. fat), 13mg chol., 52mg sod., 12g carb. (7g sugars, 0 fiber), 1g pro.*

MEMORABLE BISCOTTI

The enticing aroma of anise filled the kitchen and wafted through the house as Mom baked these crisp cookies when I was a girl. Mom always kept a big glass jar filled so we had a supply of these traditional treats on hand.
—Cookie Curci, San Jose, CA

PREP: 20 min. • **BAKE:** 55 min. + cooling
MAKES: about 2½ dozen

- 1 cup butter, softened
- 1 cup sugar
- 3 large eggs, room temperature
- 1 tsp. vanilla extract
- 1 tsp. anise extract
- 3 cups all-purpose flour
- 1 Tbsp. baking powder
- ½ tsp. salt
- 1 cup chopped almonds

1. Preheat oven to 300°. In a large bowl, cream the butter and sugar until light and fluffy, 5-7 minutes. Add eggs, 1 at a time, beating well after each addition. Beat in extracts. Combine the flour, baking powder and salt; gradually add to the creamed mixture and mix well. Stir in almonds.
2. Line a baking sheet with foil; grease the foil. Divide dough in half. On the foil, form each portion into an 11x3-in. rectangle.
3. Bake for 35 minutes or until lightly browned. Carefully remove to wire racks; cool for 15 minutes. Increase heat to 325°.
4. Transfer rectangles to a cutting board; cut diagonally with a serrated knife into ¾-in. slices. Place the cut side down on ungreased baking sheets.
5. Bake for 10 minutes. Turn and bake 10 minutes longer or until firm. Remove to wire racks to cool completely. Store in an airtight container.
1 COOKIE: *159 cal., 9g fat (4g sat. fat), 35mg chol., 144mg sod., 17g carb. (7g sugars, 1g fiber), 3g pro.*

PINEAPPLE COCONUT TASSIES

These Hawaiian-style cookies may sound and look fancy, but they're easy to make—and their simplicity makes them an ideal choice for baking with children. My granddaughter enjoys helping me measure ingredients. Children also can help shape the dough into balls, then you can finish them together.
—Connie Shuff, York, PA

PREP: 40 min.
BAKE: 20 min./batch + cooling
MAKES: 40 cookies

- 1 cup unsalted butter, softened
- ½ cup confectioners' sugar
- 1 tsp. vanilla extract
- 2 cups cake flour
- 2 Tbsp. cornstarch
- ½ tsp. salt

FILLING
- 1½ cups sweetened shredded coconut
- 1 cup pineapple ice cream topping
- ½ cup sugar
- ¼ cup chopped macadamia nuts
- 1 large egg
- 2 tsp. cornstarch

ICING
- ½ cup confectioners' sugar
- 1 Tbsp. 2% milk
- ½ tsp. coconut extract

1. Preheat oven to 350°. Cream butter and confectioners' sugar until light and fluffy, 5-7 minutes. Beat in vanilla. In another bowl, whisk flour, cornstarch and salt; gradually beat into the creamed mixture. Shape dough into 1-in. balls; press evenly onto the bottoms and up the sides of 40 greased and floured mini muffin cups.
2. In a small bowl, mix coconut, ice cream topping, sugar, macadamia nuts, egg and cornstarch. Place 1 Tbsp. filling in each cup. Bake until edges are golden and the filling is puffed, 20-25 minutes. Let cool in pans for 5-10 minutes, then carefully remove to wire racks to cool.
3. In a small bowl, combine the icing ingredients. Drizzle icing over cookies; let set completely.
1 COOKIE: *136 cal., 7g fat (4g sat. fat), 17mg chol., 48mg sod., 19g carb. (9g sugars, 0 fiber), 1g pro.*

BROWNED-BUTTER PISTACHIO COOKIES

California produces 99% of the pistachios in the U.S., so these simple, show-stopping cookies are especially popular there. They just melt in your mouth and the pistachios and bay leaves add a subtle, unique flavor.
—Stephanie Sutphin, Radford, VA

PREP: 1 hour + chilling
BAKE: 15 min./batch + cooling
MAKES: 6 dozen

- 1 cup butter, cubed
- 6 bay leaves
- 3 cups confectioners' sugar, divided
- 2 large egg yolks, room temperature
- 2 tsp. vanilla extract, divided
- 1½ cups all-purpose flour
- ¾ cup pistachios, toasted and finely chopped, divided
- 2 Tbsp. water
- 1 tsp. flaky sea salt, such as Maldon

1. In a small heavy saucepan, melt butter over medium heat. Add bay leaves; heat until golden brown, 5-7 minutes, stirring constantly. Transfer to a large bowl; discard bay leaves. Cool completely until butter is solid.
2. Add 1 cup confectioners' sugar to butter; cream until light and fluffy. Beat in egg yolks and 1 tsp. vanilla. Gradually beat in flour; stir in ½ cup pistachios. Cover and refrigerate until firm enough to roll, about 1 hour.
3. Preheat oven to 350°. On a lightly floured surface, roll dough to ¼-in. thickness. Cut into 1½-in. diamonds. Place 2 in. apart on parchment-lined baking sheets. Bake until edges just begin to brown, 12-15 minutes. Remove from pans to wire racks to cool completely.
4. For glaze, mix water, remaining 2 cups confectioners' sugar and remaining 1 tsp. vanilla; stir until smooth. Dip cookies in glaze, allowing excess to drip off. Place on waxed paper; sprinkle with sea salt and remaining pistachios. Let stand until set. Store in an airtight container.
1 COOKIE: *61 cal., 3g fat (2g sat. fat), 12mg chol., 53mg sod., 7g carb. (5g sugars, 0 fiber), 1g pro.*

FROSTED BUTTER RUM BRICKLE BITES

Rum, real butter and toffee bits turned these cookies into my husband's new favorite. If you'd like them less sweet, skip the frosting and sprinkle with confectioners' sugar while the cookies are still warm.
—Cindy Nerat, Menominee, MI

PREP: 35 min.
BAKE: 10 min./batch + cooling
MAKES: about 4 dozen

1 cup butter, softened
¾ cup confectioners' sugar
2 tsp. rum extract
½ tsp. salt
2 cups all-purpose flour
1 pkg. (8 oz.) brickle toffee bits
ICING
⅓ cup butter, cubed
2 cups confectioners' sugar
½ tsp. rum extract
2 to 3 Tbsp. 2% milk

1. Preheat oven to 375°. Beat the first 4 ingredients until blended. Beat in flour. Stir in toffee bits. Shape dough into 1-in. balls; place 2 in. apart on parchment-lined baking sheets.
2. Bake until edges are light brown and toffee bits begin to melt, 8-10 minutes. Cool on pans 5 minutes. Remove to wire racks to cool completely.
3. In a small heavy saucepan, melt the butter over medium heat. Heat until golden brown, about 5 minutes, stirring constantly. Remove from the heat; stir in confectioners' sugar, rum extract and enough milk to reach desired consistency. Spread over cookies.

1 COOKIE: 112 cal., 6g fat (4g sat. fat), 15mg chol., 89mg sod., 13g carb. (9g sugars, 0 fiber), 1g pro.

Holiday Helper
You'll know these are done when the toffee bits around the edges just start to melt and the cookies' edges are lightly browned. This thick, buttery icing with its toasty flavor would also enhance pecan shortbreads or pumpkin cookies. If you like, you can use real rum instead of extract!

MEXICAN CINNAMON COOKIES

My extended family shares a meal every Sunday. The aunts and uncles take turns bringing everything from main dishes to desserts like this traditional Mexican cinnamon cookie called reganadas.
—Adan Franco, Milwaukee, WI

PREP: 25 min. + standing
BAKE: 10 min./batch • **MAKES:** 12 dozen

2 cups lard, room temperature
4 cups all-purpose flour
3 tsp. baking powder
1½ tsp. ground cinnamon
Dash salt
1 large egg, separated, room temperature
¾ cup sugar
COATING
⅔ cup sugar
4 tsp. ground cinnamon
Confectioners' sugar, optional

1. Preheat oven to 375°. In a large bowl, beat lard until creamy. In another bowl, whisk flour, baking powder, cinnamon and salt; gradually beat into lard.
2. In a small bowl, beat egg white on high speed until stiff peaks form. Gently whisk in sugar and egg yolk. Gradually beat into lard mixture. Turn onto a lightly floured surface; knead gently 8-10 times.
3. Divide dough into 6 portions. On a lightly floured surface, roll each portion into a 24-in.-long rope; cut diagonally into 1-in. pieces. Place 1 in. apart on ungreased baking sheets. Bake until edges are light brown, 8-10 minutes. Cool on pans for 2 minutes.
4. For the coating, in a small bowl, mix sugar and cinnamon. Roll warm cookies in cinnamon sugar mixture or confectioners' sugar. Cool on wire racks.

1 COOKIE: 47 cal., 3g fat (1g sat. fat), 4mg chol., 10mg sod., 5g carb. (2g sugars, 0 fiber), 0 pro.

GOOEY BUTTER COOKIES

As a native of St. Louis, I wanted to make a cookie version of the famous gooey butter cake. Although many of the gooey butter cake recipes use a cake mix, my cookies are made from scratch.
—Julia TenHoeve, Richmond, VA

PREP: 25 min. + chilling
BAKE: 10 min./batch
MAKES: 5 dozen

½ cup butter, softened
1   pkg. (8 oz.) cream cheese, softened
1½ cups sugar
1   large egg, room temperature
1¼ tsp. vanilla extract
2¼ cups all-purpose flour
½   cup nonfat dry milk powder
3   tsp. baking powder
½   cup confectioners' sugar

1. Preheat oven to 350°. Beat the butter, cream cheese and sugar until blended. Beat in egg and vanilla. In a second bowl, whisk flour, milk powder and baking powder; gradually beat into the creamed mixture. Chill dough for 30 minutes or until slightly firm.
2. Scoop level tablespoons of dough; roll in confectioners' sugar. Place 1 in. apart on parchment-lined baking sheets. Bake until light brown, 10-12 minutes. Remove from pans to wire racks to cool.
1 COOKIE: 70 cal., 3g fat (2g sat. fat), 11mg chol., 50mg sod., 10g carb. (6g sugars, 0 fiber), 1g pro.

MINTY AVOCADO CHRISTMAS COOKIES

Best known in the Southwest, avocado cookies are becoming more popular now that avocados are available year-round. These minty cookies are tasty, especially during the holidays.
—Pat Dazis, Charlotte, NC

PREP: 20 min.
BAKE: 10 min./batch + cooling
MAKES: 7 dozen

2½ cups all-purpose flour
1   tsp. baking powder
½   tsp. baking soda
1   tsp. salt
1   cup pureed avocado
    (about 2 small avocados)
½   cup unsalted butter, softened
1   cup packed brown sugar
½   cup sugar
2   large eggs, room temperature
1½ tsp. mint extract
1   cup semisweet chocolate chips
1   pkg. (10 oz.) Andes crème de menthe baking chips
2   drops green food coloring, optional

1. Preheat oven to 350°. In large bowl, sift flour, baking powder, baking soda and salt; set aside.
2. In another large bowl, cream avocado, butter and sugars. Add eggs and mint extract. Gradually add the flour mixture to the creamed mixture, beating well; stir in semisweet and Andes chips. Add green food coloring if desired.
3. Drop by tablespoonfuls on parchment-lined baking sheets. Bake until the edges start to brown, 10-12 minutes. Cool on pans for 2 minutes, then remove to wire racks to cool completely.
1 COOKIE: 72 cal., 3g fat (2g sat. fat), 7mg chol., 46mg sod., 10g carb. (7g sugars, 1g fiber), 1g pro.

Holiday Helper

To make these cookies chocolaty, substitute ¼ cup cocoa powder for 2 Tbsp. of the flour. For the best flavor, add the cocoa powder after the eggs to bloom the chocolate. Don't go overboard on the cocoa, or the cookies may be crumbly.

SOURDOUGH OATMEAL CHOCOLATE CHIP COOKIES

My husband's family has been passing down sourdough recipes for more than 100 years. They brought them from Europe and added some American jazz over the years.
—Lisa Raymond, St. Joseph, IL

PREP: 20 min. • **BAKE:** 10 min./batch • **MAKES:** 4 dozen

- 1¼ cups packed brown sugar
- 1 cup butter, softened
- 2 cups Sourdough Starter
- 1 tsp. vanilla extract
- 2 cups all-purpose flour
- 1 tsp. baking soda
- 3½ cups quick-cooking oats
- 1½ cups semisweet chocolate chips
- ½ cup toasted chopped pecans, optional

1. Preheat oven to 350°. In a large bowl, cream brown sugar and butter until light and fluffy, 5-7 minutes. Add Sourdough Starter and vanilla; mix well. In another bowl, whisk the flour and baking soda; gradually beat into creamed mixture. Stir in oats, chocolate chips and, if desired, pecans.
2. Drop dough by tablespoonfuls 2 in. apart onto parchment-lined baking sheets. Press lightly on each cookie to flatten. Bake until set but still soft, 10-12 minutes. Cool on pans 3 minutes. Serve warm or remove to wire racks to cool completely. Store in an airtight container.
1 COOKIE: *122 cal., 6g fat (3g sat. fat), 10mg chol., 59mg sod., 17g carb. (9g sugars, 1g fiber), 2g pro.*

SOURDOUGH STARTER

In a covered 4-qt. glass or ceramic container, mix 2 cups all-purpose flour and 1 package (¼ oz.) yeast. Gradually stir in 2 cups warm (110°-115°) water until smooth. Cover loosely with a kitchen towel; let stand in a warm place 2-4 days or until mixture is bubbly and sour smelling and a clear liquid has formed on top. (Starter may darken, but if starter turns another color or develops an offensive odor or mold, discard it and start over.) Cover tightly and refrigerate starter until ready to use. Use and replenish starter, or nourish it, once every 1-2 weeks.

TO USE AND REPLENISH:
Stir in any liquid on top. Remove starter needed; bring to room temperature before using. For each ½ cup starter removed, add ½ cup flour and ½ cup warm water to the remaining starter and stir until smooth. Cover loosely and let stand in a warm place 1-2 days or until light and bubbly. Stir; cover tightly and refrigerate.

TO NOURISH:
Remove half of the starter. Stir in equal parts of flour and warm water; cover loosely and let stand in a warm place 1-2 days or until light and bubbly. Stir; cover tightly and refrigerate.

TRAVEL-WORTHY TREATS

*Whether you're preparing a care package to ship
to loved ones far away or filling a tin to carry with you
on your holiday travels, you want treats that will hold up
to the journey and still taste fresh when they arrive!*

SPICED RUM FRUITCAKE

This fruitcake not only can be made weeks ahead, it tastes better that way! You can substitute Brazil nuts, pecans and hazelnuts for the walnuts—or use a combination of nuts if you prefer.
—Jason Boor, Manchester, NY

- -

PREP: 25 min. • **BAKE:** 1¼ hours + cooling
MAKES: 1 loaf (16 pieces)

- ¾   cup all-purpose flour
- ½   tsp. baking powder
- ¼   tsp. salt
- 2   cups chopped walnuts
- 1   pkg. (8 oz.) pitted dates, chopped
- 1   cup maraschino cherries, halved
- ½   cup dried mangoes, chopped
- 3   large eggs, room temperature
- ¾   cup packed brown sugar
- 1   cup spiced rum, divided

1. Preheat oven to 300°. Line a 9x5-in. loaf pan with parchment, letting ends extend up sides of pan; grease and set aside.

2. In a large bowl, mix the flour, baking powder and salt. Add the walnuts, dates, cherries and mangoes; toss to coat. In a small bowl, whisk the eggs, brown sugar and ½ cup rum until blended; stir into fruit mixture. Transfer to prepared pan.

3. Bake until a toothpick inserted in the center comes out clean, 1¼-1½ hours. Cool in pan on a wire rack 20 minutes. Slowly pour remaining ½ cup rum over cake. Cool completely. Wrap tightly and store in a cool, dry place overnight. Cut with a serrated knife.

1 PIECE: *256 cal., 11g fat (1g sat. fat), 35mg chol., 96mg sod., 35g carb. (25g sugars, 3g fiber), 4g pro.*

Holiday Helper
Try leftover slices toasted and spread with spiced cream cheese. Fruitcake can be stored in the refrigerator for 2-3 months.

TOFFEE-COATED PEANUTS

A handful is never enough when you serve these mouthwatering nuts, so be sure to make plenty! The sweet toffee coating is enhanced with cinnamon and nutmeg.
—Julia Spence, New Braunfels, TX

- -

PREP: 10 min. • **BAKE:** 20 min. + cooling
MAKES: 3 cups

- ¼   cup sugar
- 2   Tbsp. butter, melted
- 2   Tbsp. corn syrup
- 1¼ tsp. ground cinnamon
- ¼   tsp. salt
- ¼   tsp. ground nutmeg
- 2   cups unsalted dry roasted peanuts

1. Preheat oven to 300°. In a large bowl, combine the sugar, butter, corn syrup, cinnamon, salt and nutmeg. Add the peanuts; toss to coat. Transfer to a greased 15x10x1-in. baking pan.

2. Bake until bubbly and golden brown, stirring once, 20-25 minutes. Cool in pan on a wire rack; break apart if necessary. Store in an airtight container.

¼ CUP: *186 cal., 14g fat (3g sat. fat), 5mg chol., 66mg sod., 12g carb. (6g sugars, 2g fiber), 6g pro.*

MACADAMIA-COCONUT CANDY CLUSTERS

My creamy candies are super easy to make and are ideal for bake sales, holiday gifts or cookie platters. They are a nice change from milk or dark chocolate clusters.
—*Lori Bondurant, Paducah, KY*

- -

PREP: 25 min. + standing • **MAKES:** 2 dozen

1 pkg. (10 to 12 oz.) white baking chips
2 tsp. shortening
1 cup sweetened shredded coconut, toasted
½ cup crisp rice cereal
½ cup chopped macadamia nuts, toasted

1. In a microwave, melt the baking chips and shortening; stir until smooth. Add the coconut, cereal and nuts.
2. Drop by tablespoonfuls onto waxed paper; let stand until set. Store in an airtight container at room temperature.
1 PIECE: *108 cal., 8g fat (4g sat. fat), 2mg chol., 34mg sod., 10g carb. (9g sugars, 0 fiber), 1g pro.*

LEMON BARK

I wasn't a fan of white chocolate until I made this candy. It's tangy, sweet and creamy all at the same time.
—*Diana Wing, Bountiful, UT*

- -

PREP: 10 min. + chilling • **MAKES:** 1¾ lbs.

2 pkg. (10 to 12 oz. each) white baking chips
1 cup crushed hard lemon candies, divided

1. Line a 15x10x1-in. pan with foil; set aside. In the top of a double boiler or in a metal bowl over barely simmering water, melt baking chips; stir until smooth. Stir in ⅔ cup crushed candies; spread into the prepared pan. Sprinkle with remaining ⅓ cup candies. Cool. Refrigerate until set, about 1 hour.
2. Break into pieces. Store in an airtight container.
1 OZ.: *122 cal., 7g fat (4g sat. fat), 4mg chol., 20mg sod., 15g carb. (14g sugars, 0 fiber), 1g pro.*

CALLAHAN CHRISTMAS WREATHS

When my family asked for old-fashioned Norwegian wreath cookies, I studied several recipes for ideas and then added my own touches to create a special version.
—Cassidy Callahan, Fitchburg, MA

PREP: 30 min. • **BAKE:** 10 min./batch
MAKES: 2½ dozen

- ½ cup butter, softened
- ½ cup shortening
- 1 cup sugar
- 2 large eggs, room temperature
- 2 tsp. grated orange zest
- ½ tsp. almond extract
- 3 cups all-purpose flour
  Green food coloring
  Red and green candied cherries

1. Preheat oven to 400°. In a large bowl, cream butter, shortening and sugar until light and fluffy, 5-7 minutes. Beat in eggs, orange zest and extract. Gradually beat in flour. Divide dough in half; tint 1 portion green with food coloring.

2. For each wreath, shape two 6-in. ropes using 2 tsp. plain dough for the first and 2 tsp. green dough for the other. Place the 2 ropes side by side; press together lightly, then twist several times. Shape into a circle, pinching ends to seal. Place 2 in. apart on ungreased baking sheets. Repeat with the remaining dough.

3. Cut the candied cherries into small pieces and place on wreaths to decorate as desired, pressing lightly to adhere. Bake cookies until set and bottoms are light brown, 6-8 minutes.

4. Remove from pans to wire racks to cool. Store in an airtight container.

1 COOKIE: *133 cal., 7g fat (3g sat. fat), 21mg chol., 29mg sod., 16g carb. (7g sugars, 0 fiber), 2g pro.*

> ### Holiday Helper
> Food coloring comes in several forms—liquid, liquid gel and gel paste. Gels produce more vivid colors, but they can be hard to work into cookie dough, so liquid is best for this recipe.

CHERRY PISTACHIO BARK

Flecked with red cherry bits, these diamond-shaped pieces are lovely on a sweets tray. Plus, they come together quickly with only four ingredients.
—Beth Jenkins-Horsley, Belmont, NC

PREP: 15 min. + chilling • **MAKES:** 3 lbs.

- 2 pkg. (10 to 12 oz. each) vanilla or white chips
- 12 oz. white candy coating, chopped
- 1¼ cups dried cherries, chopped
- 1¼ cups pistachios, chopped

1. Line a 15x10x1-in. pan with foil; set aside. In a microwave-safe bowl, melt chips and candy coating; stir until smooth. Stir in the cherries and pistachios. Spread into prepared pan. Refrigerate until firm, 15-20 minutes.

2. Break or cut into pieces. Store in an airtight container.

1 OZ.: *133 cal., 7g fat (4g sat. fat), 2mg chol., 25mg sod., 16g carb. (15g sugars, 0 fiber), 1g pro.*

PARMESAN-PRETZEL CRISPS

I love this recipe because I usually have the ingredients on hand and it is so easy to prepare. It's one of those snacks that makes guests think you've gone the extra mile.
—Pauline Porterfield, Roxboro, NC

PREP: 10 min. • **BAKE:** 10 min./batch
MAKES: about 3 dozen

- 1½ cups shredded Parmesan cheese
- ¼ cup finely crushed pretzels
- ⅛ tsp. crushed red pepper flakes
  Optional: Pizza sauce and sliced fresh basil

1. Preheat oven to 350°. Toss together cheese, pretzels and red pepper flakes. Place 2 tsp. mixture in each greased nonstick mini muffin cup.

2. Bake until golden brown, 10-15 minutes. If desired, serve with pizza sauce and fresh basil.

1 CRISP: *16 cal., 1g fat (1g sat. fat), 2mg chol., 66mg sod., 1g carb. (0 sugars, 0 fiber), 1g pro.*

SHARI'S EXTRA-SPICY GINGERSNAPS

My family loves spicy foods. I created this recipe so that we could enjoy some spicy heat even in a cookie. If you too crave the heat, use the full amount of cayenne pepper.
—Shari Upchurch, Lawrenceville, GA

PREP: 30 min. + chilling
BAKE: 10 min./batch • **MAKES:** 5 dozen

- ¾ cup butter, softened
- 1 cup packed brown sugar
- ¼ cup molasses
- 1 large egg, room temperature
- 2 cups all-purpose flour
- 2 tsp. ground ginger
- 1 tsp. baking soda
- 1 tsp. ground cinnamon
- ½ tsp. ground mustard
- ½ tsp. white pepper
- ½ tsp. ground cardamom
- ¼ to ½ tsp. cayenne pepper
- ¼ tsp. ground cloves
- ¼ tsp. salt
- 4½ tsp. finely chopped crystallized ginger
- 3 Tbsp. sugar

1. In a large bowl, cream butter and brown sugar until light and fluffy, 5-7 minutes. Beat in molasses and egg.
2. Combine the flour, ground ginger, baking soda, cinnamon, mustard, white pepper, cardamom, cayenne, cloves and salt; gradually add to creamed mixture and mix well. Stir in crystallized ginger. Cover and refrigerate until easy to handle, about 1½ hours.
3. Preheat oven to 350°. Shape dough into 1-in. balls; roll in sugar. Place balls 3 in. apart on ungreased baking sheets. Bake until set, 8-10 minutes. Cool 2 minutes before removing from pans to wire racks to cool completely. Store in an airtight container.

1 COOKIE: *58 cal., 2g fat (1g sat. fat), 10mg chol., 50mg sod., 9g carb. (5g sugars, 0 fiber), 1g pro.*

STOVETOP APPLE BUTTER

The taste of homemade apple butter is worth the time it takes to make. My dad's family made theirs in the backyard in a big copper kettle over a fire of burning hedge wood. It took 6 bushels of apples, 60 pounds of sugar, four cinnamon sticks, a lemon slice and some nine hours of constant stirring to make 18 gallons of apple butter—about a year's supply!
—Rev. Willis Piepenbrink, Oshkosh, WI

PREP: 25 min. • **COOK:** 8 hours
MAKES: 4 cups

- 6 to 7 lbs. tart apples, unpeeled and quartered
- 3 cups water
- 3½ cups sugar
- 1 tsp. ground cinnamon
- 1 cinnamon stick (3 in.)

1. In a Dutch oven or large stockpot, bring apples and water to a boil. Reduce heat and simmer until apples are tender. Press cooked apples through a colander or food mill. Discard peels.
2. Return pureed apples to Dutch oven. Stir in sugar, cinnamon and cinnamon stick. Simmer, uncovered, stirring frequently, until the consistency is very thick and the color is dark brown, about 8 hours. Freeze in containers.

2 TBSP.: *135 cal., 0 fat (0 sat. fat), 0 chol., 0 sod., 35g carb. (31g sugars, 2g fiber), 0 pro.*

Holiday Helper
If you like, you can place this apple butter in canning jars and process it in a boiling water bath for 15 minutes. The recipe makes 4 half pint jars.

CHEESY CAJUN CORNBREAD BISCOTTI

This savory cookie is the bestseller at our Christmas cookie bazaar. Everyone requests the tasty biscotti every year. They're simple but very delicious. I also serve them year-round as an appetizer.
—Paula Marchesi, Auburn, PA

- -

PREP: 20 min. • **BAKE:** 35 min. + cooling
MAKES: 3 dozen

- 2 pkg. (8½ oz. each) cornbread/muffin mix
- ¾ cup grated Parmigiano-Reggiano cheese
- 2 tsp. Cajun seasoning
- 1 tsp. minced fresh chives
- ½ tsp. pepper
- ¼ cup cold butter, cubed
- ¼ cup buttermilk
- 2 large eggs, beaten

TOPPING
- 1 large egg, beaten
- ¼ cup grated Parmigiano-Reggiano cheese

1. Preheat oven to 350°. Place cornbread mix, cheese, Cajun seasoning, chives and pepper in a food processor; pulse until blended. Add butter; continue pulsing until crumbly. Add buttermilk and eggs to form a moist dough (dough will be thick).
2. Divide dough in half. On a parchment-lined baking sheet, shape each portion into an 8x4-in. rectangle. Brush with beaten egg; sprinkle with cheese. Bake until light brown, 18-20 minutes. Cool on pans on wire racks until firm, about 10 minutes.
3. Reduce oven setting to 300°. Transfer baked rectangles to a cutting board. Using a serrated knife, cut crosswise into ½-in. slices. Place slices on baking sheets, cut side down.
4. Bake until golden brown, 14-16 minutes. Remove from pans to wire racks to cool completely. Store in airtight containers.
1 COOKIE: 83 cal., 4g fat (2g sat. fat), 21mg chol., 191mg sod., 10g carb. (3g sugars, 1g fiber), 2g pro.

JOT IT DOWN

Create a butcher-paper message board to keep family notes rolling! Exact measurements and size of screws will be determined by the board and hooks you choose.

WHAT YOU'LL NEED
- Wooden board
- Drill and drill bits
- Screwdriver and screws
- 2 curtain rod hooks
- Saw
- Wooden dowel (½ to ¾ in. diameter)
- 2 paint stir sticks
- Wood stain
- Hammer and brad nails
- Butcher paper roll (unwaxed)

INSTRUCTIONS
1. Pre-drill holes in the board for hooks. Screw hooks into place.
2. Cut dowel to desired length.
3. Stain dowel and stir sticks to a color of your choice; let dry.
4. Nail ends of stir sticks into place horizontally on upper and lower portions of board.
5. Slide a butcher paper roll onto the dowel; set the dowel into place on the hooks. Feed the paper behind the stir sticks.

CURRIED CRANBERRY SNACK MIX

I started making up different snack mixes because whenever my friends and I meet up for drinks, we always want a mix to munch on. This one has been requested over and over. Now I include it with most all holiday gifts.
—Robin Haas, Cranston, RI

- -

PREP: 10 min. • **COOK:** 15 min. + cooling
MAKES: 4 qt.

- 6 cups Corn Chex
- 3 cups Rice Chex
- 1 can (6 oz.) french-fried onions
- 2 cups miniature pretzels
- 1½ cups honey-roasted peanuts
- ⅓ cup butter, cubed
- 3 Tbsp. honey
- 2 Tbsp. honey mustard
- 1½ tsp. curry powder
- 1 tsp. garlic powder
- 1½ cups dried cranberries

1. In a large bowl, combine the first 5 ingredients. Place the butter, honey, honey mustard, curry powder and garlic powder in a small microwave-safe bowl. Microwave, uncovered, on high for 1-1½ minutes, stirring every 30 seconds or until mixture is smooth. Pour over cereal mixture and toss to coat.
2. Place half of the mixture in a large microwave-safe bowl. Microwave, uncovered, on high for 2-3 minutes, stirring after each minute. Stir in ¾ cup cranberries. Immediately spread onto waxed paper; cool completely. Repeat with remaining cereal mixture and ¾ cup cranberries. Store in an airtight container.

¾ **CUP:** 234 cal., 12g fat (4g sat. fat), 8mg chol., 307mg sod., 30g carb. (11g sugars, 2g fiber), 4g pro.

Holiday Helper

Curry isn't a single spice, but rather it's a blend of many different spices—and those spices vary depending on the region. Indian, Thai, Jamaican and North African cuisines—and various regional subsets—all have their own curries. Curry powder imparts a distinctive flavor and rich golden color to recipes and can be found in both mild and hot versions. Most cooks season dishes lightly with curry powder and add more as desired to reach an acceptable spice level.

GINGERBREAD CHRISTMAS CARDS

'Tis the season for mailing out cards and gift packages stuffed with homemade cookies. Why not save time and combine the two? Royal icing is the perfect backdrop to customize a heartfelt holiday greeting.
—Taste of Home *Test Kitchen*

PREP: 2 hours + standing
BAKE: 15 min./batch + cooling
MAKES: 2 dozen

- 1⅓ cups packed brown sugar
- 1⅓ cups molasses
- 2 cups cold butter, cubed
- 2 large eggs, room temperature, lightly beaten
- 8 cups all-purpose flour
- 3 Tbsp. ground ginger
- 2 Tbsp. ground cinnamon
- 4 tsp. baking soda
- 2 tsp. ground allspice
- 2 tsp. ground cloves
- 1 tsp. salt
- 1 tsp. ground cardamom

ROYAL ICING AND DECORATIONS
- 3¾ cups confectioners' sugar
- 3 Tbsp. meringue powder
- 5 Tbsp. warm water
- Edible food writing pens, optional

1. In a large saucepan over medium heat, bring brown sugar and molasses just to a boil, stirring constantly. Remove from the heat; stir in butter until melted. Stir in eggs until blended. Combine the remaining dough ingredients; stir into the brown sugar mixture. Divide dough into 4 portions. Refrigerate 30 minutes or until firm enough to roll.

2. Preheat oven to 325°. On a lightly floured surface, roll out each portion of dough to ⅛-in. thickness. Cut with a floured 3x5-in. rectangular cookie cutter. Place 2 in. apart on greased baking sheets. Bake until set, 10-12 minutes. Remove to wire racks to cool.

3. For icing, in a large bowl, combine confectioners' sugar, meringue powder and water; beat on low speed just until combined. Beat on high for 4-5 minutes or until stiff peaks form. Add additional water as necessary to achieve desired consistency. Keep icing covered at all times with a damp cloth. If necessary, beat again on high speed to restore texture.

4. Frost cookies and let dry completely. Decorate cookies as desired using edible writing pens.

1 COOKIE: *472 cal., 16g fat (10g sat. fat), 56mg chol., 456mg sod., 77g carb. (44g sugars, 2g fiber), 6g pro.*

SNACKERS

These crispy, chewy treats pack lots of peanut flavor. They're our favorite travel snack. I always make a double batch so we have some left when we reach our destination.
—W.H. Gregory, Roanoke, VA

TAKES: 20 min. • **MAKES:** about 1½ dozen

- 3 cups Crispix cereal
- ½ cup salted peanuts
- ⅓ cup packed brown sugar
- ⅓ cup corn syrup
- ¼ cup peanut butter

In a large bowl, combine cereal and peanuts; set aside. In a microwave-safe bowl, combine brown sugar and corn syrup. Microwave until sugar is dissolved, 30-60 seconds, stirring several times. Immediately stir in peanut butter until smooth. Pour over cereal mixture and toss to coat. Drop by rounded tablespoonfuls onto waxed paper. Cool.

1 PIECE: *97 cal., 4g fat (1g sat. fat), 0 chol., 65mg sod., 15g carb. (10g sugars, 1g fiber), 2g pro.*

> ### Holiday Helper
> If you prefer, you can use unsalted peanuts for this recipe, and adjust the salt level to taste.

SPICY PECAN BRITTLE

This delectable combination of spicy, salty, and sweet flavors is easy to make and package as gifts. Do not use pure maple syrup, as it burns at a lower temperature than corn syrup (the main ingredient in pancake syrup). If you don't have maple-flavored pancake syrup, use corn syrup and add maple extract.
—Beth McGee, Pinckney, MI

PREP: 10 min. • **COOK:** 40 min. + cooling
MAKES: 1¼ lbs.

- 1 **tsp. plus ½ cup butter**
- ½ **tsp. salt**
- ¼ **tsp. baking soda**
- ¼ **tsp. cayenne pepper**
- 1 **cup sugar**
- ½ **cup water**
- ¼ **cup light corn syrup**
- ¼ **cup maple pancake syrup**
- 1¼ **cups chopped pecans**

1. Line a 15x10x1-in. baking pan with foil. Grease foil with 1 tsp. butter; set aside. In a small bowl, combine salt, baking soda and cayenne pepper; set aside.
2. In a large heavy saucepan, combine sugar, water and syrups. Bring to a boil, stirring constantly to dissolve sugar. Using a pastry brush dipped in water, wash down the sides of the pan to eliminate sugar crystals. Cook, without stirring, over medium heat until a candy thermometer reads 260° (hard-ball stage). Stir in pecans and the remaining ½ cup butter; cook until thermometer reads 300° (hard-crack stage), stirring frequently, about 9 minutes longer.
3. Remove from heat; stir in baking soda mixture (mixture will foam). Immediately pour onto prepared pan, spreading as thin as possible. Cool completely.
4. Break brittle into pieces. Store between layers of waxed paper in an airtight container.
1 OZ.: *151 cal., 10g fat (3g sat. fat), 13mg chol., 123mg sod., 17g carb. (15g sugars, 1g fiber), 1g pro.*

SESAME CHEESE CRACKERS

Enjoy these irresistible homemade crackers with soups, or munch on them by themselves. The cayenne pepper adds a bit of a kick, so add as much or as little pepper as you like.
—Margaret Inlow, Joliet, IL

PREP: 25 min. + chilling • **BAKE:** 15 min.
MAKES: 77 crackers

- 1 **cup all-purpose flour**
- ½ **tsp. salt**
- ⅛ **to ¼ tsp. cayenne pepper**
- 6 **Tbsp. cold butter**
- 1 **cup finely shredded cheddar cheese**
- ¼ **cup sesame seeds, toasted**
- 6 **to 7½ tsp. ice water, divided**
- ½ **tsp. soy sauce**

1. In a small bowl, whisk flour, salt and cayenne; cut in butter until mixture resembles coarse crumbs. Stir in cheese and sesame seeds. Combine 3 tsp. water and the soy sauce; stir into dry ingredients with a fork. Stir in enough remaining water until dough forms a ball. Wrap and refrigerate until firm, 1 hour.
2. Preheat oven to 400°. On a floured surface, roll dough into a 14x11-in. rectangle. Cut into 2x1-in. strips. Place strips on lightly greased baking sheets. Bake until golden brown, 12-15 minutes. Remove to wire racks to cool.
1 CRACKER: *23 cal., 2g fat (1g sat. fat), 4mg chol., 38mg sod., 2g carb. (0 sugars, 0 fiber), 1g pro.*

OUR FAVORITE THINGS

So what do we at Taste of Home serve up for our own holiday celebrations? This chapter spotlights some treasured recipes created by staff members and our Test Kitchen experts.

REINDEER SNACK MIX

Rudolph and his pals will be dashing, dancing and prancing to gobble up this savory snack mix. Humans also will enjoy the buttery, perfectly seasoned and wonderfully crunchy combination.
—Taste of Home *Test Kitchen*

- -

PREP: 10 min. • **BAKE:** 1 hour + cooling
MAKES: 12 servings (2¼ qt.)

- 2 cups Bugles
- 2 cups pretzel sticks
- 2 cups cheese-flavored snack crackers
- 1 cup bite-sized shredded wheat
- 1 cup Corn Chex
- 1 cup pecan halves
- ½ cup butter, cubed
- 1 Tbsp. maple syrup
- 1½ tsp. Worcestershire sauce
- ¾ tsp. Cajun seasoning
- ¼ tsp. cayenne pepper

1. Preheat oven to 250°. Place the first 6 ingredients in a large bowl. In a microwave, melt butter; stir in remaining ingredients. Drizzle over snack mixture; toss to combine. Transfer to an ungreased 15x10x1-in. pan.
2. Bake 1 hour, stirring every 15 minutes. Cool completely before storing in an airtight container.
¾ CUP: *239 cal., 16g fat (6g sat. fat), 21mg chol., 331mg sod., 22g carb. (2g sugars, 2g fiber), 3g pro.*

CRUNCHY HONEY-GLAZED BUTTERNUT SQUASH

I'm now required to bring this to every family gathering during the holidays because it's so awesome! Why not start a new tradition for your family?
—Sarah Farmer, Executive Culinary Director

- -

PREP: 20 min. • **BAKE:** 45 min.
MAKES: 10 servings

- ½ cup honey
- 1 tsp. dried thyme, divided
- 1 large butternut squash (about 5 lbs.), peeled, halved, seeded and thinly sliced
- 3 Tbsp. water
- ¼ cup plus 2 Tbsp. olive oil, divided
- 1½ tsp. salt, divided
- 1½ tsp. pepper, divided
- ½ cup panko bread crumbs

1. Preheat oven to 375°. In a large saucepan, heat honey and ½ tsp. thyme, stirring occasionally, over low heat until fragrant, 3-4 minutes.
2. Meanwhile, in a large microwave-safe dish, combine the squash and water; microwave, covered, on high until squash is tender, 6-8 minutes. Drain. Add ¼ cup olive oil, 1 tsp. salt and 1 tsp. pepper; toss to coat.
3. On a flat surface, stack squash slices. Arrange stacks on their sides in a greased 9-in. square baking dish. (To make stacking easier, set baking dish on end; fill with squash stacks. When dish is full, return to original position.) Drizzle 3 Tbsp. honey mixture over squash.
4. Bake until the squash is tender, 45-50 minutes. In a small skillet, heat remaining 2 Tbsp. oil over medium heat. Add bread crumbs; toss with remaining ½ tsp. thyme, ½ tsp. salt and ½ tsp. pepper. Cook and stir until golden brown, about 5 minutes. Sprinkle over baked squash; if desired, drizzle with additional honey mixture.
1 SERVING: *237 cal., 8g fat (1g sat. fat), 0 chol., 373mg sod., 43g carb. (20g sugars, 8g fiber), 3g pro.*

Holiday Helper
If you like some heat, spice this up by adding 1 or 2 sliced Thai chile peppers to the honey mixture when heating. Be careful, though—these peppers are spicy! Swap sweet potatoes for the squash, or make it with both.

CRAN-APPLE PIE

Our home economists capture delectable harvest flavors in this pretty lattice pie that's perfect for a holiday table.
—James Schend, Deputy Editor, Culinary

- -

PREP: 40 min. + chilling
BAKE: 50 min. + cooling • **MAKES:** 8 servings

- 2 cups all-purpose flour
- 1 cup cake flour
- 3 Tbsp. sugar
- 1¼ tsp. salt
- ½ tsp. baking powder
- 8 Tbsp. lard, cut into small cubes
- 8 Tbsp. unsalted butter, cut into small cubes
- 1 large egg yolk
- 10 to 12 Tbsp. ice water

FILLING
- 5 cups thinly sliced peeled tart apples
- ¾ cup plus 2 Tbsp. apple juice, divided
- ¾ cup sugar
- ¾ tsp. ground cinnamon
- ¼ tsp. salt
- ¼ tsp. ground nutmeg
- 3 Tbsp. cornstarch
- 2 cups fresh cranberries

EGG WASH
- 1 large egg, lightly beaten
- 1 Tbsp. 2% milk

1. In a large bowl, combine all-purpose flour, cake flour, sugar, salt and baking powder; cover and freeze 30 minutes. Place lard and butter in a separate bowl; freeze 30 minutes. Place flour mixture in a food processor; pulse until blended. Add lard and butter; pulse until mixture is the size of peas.

2. Transfer flour mixture to a large bowl. Mix together egg yolk and 10 Tbsp. ice water; gradually add to flour mixture. Toss with a fork until the dough holds together when pressed, adding more water if needed. Divide dough into thirds. Shape each into a disk; wrap and refrigerate for 1 hour or overnight.

3. In a large saucepan, combine apples, ¾ cup apple juice, the sugar, cinnamon, salt and nutmeg; bring to a boil over medium heat, stirring occasionally. Combine cornstarch and remaining 2 Tbsp. juice until smooth; add to saucepan. Return to a boil, stirring

constantly. Cook and stir 1 minute or until thickened. Remove from the heat; let cool to room temperature. Stir in the cranberries.

4. On a lightly floured surface, roll 1 dough portion into a ⅛-in.-thick circle; transfer to a 9-in. pie plate. Trim crust even with rim. Pour fruit filling into crust.

5. Roll out second portion of dough; make a lattice crust. Place over filling. Trim and seal edge.

6. Roll out last third of dough to a 14x4-in. rectangle. Cut four 14x¼-in. strips. Place 2 strips side by side; twist together. Repeat with remaining 2 strips. Combine egg and milk; lightly brush lattice and edge of crust with egg wash. Place twists along edge of crust; press lightly to adhere.

7. For decorative cutouts, cut remaining dough out with a 1½-in. leaf-shaped cookie cutter. With a sharp knife, lightly score cutouts to resemble veins on leaves. Overlap cutouts on top of the lattice and along the edge of the pie; use egg wash to adhere. Refrigerate pie until crust is well chilled, about 30 minutes.

8. Preheat oven to 400°. Brush cutouts with egg wash. Cover edge loosely with foil coated with cooking spray. Bake 20 minutes. Remove foil; bake until crust is golden brown and filling is bubbly, 30-40 minutes longer. Cool on a wire rack.

1 PIECE: *489 cal., 22g fat (6g sat. fat), 23mg chol., 307mg sod., 67g carb. (30g sugars, 3g fiber), 6g pro.*

THE BEST EVER CHILI

After my honeymoon in New Mexico, inspired by the fragrant chile peppers at the Santa Fe farmers market, I introduced my family to this spicy, meaty chili with a touch of masa harina. It takes a little extra work, but is totally worth the effort!
—Sarah Farmer, Executive Culinary Director

- -

PREP: 20 min. + standing
COOK: 1 hour 20 min.
MAKES: 8 servings (3½ qt.)

- 3   dried ancho or guajillo chiles
- 1   to 2 cups boiling water
- 2   Tbsp. tomato paste
- 3   garlic cloves
- ¼   cup chili powder
- 1½ tsp. smoked paprika
- 2   tsp. ground cumin
- 1   lb. ground beef
- 1½ tsp. Montreal steak seasoning
- 2   lbs. beef tri-tip roast, cut into ½-in. cubes
- 2   tsp. salt, divided
- 2   tsp. coarsely ground pepper, divided
- 2   Tbsp. canola oil, divided
- 1   large onion, chopped (about 2 cups)
- 1   poblano pepper, seeded and chopped
- 1   tsp. dried oregano
- 1½ tsp. crushed red pepper flakes
- 3   cups beef stock
- 1   bottle (12 oz.) beer
- 2   cans (14½ oz. each) fire-roasted diced tomatoes, undrained
- 1   can (16 oz.) kidney beans, drained
- 3   Tbsp. masa harina
     Optional: American cheese slices, sour cream, shredded cheddar cheese, diced red onion, sliced jalapenos, cilantro and corn chips

1. Combine chiles and enough boiling water to cover; let stand until softened, about 15 minutes. Drain, reserving ⅓ cup of the soaking liquid. Discard stems and seeds. Process chiles, tomato paste, garlic and reserved liquid until smooth.
2. In a small skillet, toast chili powder, paprika and cumin over medium heat until aromatic, 3-4 minutes; remove and set aside. In a Dutch oven, cook and stir ground beef and steak seasoning over medium-high heat until beef is no longer pink, about 5 minutes; remove and drain.

3. Sprinkle steak cubes with 1 tsp. each salt and pepper. In the same Dutch oven, brown steak in batches in 1 Tbsp. oil over medium-high heat; remove and set aside.
4. Saute onion and poblano pepper in the remaining 1 Tbsp. oil until tender, about 5 minutes. Stir in toasted spices, oregano and pepper flakes. Add the cooked meats along with stock, beer, tomatoes, beans, remaining 1 tsp. salt and 1 tsp. pepper, and the chile paste mixture. Cook over medium heat 20 minutes.
5. Reduce heat to low. Stir in masa harina and simmer 30-45 minutes longer. Serve with desired toppings.
1¾ CUPS: 473 cal., 20g fat (6g sat. fat), 103mg chol., 1554mg sod., 29g carb. (8g sugars, 7g fiber), 41g pro.

Holiday Helper

Adding the masa harina at the end helps thicken the chili and give it a subtle corn flavor. While this chili is fantastic right out of the pot, as with a lot of soups, stews and other chilis, it tastes even better the next day. For a smart make-ahead option, double the batch and freeze the leftovers in individual portions. They'll keep for at least 6 months.

BISCOFF DRINKING CHOCOLATE

This is a deliciously different version of hot chocolate your family will love. When you're ready to serve, you can top each cup with a whole cookie or crumbled cookie pieces for a sweet touch.
—James Schend, Deputy Editor, Culinary

- -

TAKES: 20 min. • **MAKES:** 5 cups

- 4   cups half-and-half cream
- 7   oz. 70% cacao dark chocolate, chopped
- 2   oz. milk chocolate, chopped
- ⅓   cup Biscoff creamy cookie spread
     Dash salt
     Sweetened whipped cream and Biscoff cookies

In a large saucepan, heat cream over medium heat until bubbles form around side of pan (do not boil). Remove from the heat; whisk in the chocolates, cookie spread and salt until smooth. Return to heat; cook and stir until heated through. Immediately pour into mugs; top with whipped cream and cookies.
1 CUP: 582 cal., 41g fat (24g sat. fat), 105mg chol., 130mg sod., 46g carb. (39g sugars, 4g fiber), 10g pro.

FOCACCIA SANDWICHES

Slices of this pretty sandwich make any casual get-together more special. Add or change ingredients to your taste.
—Peggy Woodward, Senior Food Editor

TAKES: 15 min. • **MAKES:** 2 dozen

- ⅓ cup mayonnaise
- 1 can (4¼ oz.) chopped ripe olives, drained
- 1 focaccia bread (about 12 oz.), split
- 4 romaine leaves
- ¼ lb. shaved deli ham
- 1 medium sweet red pepper, thinly sliced into rings
- ¼ lb. shaved deli turkey
- 1 large tomato, thinly sliced
- ¼ lb. thinly sliced hard salami
- 1 jar (7 oz.) roasted sweet red peppers, drained
- 4 to 6 slices provolone cheese

In a small bowl, combine mayonnaise and olives; spread over the bottom half of bread. Layer with remaining ingredients; replace bread top. Cut into 24 pieces; secure with toothpicks.

NOTE: *A rectangular-shaped focaccia bread, measuring about 12x8 in., works best for this sandwich.*

1 PIECE: *113 cal., 6g fat (2g sat. fat), 13mg chol., 405mg sod., 9g carb. (1g sugars, 1g fiber), 5g pro.*

PUMPKIN PECAN WHOOPIE PIES

These whoopie pies are full of pumpkin flavor—a perfect seasonal treat! For a finishing touch, I like to roll the outside edges in mini chocolate chips or chopped nuts and dust with cinnamon sugar.
—Rashanda Cobbins, Food Editor

PREP: 30 min. + chilling
BAKE: 10 min./batch + cooling
MAKES: 20 servings

- 3¼ cups all-purpose flour
- 1½ cups sugar
- 2 tsp. baking powder
- 2 tsp. baking soda
- 1½ tsp. ground cinnamon
- 1 tsp. ground nutmeg
- 1 tsp. ground cloves
- ½ tsp. salt
- 5 large eggs, room temperature
- 1 can (15 oz.) pumpkin
- ½ cup water
- ½ cup canola oil
- 1 tsp. vanilla extract

FILLING
- 6 Tbsp. all-purpose flour
- 1 dash salt
- 1 cup plus 2 Tbsp. unsweetened almond milk
- 1½ cups shortening
- 3 cups confectioners' sugar
- 3 tsp. vanilla extract

Optional: Toasted chopped pecans, miniature semisweet chocolate chips and ground cinnamon

1. Preheat oven to 350°. In a large bowl, combine flour, sugar, baking powder, baking soda, cinnamon, nutmeg, cloves and salt. In another bowl, whisk the eggs, pumpkin, water, oil and vanilla. Stir into the dry ingredients just until moistened.
2. Drop by 2 tablespoonfuls 2 in. apart onto parchment-lined baking sheets. Bake for 8-10 minutes. Remove to wire racks to cool completely.
3. For filling, combine the flour and salt in a small saucepan. Gradually whisk in milk until smooth; bring to a boil over medium-high heat. Reduce heat to medium; cook and stir until thickened, about 2 minutes. Refrigerate, covered, until completely cooled.
4. In another bowl, beat shortening, confectioners' sugar and vanilla until smooth. Add cooled milk mixture; beat until light and fluffy, about 7 minutes. Spread about 3 Tbsp. filling on the bottom of half the cookies; cover with the remaining cookies. Store in the refrigerator. If desired, roll filled pies in pecans or chocolate chips and sprinkle with additional cinnamon.

1 WHOOPIE PIE: *424 cal., 22g fat (5g sat. fat), 47mg chol., 277mg sod., 53g carb. (34g sugars, 1g fiber), 4g pro.*

DUTCH-OVEN RAISIN WALNUT BREAD

On a cold day, nothing is better than a warm, crusty bread filled with raisins and walnuts.
—Catherine Ward, Prep Kitchen Manager

- -

PREP: 15 min. + rising
BAKE: 50 min.
MAKES: 1 loaf (32 pieces)

  6   to 7 cups all-purpose flour
  ¼   cup sugar
  2   tsp. active dry yeast
  2   tsp. ground cinnamon
  2   tsp. salt
  1   cup raisins
  1   cup chopped walnuts
  3   cups cool water (70° to 75°)

1. In a large bowl, whisk 6 cups flour, the sugar, yeast, cinnamon and salt. Stir in raisins and walnuts; add water and enough of the remaining flour to form a moist, shaggy dough. Do not knead. Cover and let rise in a cool place until doubled, 7-8 hours.

2. Preheat oven to 450°; place a Dutch oven with lid onto center rack and heat for at least 30 minutes. Once Dutch oven is heated, turn dough onto a generously floured surface. Using a metal scraper or spatula, quickly shape into a round loaf. Gently place loaf on top of a piece of parchment.

3. Using a sharp knife, make a slash (¼ in. deep) across top of loaf. Using the parchment, immediately lower bread into heated Dutch oven. Cover; bake for 30 minutes.

4. Uncover; bake until loaf is deep golden brown and sounds hollow when tapped, 20-30 minutes longer, partially covering if it is browning too much. Remove loaf from Dutch oven and cool on wire rack.

1 PIECE: *130 cal., 3g fat (0 sat. fat), 0 chol., 149mg sod., 24g carb. (4g sugars, 1g fiber), 3g pro.*

> ## *Holiday Helper*
> This soft, gentle dough should be baked immediately after shaping. Preheating the Dutch oven and working quickly are keys to success.

NO-BAKE CHRISTMAS WREATH TREATS

Cornflakes take the place of traditional rice cereal in these sweet no-bake treats. Dressed up with green food coloring and red candies, they're a pretty addition to cookie platters and dessert buffets.
—Taste of Home *Test Kitchen*

- -

PREP: 20 min. + standing • **COOK:** 5 min.
MAKES: 8 servings

  20   large marshmallows
  2   Tbsp. butter
       Green food coloring
  3   cups cornflakes
       Red M&M's minis (about 2 Tbsp.)

1. Place marshmallows and butter in a microwave-safe bowl; microwave, uncovered, on high until the butter is melted and marshmallows are puffed, about 45 seconds. Tint with green food coloring. Stir in cornflakes.

2. On a waxed paper-lined baking sheet, divide mixture into 8 portions. With buttered hands, working quickly, shape each portion into a 3-in. wreath. Decorate immediately with M&M's, pressing to adhere. Let stand until set.

1 WREATH: *134 cal., 4g fat (2g sat. fat), 9mg chol., 116mg sod., 25g carb. (13g sugars, 0 fiber), 1g pro.*

BAKED FETA PASTA

There's a reason this recipe went viral on TikTok! It's simple to throw together and incredibly creamy and delicious—just the thing for a busy week when you've got a ton of other things going on!
—Sarah Tramonte, Associate Culinary Producer

PREP: 5 min. • **BAKE:** 30 min. • **MAKES:** 8 servings

- 2   pints cherry tomatoes
- 3   garlic cloves, halved
- ½   cup olive oil
- 1   pkg. (8 oz.) block feta cheese
- 1   tsp. sea salt
- ¼   tsp. coarsely ground pepper
- 1   pkg. (16 oz.) rigatoni or other short pasta
      Fresh basil leaves, coarsely chopped

1. Preheat oven to 400°. In a 13x9-in. baking dish, combine the tomatoes, garlic and ¼ cup olive oil. Place the block of feta in the center, moving tomatoes so the cheese is sitting on the pan bottom. Drizzle feta with remaining ¼ cup oil and sprinkle with salt and pepper. Bake until tomato skins start to split and the garlic has softened, 30-40 minutes.
2. Meanwhile, cook pasta according to package directions for al dente. Drain, reserving 1 cup pasta water.
3. Stir feta mixture, lightly pressing tomatoes, until combined. Add pasta and toss to combine. Stir in enough reserved pasta water to achieve desired consistency. Sprinkle with basil.
1 SERVING: *373 cal., 16g fat (6g sat. fat), 25mg chol., 507mg sod., 46g carb. (5g sugars, 3g fiber), 12g pro.*

BAKER'S DOZEN YEAST ROLLS

A yummy honey-garlic topping turns these easy dinner rolls into something extra special.
—Taste of Home *Test Kitchen*

PREP: 25 min. + rising • **BAKE:** 15 min. • **MAKES:** 13 rolls

- 2   to 2½ cups all-purpose flour
- 2   Tbsp. sugar
- 1   pkg. (¼ oz.) quick-rise yeast
- ½   tsp. salt
- ¾   cup warm water (120° to 130°)
- 2   Tbsp. plus 4 tsp. butter, melted, divided
- ¾   cup shredded sharp cheddar cheese
- 2   tsp. honey
- ⅛   tsp. garlic salt

1. In a large bowl, combine 1½ cups flour, the sugar, yeast and salt. Add water and 2 Tbsp. butter; beat on medium speed for 3 minutes or until smooth. Stir in cheese and enough remaining flour to form a soft dough.
2. Turn onto a lightly floured surface; knead until smooth and elastic, 4-6 minutes. Cover and let rest for 10 minutes. Divide dough into 13 pieces; shape each piece into a ball. Place balls in a greased 9-in. round baking pan. Cover and let rise in a warm place until doubled, about 30 minutes.
3. Preheat oven to 375°. Bake rolls 11-14 minutes or until lightly browned. Combine honey, garlic salt and remaining 4 tsp. butter; brush over rolls. Remove from pan to wire rack to cool.
1 ROLL: *131 cal., 5g fat (3g sat. fat), 15mg chol., 169mg sod., 18g carb. (3g sugars, 1g fiber), 4g pro.*

HOMEMADE LEMON CURD

Lemon curd is a scrumptious spread for scones, biscuits or other baked goods. You can find it in stores with the jams and jellies, but we like making it from scratch.
—Mark Hagen, Executive Editor

- -

PREP: 20 min. + chilling • **MAKES:** 1⅔ cups

3 large eggs
1 cup sugar
½ cup fresh lemon juice (about 2 lemons)
¼ cup butter, cubed
1 Tbsp. grated lemon zest

In a small heavy saucepan over medium heat, whisk eggs, sugar and lemon juice until blended. Add butter and lemon zest; cook, whisking constantly, until mixture is thickened and coats the back of a metal spoon. Transfer to a small glass bowl; cool for 10 minutes. Cover with plastic wrap, smoothing the wrap against the surface of the curd to prevent a skin from forming. Refrigerate until cold.

2 TBSP.: *110 cal., 5g fat (3g sat. fat), 52mg chol., 45mg sod., 16g carb. (16g sugars, 0 fiber), 2g pro.*

Holiday Helper

- Don't use aluminum or unlined copper pans when making curd; they could react with the acid in the lemons, discoloring the curd and leaving a metallic aftertaste.
- This recipe and method will work with any citrus fruit; try it with limes, oranges or grapefruit for a little variety. Blood oranges will produce a lovely, rose-colored curd.
- Lemon curd can be made up to 7 days in advance and kept in the refrigerator. To freeze curd, place it in an airtight container and store in the freezer for up to 2 months. Thaw it in the fridge overnight, and use up within 1 week.

CLASSIC CHEESECLOTH TURKEY

This turkey uses a classic method, wine-soaked cheesecloth, to give you the juiciest turkey and most flavorful gravy you've ever tasted! The cheesecloth not only adds an extra layer of flavor but also locks in moisture, reducing the need for basting as often. Pair with your favorite sides for a complete meal.
—Rashanda Cobbins, Food Editor

PREP: 30 minutes
BAKE: 3¾ hours + standing
MAKES: 24 servings (4 cups gravy)

- 1 turkey (14 to 16 lbs.)
- ½ cup butter, softened
- 3 Tbsp. minced fresh thyme
- 3 Tbsp. minced fresh sage
- 1 tsp. salt
- 1 tsp. pepper
- 2 celery ribs, quartered
- 1 medium onion, chopped
- 1 medium carrot, quartered
- 1 cup butter, cubed
- 2 cups white wine

GRAVY
- 2 to 3 cups chicken broth
- 5 Tbsp. all-purpose flour

1. Preheat oven to 325°. Remove giblets from turkey; cover and refrigerate for gravy. Pat turkey dry; place breast side up on a rack in a roasting pan. In small bowl, combine softened butter, thyme and sage. With fingers, carefully loosen skin from turkey breast; rub butter mixture under the skin. Sprinkle salt and pepper over turkey and inside cavity; fill cavity with celery, onion and carrot.
2. In a large saucepan, melt cubed butter; stir in wine. Saturate a 4-layered, 17-in. square of cheesecloth in the butter mixture; drape over turkey. Bake turkey, uncovered, 3 hours; baste with wine mixture every 30 minutes, keeping cheesecloth moist at all times.
3. Remove and discard the cheesecloth. Bake turkey until a thermometer inserted in the thigh reads 170°-175°, basting occasionally with the pan drippings, 45 minutes to 1¼ hours longer. (Cover loosely with foil if the turkey browns too quickly).

4. Remove turkey to a serving platter. Discard vegetables from cavity. Pour drippings and loosened brown bits into a measuring cup. Skim fat, reserving ⅓ cup. Add enough broth to remaining drippings to measure 4 cups. Cover turkey and let stand 20 minutes before carving.
5. For gravy, chop reserved giblets. In a large saucepan, saute giblets in reserved fat until browned. Stir in flour until blended; gradually stir in broth mixture. Bring to a boil; cook and stir 2 minutes or until thickened. Serve with turkey.

6 OZ. COOKED TURKEY WITH ABOUT 3 TBSP. GRAVY: *354 cal., 16g fat (5g sat. fat), 149mg chol., 302mg sod., 3g carb. (1g sugars, 0 fiber), 43g pro.*

> ### Holiday Helper
> Cheesecloth comes in a variety of grades based on the looseness or tightness of the weave. For this recipe, any grade works because the cheesecloth is primarily acting to keep moisture consistently on the turkey as it bakes.

SPICED AMARETTO CRANBERRY SAUCE

Looking to elevate your holiday cranberry sauce? Try adding a touch of amaretto. The almond flavor supplies a distinctive note that will have people guessing what you've added.
—James Schend, Deputy Editor, Culinary

TAKES: 25 min. • **MAKES:** 2 cups

- 2 cups fresh or frozen cranberries
- ½ cup maple syrup
- ½ cup honey
- 1 Tbsp. grated orange zest
- 1 tsp. apple pie spice
- ¼ cup amaretto
  Toasted sliced almonds, optional

In a large saucepan, combine cranberries, syrup, honey, orange zest and pie spice. Cook over medium heat until the berries pop, about 15 minutes. Stir in amaretto; cook 5 minutes. Cover and store in the refrigerator. If desired, top with almonds before serving.

2 TBSP.: *78 cal., 0 fat (0 sat. fat), 0 chol., 2mg sod., 18g carb. (17g sugars, 1g fiber), 0 pro.*

SPANISH-STYLE PAELLA

If you enjoy cooking traditional ethnic foods, this hearty rice dish is a great one. It's brimming with generous chunks of sausage, shrimp and veggies.
—Taste of Home *Test Kitchen*

PREP: 10 min. • **COOK:** 35 min.
MAKES: 8 servings

- ½ lb. Spanish chorizo links, sliced
- ½ lb. boneless skinless chicken breasts, cubed
- 1 Tbsp. olive oil
- 1 garlic clove, minced
- 1 cup uncooked short grain rice
- 1 cup chopped onion
- 1½ cups chicken broth
- 1 can (14½ oz.) stewed tomatoes, undrained
- ½ tsp. paprika
- ¼ tsp. ground cayenne pepper
- ¼ tsp. salt
- 10 strands saffron, crushed or ⅛ tsp. ground saffron
- ½ lb. uncooked medium shrimp, peeled and deveined
- ½ cup sweet red pepper strips
- ½ cup green pepper strips
- ½ cup frozen peas
  Optional: Minced fresh parsley and lemon wedges

1. In a large saucepan or skillet over medium-high heat, cook sausage and chicken in oil for 5 minutes or until sausage is lightly browned and chicken is no longer pink, stirring frequently. Add garlic; cook 1 minute longer. Drain if necessary.
2. Stir in rice and onion. Cook until the onion is tender and rice is lightly browned, stirring frequently. Add broth, tomatoes, paprika, cayenne, salt and saffron. Bring to a boil. Reduce heat to low; cover and cook for 10 minutes.
3. Stir in the shrimp, peppers and peas. Cover and cook 10 minutes longer or until rice is tender, shrimp turn pink and liquid is absorbed. If desired, top with fresh parsley and lemon wedges.
1 CUP: *237 cal., 7g fat (2g sat. fat), 62mg chol., 543mg sod., 27g carb. (5g sugars, 2g fiber), 16g pro.*

BOK CHOY SALAD

Depending on what I have at home, I sometimes use only the sunflower kernels or almonds in this salad. The recipe makes a big amount, perfect for get-togethers.
—Stephanie Marchese, *Executive Director*

TAKES: 25 min. • **MAKES:** 10 servings

- 1 head bok choy, finely chopped
- 2 bunches green onions, thinly sliced
- 2 pkg. (3 oz. each) ramen noodles, broken
- ¼ cup slivered almonds
- 2 Tbsp. sunflower kernels
- ¼ cup butter

DRESSING
- ⅓ to ½ cup sugar
- ½ cup canola oil
- 2 Tbsp. cider vinegar
- 1 Tbsp. soy sauce

1. In a large bowl, combine bok choy and green onions. Save seasoning packet from ramen noodles for another use. In a large skillet, saute the noodles, almonds and sunflower kernels in butter until browned, about 7 minutes. Remove from the heat; cool to room temperature. Add to bok choy mixture.
2. In a jar with a tight-fitting lid, combine the dressing ingredients; shake well. Just before serving, drizzle over salad and toss to coat.
¾ CUP: *240 cal., 19g fat (5g sat. fat), 12mg chol., 386mg sod., 16g carb. (8g sugars, 2g fiber), 4g pro.*

Holiday Helper

When making a raw salad, look for baby bok choy—it will give your dish maximum flavor. If using regular bok choy, discard the root end; if using baby bok choy, that end is edible, too!

MELTING SNOWMAN

After an afternoon of sledding, kids will love to warm up with hot chocolate and these special snowman toppers. The snowmen will disappear as they sip and so will the chill on their fingers and toes!
—Taste of Home *Test Kitchen*

- -

PREP: 10 min. + freezing • **MAKES:** 1 dozen

- ¾ cup whipped topping
  Miniature semisweet chocolate chips
  Orange jimmies
  Hot cocoa

Using a small cookie scoop, drop tablespoons of whipped topping onto a waxed paper-lined baking sheet. Decorate with chocolate chips and jimmies to create faces. Freeze until firm. Place a snowman on top of a mug of hot cocoa just before serving.
1 SNOWMAN: 13 cal., 1g fat (1g sat. fat), 0 chol., 0 sod., 1g carb. (1g sugars, 0 fiber), 0 pro.

> ### *Holiday Helper*
> You can make these little snowmen in advance and have them ready for when the weather turns icy. Once they're frozen, they'll keep in the freezer for up to 1 month.

YETI COOKIES

When the weather outside is frightful, these smiley guys are so delightful. Let it snow!
—Shannon Norris, Senior Food Stylist

- -

PREP: 45 min. + chilling
BAKE: 10 min./batch + cooling
MAKES: 1½ dozen

- ½ cup butter, softened
- ½ cup sugar
- 1 large egg, room temperature
- ¾ tsp. vanilla extract
- ¼ tsp. almond extract
- 1¾ cups all-purpose flour
- ½ tsp. ground cinnamon
- ¼ tsp. salt
- ¼ tsp. baking powder
- 1 can (16 oz.) vanilla frosting
- 1 cup white sprinkles
- ¾ cup blue decorating icing
- ¼ cup black decorating icing
- 36 candy eyes
  Optional: Additional sprinkles and candies

1. In a large bowl, cream butter and sugar until light and fluffy, 5-7 minutes. Beat in egg and extracts. In another bowl, whisk flour, cinnamon, salt and baking powder; gradually beat into the creamed mixture. Shape into a disk; cover and refrigerate until firm enough to roll, about 1 hour.
2. On a lightly floured surface, roll the dough to ⅛-in. thickness. Cut with a floured 4-in. gingerbread man cookie cutter. Place 1 in. apart on ungreased baking sheets. Bake at 350° until light brown, 9–11 minutes. Remove from pans to wire racks to cool completely.
3. Spread cookies with vanilla frosting; decorate with sprinkles. Add face, hands and feet with blue icing; add mouth with black icing. Use additional sprinkles for teeth; add eyes. If desired, add additional sprinkles or candies for decoration.
TO MAKE AHEAD: *Dough can be made 2 days in advance. Store in an airtight container in the refrigerator.*
1 COOKIE: *345 cal., 14g fat (6g sat. fat), 24mg chol., 173mg sod., 52g carb. (36g sugars, 0 fiber), 2g pro.*

MILE-HIGH CHICKEN POTPIE

Classic chicken potpie gets extra homey when it's loaded with a creamy filling and baked tall in a springform pan. This deep-dish marvel is perfect for special family dinners.
—*Shannon Norris, Senior Food Stylist*

- -

PREP: 40 min. + chilling
BAKE: 50 min. + cooling
MAKES: 6 servings

- 1 large egg, separated
- 4 to 6 Tbsp. cold water, divided
- 2 cups all-purpose flour
- ¼ tsp. salt
- ⅔ cup cold butter, cubed

FILLING
- 3 Tbsp. butter
- 2 medium potatoes, peeled and cut into ½-in. cubes
- 4 medium carrots, thinly sliced
- 2 celery ribs, finely chopped
- ¼ cup finely chopped onion
- 3 Tbsp. all-purpose flour
- 2 Tbsp. chicken bouillon granules
- 1½ tsp. dried tarragon
- ½ tsp. coarsely ground pepper
- 1½ cups half-and-half cream
- 2½ cups cubed cooked chicken
- 1½ cups fresh peas or frozen peas
- ½ to 1 tsp. celery seed

1. In a small bowl, beat egg yolk with 2 Tbsp. water. In a large bowl, combine flour and salt; cut in butter until crumbly. Gradually add yolk mixture, tossing with a fork; add additional cold water 1 Tbsp. at a time, as needed, until dough forms a ball. Divide dough into 2 portions, 1 with three-quarters of the dough and 1 with the remainder. Shape each into a disk; cover and refrigerate 1 hour or overnight.
2. For filling, in a Dutch oven, melt butter. Saute potatoes, carrots, celery and onion until crisp-tender, 5-7 minutes. Stir in flour, bouillon, tarragon and pepper. Gradually stir in cream. Bring to a boil; cook and stir until thickened, about 2 minutes. Stir in chicken and peas; set aside to cool completely.
3. On a lightly floured surface, roll out larger portion of dough to fit bottom and up the side of an 8-in. springform pan. Place dough in pan; add cooled filling. Roll remaining dough to fit over the top. Place over filling. Trim, seal and flute edge. Cut slits in top. Chill for at least 1 hour.
4. Lightly beat egg white with 1 tsp. water. Brush over top crust; sprinkle with celery seed. Place pie on a rimmed baking tray.
5. Bake at 400° until crust is golden brown and filling is bubbly, 50-55 minutes. Cool on a wire rack for at least 30 minutes before serving.
1 PIECE: *700 cal., 38g fat (22g sat. fat), 183mg chol., 1282mg sod., 58g carb. (8g sugars, 6g fiber), 29g pro.*

BAKED HAM WITH HONEY-CHIPOTLE GLAZE

Your holiday celebration will be so simple to orchestrate with this sweet, smoky ham recipe at your fingertips. It feeds a crowd and tastes fantastic.
—Taste of Home *Test Kitchen*

- -

PREP: 10 min. • **BAKE:** 2 hours
MAKES: 16 servings

- 1 fully cooked bone-in ham (8 to 10 lbs.)
- 1 cup packed brown sugar
- 3 Tbsp. honey
- 2 Tbsp. cider vinegar
- 2¼ cups ginger ale
- 4 chipotle peppers in adobo sauce, minced
- 3 garlic cloves, minced
- 1½ tsp. Dijon mustard
- ¾ tsp. ground cinnamon
- ¾ tsp. ground cumin

1. Preheat oven to 325°. Place ham on a rack in a roasting pan. Using a sharp knife, score surface of the ham with ½-in.-deep cuts in a diamond pattern. Bake, uncovered, 1½ hours.
2. Meanwhile, for glaze, in a small saucepan, mix brown sugar, honey, vinegar and ginger ale. Bring to a boil; cook until mixture is reduced by half, about 15 minutes. Stir in remaining ingredients. Reduce heat; simmer, uncovered, 5 minutes. Remove from heat. Reserve 1 cup mixture for sauce; keep warm.
3. Brush ham with some of the remaining glaze. Bake, uncovered, until a thermometer reads 140°, about 30 minutes, brushing twice with additional glaze. Serve with reserved sauce.
5 OZ. COOKED HAM WITH 1 TBSP. SAUCE: *270 cal., 6g fat (2g sat. fat), 100mg chol., 1234mg sod., 21g carb. (20g sugars, 0 fiber), 33g pro.*
BAKED HAM WITH HONEY-ORANGE GLAZE: *Omit glaze ingredients. Bake ham as directed. Meanwhile, combine ¼ cup packed brown sugar, ¼ cup orange juice, 2 Tbsp. honey, 1 Tbsp. stone-ground mustard, 2 tsp. dried basil, 1 tsp. orange zest and ⅛ tsp. ground cloves. Baste ham and proceed as recipe directs.*

Getting Ready for the Holidays

PARTY TIMELINE

This useful checklist will help you budget your time wisely and keep your party on schedule.

1 MONTH PRIOR:

☐ Choose date and time.

☐ Set budget.

☐ Determine guest list.

3 WEEKS PRIOR:

☐ Send out invitations (ask about any food allergies).

☐ Check to make sure you have enough chairs, linens, serving dishes and utensils. Rent or buy more if needed.

☐ Arrange for a helper (this would be a good thing to ask an older child or teenager to do).

2 WEEKS PRIOR:

☐ Plan the menu; create a master shopping list.

☐ Make a large grocery shopping trip to buy nonperishables and ingredients for freezer-friendly dishes. Prepare and freeze any dishes that can be made in advance.

1 WEEK PRIOR:

☐ Follow up with any guests who haven't responded.

☐ Clean the house thoroughly; put away breakable items.

☐ Stock the bar.

☐ Choose the music.

2 TO 3 DAYS PRIOR:

☐ Notify neighbors if cars will be parked on the street.

☐ Clean glassware, china and silverware. Clean and iron table linens.

☐ Think about the party space: Where will coats go? Where are the trash cans? How will people move around your house? Move furniture if necessary. Set up cleanup stations (salt, stain remover, club soda, clean cloths) to have at the ready.

☐ Put up decorations.

☐ Finish grocery shopping.

1 DAY PRIOR:

☐ Buy flowers.

☐ Finish as much of the cooking and prep work as possible.

☐ Do a quick cleanup of the house. Check the guest bathroom—empty trash and set out fresh hand towels.

DAY OF:

☐ Chill wine, set up the bar, and slice lemons and any other garnishes.

☐ Set the table and/or buffet.

☐ Finish any cooking.

☐ Set aside space for dirty dishes.

☐ Take out trash; have trash cans and extra garbage bags ready.

HOW TO SET THE TABLE

- The dinner plate is the center of the place setting; everything else is positioned around it. Arrange the flatware in the order in which it will be used.

- Forks go to the left of the plate. If you're serving a salad, place a small salad fork to the left of the dinner fork. Place the napkin under the forks or on the plate.

- The knife and spoons go to the right of the plate. Place the knife with the sharp edge toward the plate. The soupspoon goes outside of the teaspoon. If soup is to be served, set the bowl on the plate.

- The desert utensil—whether a fork or a spoon—can either be placed horizontally above the plate or be brought out when dessert is served.

- Smaller plates for salad or bread go above and to the left of the forks. Position the butter plate with the butter spreader across the plate.

- Cup and saucer go above the spoons with the handle to the right.

- Water and wine glasses go to the left of the coffee cup; the water glass goes on the left.

HOW MUCH FOOD & DRINK TO SERVE

Take the stress out of planning with our guide to how many drinks and how much food to stock, course by course. A good rule of thumb is to round up from these and err on the side of having too much—better to end up with a few leftovers than to leave your guests hungry.

APPETIZERS

On average, each guest will have about six appetizers (this number may double if you're having a cocktail-style event). Stock up on bulk items like nuts, pretzels and olives, both to supplement prepared appetizers and to set out before guests arrive.

Guests	Appetizers
5	30 appetizers
10	60 appetizers
20	120 appetizers

ENTREES AND SIDES

- Poultry, fish or meat: 6 oz. per serving
- Grains: 1½ oz. as a side dish, 2 oz. as a main dish casserole
- Potatoes: 5 oz.
- Vegetables: 4 oz.
- Beans: 2 oz.
- Pasta: 4 oz. (main dish)
- Bread such as buns, rolls or cornbread: 1 to 2 pieces

DESSERTS

Guests	Cake/Tart/Pastry	Creamy Dessert	Ice Cream
5	5 pieces	20 oz.	25 oz.
10	10 pieces	40 oz.	50 oz.
20	20 pieces	80 oz.	100 oz.

DRINKS

These guidelines are for parties that last two hours. Figure on 1 lb. of ice per guest.
(if serving one type of alcohol—if you're offering more, reduce the amount of each type)

Guests	Wine/Champagne	Beer	Spirits	Liqueurs	Nonalcoholic
5	3 bottles	15 bottles	1 bottle	1 bottle	5 (*if serving alcohol as well*) / 15 (*if not*)
10	5 bottles	30 bottles	2 bottles	1 bottle	10/30
20	10 bottles	60 bottles	4 bottles	2 bottles	20/60

Holiday Menus

Use these menu cards to record what you served at Christmas dinner and other seasonal gatherings. Make note of beverage pairings, ingredient substitutions or anything else you want to remember about your holiday menu.

OCCASION: _____

GUESTS: _____
_____
_____
_____
_____
_____

FOOD: _____
_____
_____
_____
_____
_____
_____
_____

DRINKS: _____
_____
_____

NOTES: _____
_____
_____
_____

OCCASION: _____

GUESTS: _____
_____
_____
_____
_____
_____

FOOD: _____
_____
_____
_____
_____
_____
_____
_____

DRINKS: _____
_____
_____

NOTES: _____
_____
_____
_____

OCCASION: _____

GUESTS: _____

_____

_____

_____

_____

FOOD: _____

_____

_____

_____

_____

_____

_____

_____

DRINKS: _____

_____

_____

NOTES: _____

_____

_____

_____

_____

_____

_____

_____

OCCASION: _____

GUESTS: _____

_____

_____

_____

_____

FOOD: _____

_____

_____

_____

_____

_____

_____

_____

DRINKS: _____

_____

_____

NOTES: _____

_____

_____

_____

_____

_____

_____

_____

Holiday Memories

FAMILY MILESTONES

What major events happened in your family this year? Births, weddings, graduations, a new home or job, or a particularly memorable vacation?

_____

_____

_____

_____

_____

_____

_____

_____

_____

_____

_____

_____

MEMORIES OF THE FEAST

What was most memorable about the time spent around the holiday table? What things did your loved ones say or do that you want to remember? Ask your family a question—what are they most thankful for, or which dish was their favorite— and record their answers!

_____

_____

_____

_____

_____

_____

_____

_____

_____

_____

_____

SPECIAL PEOPLE

Whom did you see this year that you haven't seen in a while? Who came to visit,
or hosted you? Who sent a particularly lovely card, or a favorite gift?

_____

_____

_____

_____

_____

ALL ABOUT THE COOKIES!

What cookies did you make this year, and which were your favorites?
Who is on your list for getting a cookie platter or box?

_____

_____

_____

_____

_____

RECIPE NOTES

What other recipes did you try this year? Any changes you want to make the next time round?

_____

_____

_____

_____

_____

For Next Year

GIFTS & STOCKING STUFFERS

Have a great idea for a gift for next Christmas? Make a note of it so you remember it when Christmas-shopping season rolls around.

_____

_____

_____

_____

_____

_____

_____

_____

_____

_____

_____

_____

CHRISTMAS CARD LIST

Keep track of everyone who should be on your list to get a holiday card!

_____

_____

_____

_____

_____

_____

_____

_____

_____

_____

_____

_____

_____

RECIPES TO TRY

If there are recipes you wanted to try but just didn't have time for, jot them down here so you can include them in future celebrations.

_____

_____

_____

_____

_____

_____

_____

_____

_____

_____

_____

_____

_____

_____

_____

_____

_____

_____

_____

_____

_____

_____

DECORATION IDEAS

Don't let your brainstorms be forgotten—record your ideas for festive decor here to get a jump on next year.

_____

_____

_____

_____

_____

_____

_____

_____

_____

_____

RESTOCK!

What did you use the last of that you'll need next December? Wrapping paper? Ribbon? Shipping boxes? Make a list and check back next fall.

_____

_____

_____

_____

_____

_____

_____

INDEX

This index lists every recipe in the book in alphabetical order. Just search for the titles when you want to find your favorites. On page 240, you'll find an index of the special bonus content—including tips, how-tos and more!

P. 91

P. 210

P. 103

BONUS CONTENT